ALL THE MIGHTY WORLD

The Photographs of Roger Fenton, 1852–1860

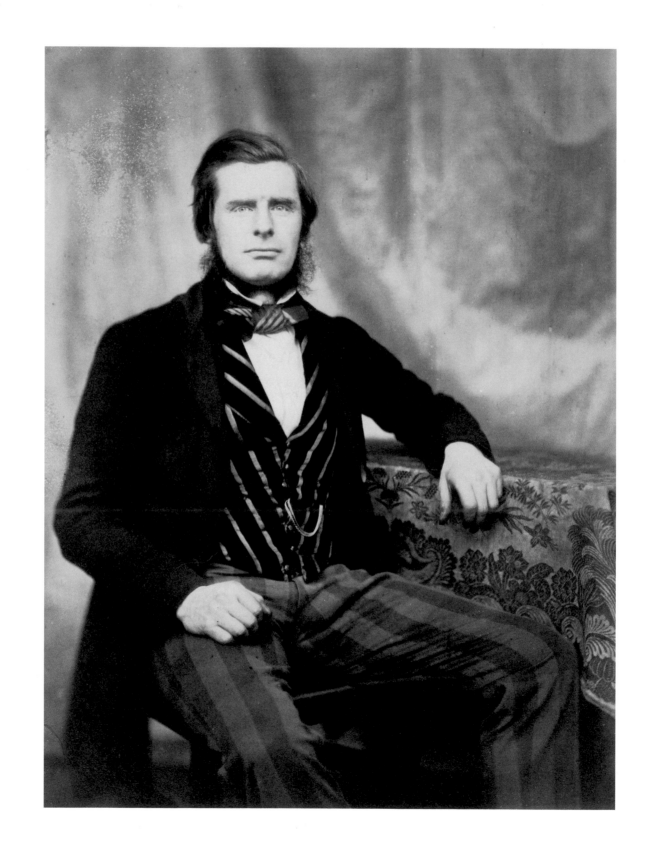

ALL THE MIGHTY WORLD

The Photographs of Roger Fenton, 1852–1860

Gordon Baldwin, Malcolm Daniel, and Sarah Greenough

With contributions by Richard Pare, Pam Roberts, and Roger Taylor

The Metropolitan Museum of Art, New York

National Gallery of Art, Washington

The J. Paul Getty Museum, Los Angeles

Yale University Press, New Haven and London

This publication accompanies the exhibition "All the Mighty World: The Photographs of Roger Fenton, 1852–1860," held at the National Gallery of Art, Washington, from October 17, 2004, to January 2, 2005; The J. Paul Getty Museum, Los Angeles, from February 1 to April 24, 2005; The Metropolitan Museum of Art, New York, from May 24 to August 21, 2005; and Tate Britain, London, from September 21, 2005, to January 2, 2006.

In New York, the exhibition is made possible by The Hite Foundation.

At the National Gallery of Art, the exhibition is made possible through the generous support of the Trellis Fund and The Ryna and Melvin Cohen Family Foundation.

The exhibition catalogue is made possible by The Andrew W. Mellon Foundation.

The exhibition is supported by an indemnity from the Federal Council on the Arts and the Humanities.

The exhibition was organized by the National Gallery of Art, Washington; The J. Paul Getty Museum, Los Angeles; and The Metropolitan Museum of Art, New York.

Published by The Metropolitan Museum of Art, New York

John P. O'Neill, Editor in Chief
Ruth Lurie Kozodoy, Editor, with Margaret Donovan
Bruce Campbell, Designer
Peter Antony and Douglas J. Malicki, Production
Minjee Cho, Desktop Publishing
Jayne Kuchna, Bibliographic Editor

New photography by Mark Morosse, the Photograph Studio, The Metropolitan Museum of Art
Map by Anandaroop Roy

Typeset in Bell and Centaur
Printed on 135 gsm Gardapat
Quadra- and duotone separations by Martin Senn
Printed and bound by EBS Editoriale Bortolazzi-Stei s.r.l., Verona

Jacket/cover illustration: Roger Fenton, *Westminster from Waterloo Bridge* (detail), ca. 1858; plate 60
Frontispiece: Roger Fenton, *Self-Portrait*, ca. 1854

LIBRARY OF CONGRESS CATALOGING-IN-PUBLICATION DATA

Baldwin, Gordon, 1939–
    All the mighty world: the photographs of Roger Fenton, 1852–1860 / Gordon Baldwin, Malcolm Daniel, and Sarah Greenough ; with contributions by Richard Pare, Pam Roberts, and Roger Taylor.
        p. cm.
    Catalog of the exhibition held Oct. 17, 2004–Jan. 2, 2005 at the National Gallery of Art, Washington, D.C.; Feb. 1, 2005–April 24, 2005 at the J. Paul Getty Museum, Los Angeles; May 24, 2005–Aug. 21, 2005 at the Metropolitan Museum of Art, New York; Sept. 21, 2005– Jan. 2, 2006 at Tate Britain.
    Includes bibliographical references and index.
    ISBN 1-58839-128-0 (hardcover) — ISBN 1-58839-129-9 (pbk.) — ISBN 0-300-10490-1 (Yale University Press)
    1. Photography, Artistic—Exhibitions. 2. Fenton, Roger, 1819–1869—Exhibitions. I. Daniel, Malcolm R. II. Greenough, Sarah, 1951– III. Fenton, Roger, 1819–1869. IV. Metropolitan Museum of Art (New York, N.Y.) V. National Gallery of Art (U.S.) VI. J. Paul Getty Museum. VII. Title.
    TR647.F46 2004
    779'.092—dc22   2004015294

Contents

Directors' Foreword

It is fitting that the first collaboration in the field of photography between The Metropolitan Museum of Art, the National Gallery of Art, and The J. Paul Getty Museum should concern a photographer so thoroughly intertwined with the broader art of his time as Roger Fenton. Trained as a painter in London and Paris, linked in aesthetic spirit to Turner and Constable, inspired by the Orientalist fantasies of Ingres and Delacroix, the landscapes of David Cox, and the still lifes of George Lance, Fenton is at home in the company of artists known and admired by our museums' visitors. He was, moreover, one of photography's supreme artists—not only of the nineteenth century or in Britain, but in the entire history of the medium. His perfect technique and unerring choice of vantage point and lighting conditions allowed him to render the smallest details while at the same time conveying a sense of monumentality, and thus to imbue his pictures with both delicacy and sublime power.

This catalogue takes its title, *All the Mighty World*, from William Wordsworth's "Lines Written a Few Miles above Tintern Abbey," an ode to nature in which the author declares himself "A lover of the meadows and the woods, / And mountains; and of all that we behold / From this green earth; of all the mighty world / Of eye and ear, both what they half-create, / And what perceive." The poet's words find an echo in the reverence for nature so evident in Fenton's landscapes, and, even more aptly, they suggest the photographer's grand ambition and broad reach. In the course of a single decade, Fenton mastered every photographic genre. He produced majestic architectural views of England's ruined abbeys and her stately homes, Romantic depictions of the countryside, moving reportage of the Crimean War (the first extensive series of war photographs), intimate portraits of Queen Victoria and her family, enchanting Orientalist tableaux, and astonishingly lush still lifes. Fenton helped shape the early progress of the medium in other ways as well. He served as the official photographer of the British Museum, being the first to hold such a position in any museum; he fought for the extension of copyright protection to photographs; and he was the principal force behind the establishment of what would eventually become the Royal Photographic Society.

Our deepest thanks go to the many individual and institutional lenders who have generously shared their prized photographs, allowing us to represent the artist at his very highest level of achievement. We are also grateful to the exhibition's curators, Sarah Greenough, Gordon Baldwin, and Malcolm Daniel, for the dedicated work that went into the organization of the exhibition and for the benefit of their scholarship and connoisseurship. Three guest authors, Roger Taylor, Pam Roberts, and Richard Pare, made important and eloquent contributions. We also thank the staffs of our three institutions and of Tate Britain for their efforts on behalf of the exhibition and catalogue. The Metropolitan Museum is very much indebted to The Hite Foundation for its generosity toward this exhibition. The Museum also thanks The Andrew W. Mellon Foundation, whose publications endowment provided support for this catalogue. The National Gallery of Art would like to express appreciation to the Trellis Fund and The Ryna and Melvin Cohen Family Foundation for their support of the exhibition, and to the Federal Council on the Arts and the Humanities for providing an indemnity for the exhibition.

Both in his own work and through his advocacy for the medium, Fenton sought to establish photography as the equal of other, long-established fine arts. A century and a half later, we derive profound pleasure from his success.

Philippe de Montebello
Director, The Metropolitan Museum of Art

Earl A. Powell III
Director, National Gallery of Art

Deborah Gribbon
Director, The J. Paul Getty Museum; Vice President, J. Paul Getty Trust

Acknowledgments

In the past decade, as interest in the history of photography has escalated exponentially, a number of nineteenth-century photographers have been the object of in-depth scholarly studies. Monographic exhibitions and publications appeared that were devoted to Édouard Baldus, Mathew Brady, Julia Margaret Cameron, Gustave Le Gray, Nadar, William Henry Fox Talbot, and Carleton Watkins, among others. Notably absent from this growing pantheon has been Roger Fenton, although an exhibition of his work showed at the Royal Academy in London in 1988 and traveled in a much-reduced scale to the Yale Center for British Art. Especially in the United States, Fenton's accomplishments have emphatically warranted further attention.

As is often the case, the idea for this catalogue and exhibition occurred simultaneously to several different people. Sarah Greenough of the National Gallery and Gordon Baldwin of The J. Paul Getty Museum had already been having conversations on the subject when The Metropolitan Museum of Art acquired The Rubel Collection, with its superb Fenton photographs. Maria Morris Hambourg of the Metropolitan Museum suggested that her colleague Malcolm Daniel join the discussion under way and that the Metropolitan Museum, the National Gallery, and the Getty embark on their first collaboration in the field of photography by organizing this important exhibition. The three curators quickly asked the noted Fenton scholars Roger Taylor, Pam Roberts, and Richard Pare to lend their expertise and to write essays for the catalogue. We have benefited enormously from the different perspectives and insights these colleagues have brought to the subject.

From the very beginning of this undertaking, energetic support has come from the leadership of our three institutions, and we are grateful to Earl A. Powell III, Director of the National Gallery of Art, Philippe de Montebello, Director of The Metropolitan Museum of Art, and Deborah Gribbon and John Walsh, the present and former Directors of The J. Paul Getty Museum, for their guidance and unwavering commitment to the project. Also deeply appreciated are the efforts at the National Gallery of Alan Shestack, Deputy Director, and D. Dodge Thompson, Chief of Exhibitions; at the Metropolitan Museum of Mahrukh Tarapor, Associate Director for Exhibitions; and at the Getty of Quincy Houghton, Head of Exhibitions and Public Programming. One of our principal objectives has been to introduce Fenton's photography to both an American and an international audience. We wish to thank Stephen Deuchar, Director of Tate Britain, for enthusiastically joining with us to bring this exhibition to London and reacquaint the British public with Fenton's art.

An exhibition and catalogue of this magnitude and complexity could not have been organized without the devoted work of many individuals. Special thanks are due to April Watson, Sara Cooling Trucksess, and Sarah Kennel in the Department of Photographs at the National Gallery; meticulous and unfailingly gracious, they have assisted with all aspects of the planning, organization, and execution of the exhibition.

We are joined by our fellow authors in expressing heartfelt gratitude to all those whose efforts made possible the realization of this catalogue, under the able leadership of John O'Neill, Editor in Chief and General Manager of Publications at the Metropolitan Museum. Ruth Kozodoy, Senior Editor, edited the essays gracefully, challenged the authors to clarify their ideas, and helped mold the book's contents into a cohesive whole. Valuable editorial work was also performed by Margaret Donovan and by Jayne Kuchna, the Bibliographic Editor. Bruce Campbell is responsible for the catalogue's elegant design, Mark Morosse of the Photograph Studio for much of the copy photography, and Martin Senn for the quadra- and duotone separations. Peter Antony, Chief Production Manager, oversaw the complex printing of the book after shepherding it, assisted by Douglas J. Malicki, through the many stages of production. Special thanks go also to Minjee Cho, Cathy Dorsey, Mary Gladue, and Anandaroop Roy.

This exhibition and publication are built on foundations laid by earlier scholars, many of whom are cited in this book's footnotes and bibliography. Special recognition should be given to Helmut and Alison Gernsheim, John Hannavy, and Valerie Lloyd for their pioneering work on Fenton. A friend, colleague, and former Curator of the Royal Photographic Society, the late Valerie Lloyd inspired all of us with her passionate dedication to Fenton's legacy. Her extensive research into his life, generously made available to Gordon Baldwin by her family, proved invaluable for the assembling of the chronology and the discovery of previously unpublished Fenton images.

In the course of our work on this project, many people have responded to our requests with a generosity that is both inspiring and humbling. We are particularly grateful to the directors and trustees of the lending institutions and to the private collectors who have magnanimously allowed their works to be included in the exhibition. In addition we especially wish to thank their curators, conservators, and registrars, whose assistance has been enormously helpful and who include Gary Thorn, Christopher Date, and Helen Sharp at The British Museum; Nicholas Olsberg, Louise Désy, Jo Anne Audet, Margaret Morris, and Marie-Chantal Anctil at the Centre Canadien d'Architecture/Canadian Centre for Architecture, Montréal; Pierre Apraxine and Maria Umali at the Gilman Paper Company Collection; Terence Suthers, Robin Diaper, Jane Stewart-Sant, and Karen Lynch at the Harewood House Trust; Mary Daniels and Irina Gorstein in Special Collections at the Frances Loeb Library, Harvard Design School; Bodo Von Dewitz at the Museum Ludwig; Paul Goodman, Jane Fletcher, Russell Roberts, and Brian Liddy at the National Museum of Photography, Film & Television, Bradford; Roy Flukinger, Barbara Brown, Debra Armstrong-Morgan, Linda Briscoe, and David Coleman at the Gernsheim Collection, Harry Ransom Center, the University of Texas at Austin; Frances Dimond, Theresa-Mary Morton, and Annaleigh Kennard at the Royal Collection, Windsor; Janet Graffius and David Knight, Stonyhurst College; Mark Haworth-Booth, Martin Barnes, David Wright, and Janet Skidmore at the Victoria and Albert Museum; and Violet Hamilton at the Wilson Centre for Photography.

At the National Gallery, special thanks are due to Carol Kelley in the Director's Office; Joe Krakora, Executive Officer, External and International Affairs; Jennifer Rich and Ann Robertson in the Department of Exhibitions; Jonathan Davis, Sarah Dennis, Karen Hellman, Marcie Hocking, and Stephen Pinson, interns in the Department of Photographs; Constance McCabe, Hugh Phibbs, Jenny Ritchie, and Jamie Stout in the Department of Conservation; Susan Arensberg and Margaret Doyle in the Department of Exhibition Programs; Elizabeth Croog and Isabelle Raval in the office of the Secretary-General Counsel; Mark Leithauser, Gordon Anson, Jame Anderson, Deborah Kirkpatrick, Nathan Peek, John Olson, Barbara Keyes, and Jeff Wilson in the Department of Design and Installation; Sally Freitag, Michelle Fondas, and Melissa Stegeman in the Office of the Registrar; Cathie Scoville in the Development Office; Chris Myers in the Office of Corporate Relations; Genevra Higginson in the Office of Special Events; Judy Metro, Sara Sanders-Buell, and Ira Bartfield in the Publishing Office; and Deborah Ziska and Mary Jane McKinven in the Press and Public Information Office.

At the Getty, thanks are due to William Griswold, Chief Curator; Weston Naef, Judith Keller, Julian Cox, Anne Lyden, Michael Hargraves, Brett Abbott, Paul Martineau, Marisa Weintraub, Valerie Graham, Edie Wu, and Ann Magee in the Department of Photographs; Marc Harnley, Ernie Mack, Lynn Kaneshiro, and Martin Salazar in the Department of Paper Conservation; Chris Hudson, Mark Greenberg, and Catherine Comeau in the Publications Department; Merritt Price, Tim McNeill, and Patrick Frederickson in the Department of Exhibition Design; Jack Ross and Christopher Foster in the Department of Photo Services; Sally Hibbard and Betsy Severance in the Registrar's Department; Pamela Johnson and

Tracy Gilbert in the Communications Department; Cathy Carpenter, Viviane Meerbergen, and Jaime Villaneda, in the Education Department; Christina Olsen and Uttara Natarajan in the Interactive Programs Department; Amber Keller in the Exhibitions Department; Ivy Okamura in the Events Department; and Bruce Metro, Mike Mitchell, Tracy Witt, and the entire team in the Preparation Department.

The Metropolitan Museum is profoundly grateful to Sybil and Lawrence Hite for their devotion to nineteenth-century British photography and to The Hite Foundation for its enlightened sponsorship of this exhibition. Also greatly appreciated is the support for the publication of this catalogue provided by The Andrew W. Mellon Foundation. At the Metropolitan, special thanks are owed to Rachel Becker for invaluable assistance with the catalogue and exhibition and to Maria Hambourg, Laura Harris, Lisa Hostetler, Nora Kennedy, and Nancy Reinhold, all in the Department of Photographs; Linda Sylling, Manager for Special Exhibitions; Martha Deese, Senior Assistant for Exhibitions; Nina Maruca, Registrar; Elly Muller, Senior Press Officer; Christine Scornavacca of the Development Office; Mike Norris and Elizabeth Hammer of the Education Department; Barbara Bridgers and Susan Bresnan of the Photograph Studio; Curators Elizabeth Barker and Laurence Kanter; and Michael Langley and Sophia Geronimus of the Design Department. The handsome presentation of the exhibited photographs is the work of Predrag Dimitrijevic of the Department of Photographs and Jed Bark of Bark Frameworks.

We also wish to give special recognition to our colleagues at Tate Britain, Sarah Munday, Judith Nesbitt, Christine Riding, and Sheena Wagstaff, for the effort they have put into presenting this exhibition in London.

Numerous other individuals gave freely of their time and eagerly of their expertise. We wish to thank Robert Flynn Johnson, Achenbach Foundation for Graphic Arts, the Fine Arts Museums of San Francisco; David Travis, Art Institute of Chicago; Peter Bunnell and Toby Jurovics, The Art Museum, Princeton University; Sylvie Aubenas, Bibliothèque Nationale de France, Paris; Pete James, Birmingham Central Library; Sally Pierce, Boston Athenaeum; Keith Sweetmore, British Records Association, London; Aidan Flood, Camden Local Studies Library, London; Jim Ganz,

Sterling and Francine Clark Art Institute, Williamstown, Massachusetts; Dr. Lindy Grant and Jeffrey Fisher, Conway Library, Courtauld Institute of Art, London, and Philip Ward-Jacson, Courtauld Institute of Art; Lynn McNabb, Guildhall Library, London; Anne Tucker and Del Zogg, Houston Museum of Fine Arts; Jennifer McDonald, Hulton Getty Archive, London; Mike Chrimes, Institution of Civil Engineers, London; Hans P. Kraus and Jennifer Parkinson of Hans P. Kraus, Jr., Inc., New York; Verna Curtis and Michelle Delaney, The Library of Congress, Washington, D.C.; Robin Darwall-Smith, Magdalen College Archive, Oxford; the Henry Moore Institute, Leeds; the staff of the Archives du Musée du Louvre, Paris; Clifford Ackley and Anne Havinga, Museum of Fine Arts, Boston; Cathy Ross and Michael J. Seaborne, Museum of London; Rachel Cognale, Museum of Modern Art, New York; David Hodge, National Maritime Museum, London; Ian Leith, National Monuments Record, Swindon; Oliver Fairclough, National Museums & Galleries of Wales; Ed Bartholomew, National Railway Museum, York; Melanie Aspey and Richard Schofield, The Rothschild Archive, London; Michael Hall, Curator to Edmund de Rothschild; Maggie Magnuson, Royal Engineers Library, Chatham, Kent; David Haberstich, National Museum of American History, Smithsonian Institution, Washington, D.C.; Paula Fleming, National Museum of Natural History, Smithsonian Institution, Washington, D.C.; Katia Busch, Société Française de Photographie, Paris; Juliet Hacking, Sotheby's, London; Peter Lord, University of Wales Centre for Advanced Welsh & Celtic Studies, Aberystwyth; Jay Kempen, Washington University Archives, Saint Louis; and Roger and Jennifer Davies; Harry and Elizabeth Ellis; Scott and Donise Ferrel; Philippe Garner; Anthony S. Hamber; Robert Hershkowitz; Charles Isaacs; Ken Jacobson; Glyn Jones; Barbara Kehoe; Randall Keynes; Briony Llewellyn; Sarah Nicholson; Peter Peecock; Maria Antonella Pellizzari; Denise Raine; Michael Rich; William Rubel; Andrew Smith; Joel Smith; Pam Solomon; Howard Stein and Lee Marks; Lindsey Stewart; Chris Taylor; Quentin Tyler; and Paul Walter.

Lenders to the Exhibition

CANADA

Montréal, Collection Centre Canadien d'Architecture/Canadian Centre for Architecture   5, 10, 25, 47, 49, 50, 54, 55, 57, 60

GERMANY

Cologne, Museum Ludwig, Collection Robert Lebeck   85

UNITED KINGDOM

Bradford, National Museum of Photography, Film & Television (RPS Collection)   6, 7, 8, 27, 28, 29, 30, 38, 39, 41, 46, 59, 65, 66, 67, 70, 75, 76, 79, 80, 86, 87, 88, 89

Clitheroe, the Governors of Stonyhurst College   73

Leeds, the Earl and Countess of Harewood, and the Trustees of Harewood House Trust   68

London, Trustees of The British Museum   40

London, Victoria and Albert Museum   44, 77

Windsor, The Royal Collection   81, 82, 83, 84

UNITED STATES

Austin, Gernsheim Collection, Harry Ransom Center, The University of Texas at Austin   19

Cambridge, Massachusetts, H. H. Richardson Collection, Frances Loeb Library, Harvard Design School   35, 36, 51, 52, 69

Los Angeles, The J. Paul Getty Museum   3, 16, 21, 24, 31, 32, 33, 37, 42, 45, 48, 53, 62, 64, 72

New York, Gilman Paper Company Collection   1, 2, 4, 11, 12, 13, 15, 20, 26, 56, 58

New York, The Metropolitan Museum of Art   22, 23, 34, 61, 78

Washington, National Gallery of Art   9

PRIVATE COLLECTIONS

Richard and Ronay Menschel   71

Private collection, London   frontispiece

Wilson Centre for Photography   14, 17, 18, 43, 63, 74

A Note on Early Photographic Techniques

In 1839, barely a dozen years before Roger Fenton took up the camera, two wholly different photographic processes were announced to the public: the daguerreotype in France and photogenic drawing in England.

The **daguerreotype** process was perfected and promoted by the painter, printmaker, and stage designer Louis-Jacques-Mandé Daguerre. In this process a highly polished silver-plated sheet of copper was sensitized with iodine fumes, exposed in a camera to record the desired object, developed over heated mercury vapors, and fixed with salt water or hypo (sodium thiosulfate). Each daguerreotype was a unique and dazzlingly detailed image. Although wildly popular in France and America, daguerreotypy was little practiced in England, where a patent restricted its use, and there is no indication that Fenton ever tried his hand at the process.

Instead, Fenton practiced various photographic techniques that all stemmed from the inventions of William Henry Fox Talbot. Prompted by Daguerre's announcement of his invention in January 1839, Talbot had scrambled to perfect and publish a completely different process, **photogenic drawing**, with which he had been experimenting for five years. His process involved immersing a sheet of fine writing paper in salt water and then, when dry, coating it with a solution of silver nitrate, thus forming light-sensitive silver chloride in the paper. Placed inside a camera, the paper darkened gradually wherever it was struck by light, eventually becoming a tonally reversed picture—what later came to be called a negative. Talbot's early exposures were lengthy, sometimes lasting hours, and the results were generally pale images in shades of yellow or purple.

In September 1840 Talbot discovered that even an exposure of mere seconds left a latent image that could be brought out—"developed," we would now say—by immersion in an "exciting liquid" (gallic acid). Paper negatives produced in this way were not absolutely transparent; their fibrous texture had a tendency to blur details and exaggerate the contrast between lights and darks, creating effects that some found more artistic than the cold precision of the daguerreotype. But the principal advantage of Talbot's **paper negative process**, which he patented as the **calotype** or **Talbotype**, was the fact that multiple positive prints could be made from a single negative.

Although protected by patent restrictions in both England and France, Talbot's calotype process was nevertheless taken up in the late 1840s by French artists, who came up with variations that in the judgment of the French courts fell outside the bounds of Talbot's patent claims. It was one such variation, Gustave Le Gray's **waxed-paper-negative** process, that Fenton saw practiced in Paris in 1851 and subsequently used for his earliest photographs. In Le Gray's process, the paper support was infused with wax prior to sensitization to create a more homogeneous texture, give added transparency to the negative, and cause the photosensitive chemicals to sit on the surface of the paper rather than being absorbed by the paper fibers. This technique not only yielded a crisper image but also allowed the photographer to prepare his negatives days or weeks in advance of their use, making it particularly practical for travel photography. Fenton utilized Le Gray's process when traveling through Russia in 1852.

By the time Fenton took up photography, there was an alternative to the paper negative process, and after returning from Russia late in 1852 he used the new method exclusively. Producing a sharper image but more complex to carry out, this **glass negative** process, also called **wet plate, wet collodion,** or **wet collodion on glass**, had been published in 1851 by Frederick Scott Archer. The new method combined the precision of the daguerreotype with the reproducibility of the calotype, and it required an exposure time of seconds rather than minutes. In this procedure the photographer coated a sheet of glass with a layer of collodion (cellulose nitrate, also called guncotton, dissolved in ether) and sensitized it in a solution of silver salts. Since the plate had to be prepared, the picture taken, and the negative developed all before the collodion dried, it was necessary to take a portable darkroom when photographing outside the studio. Despite the difficulties of this process, its results were considered so superior that by the end of the 1850s it had almost completely replaced both the calotype and the daguerreotype methods, even for campaigns such as Fenton's in the Crimea, where the use of an on-site darkroom might seem especially onerous.

While the process of taking a photograph was undergoing changes, methods for printing the image from the negative were also evolving. Prints made from paper negatives in the 1840s and early 1850s were most often **salted paper prints**, or **salt prints**. Although many individual recipes existed—each photographer learning over time that a dash of this or a few drops of that changed the sensitivity, color, or permanence of his prints—the basic process was the one outlined by Talbot. A sheet of paper sensitized with salt and silver nitrate was placed behind a negative and pressed tightly in a glass frame; the frame was set in the sun for as long as twenty minutes to "print out"; finally, the print was "fixed" in a bath of hypo (sodium thiosulfate). Salted paper prints are usually warm in color and have a velvety, matte surface because the silver particles that make up the image are nestled in and around the paper fibers. Fenton's Russian and Crimean pictures, most of his British Museum prints, and a few of his other works were produced by this method.

In the course of the 1850s, salted paper prints gradually gave way to **albumen silver prints,** or **albumen prints**—the medium Fenton used for the majority of his architectural, landscape, tableau-vivant, and still-life compositions. This type of print was made by coating a sheet of paper with a binder of egg white, then sensitizing it with silver salts and printing it in the sun in the same manner as the salt print. Albumen silver prints perfectly render the fine detail and continuous tones of glass negatives. These prints have a shinier surface than salted paper prints, and the highlights have often yellowed with age.

Whether made from a paper or a glass negative and whether a salt or an albumen print, every one of Fenton's photographs was **contact printed**: the positive print was made by direct contact with the negative and was not enlarged. Thus, Fenton's unusually large prints, about 14 x 17 inches, were printed from glass negatives of the same size; and all of the photographic manipulations, such as evenly coating and sensitizing the plate, became far more difficult as the size of the image increased. Of course, all of the attendant equipment, from the camera itself to the negative holders, trays, printing frames, and the like, took on a similarly cumbersome scale to accommodate such a large ambition.

Because both salted paper prints and albumen silver prints were recognized at the time as being subject to fading, in the 1850s many photographers worked to develop a way to print photographic images using printer's ink rather than light-sensitive chemicals. The **photogalvanograph** was one of many such **photogravure** processes. Developed by Paul Pretsch and patented in 1854, this technique combined photography and electroplating to produce an etched metal plate that could be printed, like a traditional engraving, on an intaglio press. In 1856 Fenton joined Pretsch in a failed commercial venture to exploit this process for photographic publishing. Although more permanent than traditional photographic prints, photogalvanographs lacked the finesse and tonal subtlety of chemically produced prints and often required intervention by hand.

Part of the motivation for developing a practical photogravure process had been to integrate the printing of photographic images into the pre-existing procedures of the commercial printing industry. Instead, in the late 1850s and early 1860s a whole new photographic printing industry developed, capable of mass-producing pictures for widespread distribution as individual works, tourist souvenirs, or book illustrations. Thus during the scant decade of Fenton's career, 1852 to 1860, photography underwent enormous technical changes and ultimately a shift of emphasis from handcrafted technique to industrialized production.

Malcolm Daniel

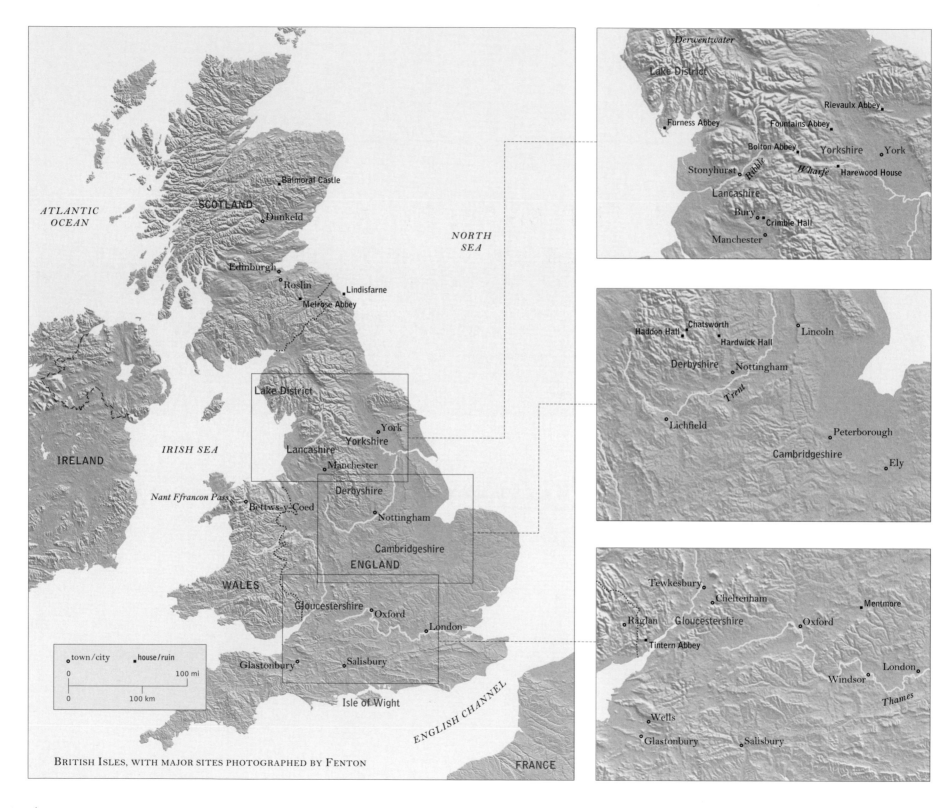

Inset map 1 (top right):

Derwentwater

Lake District

Rievaulx Abbey

Furness Abbey   Fountains Abbey

Bolton Abbey   Yorkshire   York

Stonyhurst   *Ribble*   *Wharfe*   Harewood House

Lancashire

Bury

Crimble Hall

Manchester

Inset map 2 (middle right):

Haddon Hall   Chatsworth   Lincoln

Hardwick Hall

Derbyshire   Nottingham

Trent

Lichfield   Peterborough

Cambridgeshire   Ely

Inset map 3 (bottom right):

Tewkesbury   Cheltenham   Mentmore

Raglan   Gloucestershire   Oxford

Tintern Abbey

London

Windsor

Thames

Wells

Glastonbury   Salisbury

Main map:

ATLANTIC OCEAN

SCOTLAND

Balmoral Castle

Dunkeld

NORTH SEA

Edinburgh

Roslin

Lindisfarne

Melrose Abbey

IRELAND

IRISH SEA

Lake District

York

Yorkshire

Lancashire

Manchester

Derbyshire

Nant Ffrancon Pass

Bettws-y-Coed

Nottingham

Cambridgeshire

ENGLAND

WALES

Gloucestershire

Oxford

London

Glastonbury   Salisbury

Isle of Wight

ENGLISH CHANNEL

FRANCE

○ town/city   ■ house/ruin

0   100 mi

0   100 km

BRITISH ISLES, WITH MAJOR SITES PHOTOGRAPHED BY FENTON

ALL THE MIGHTY WORLD

The Photographs of Roger Fenton, 1852–1860

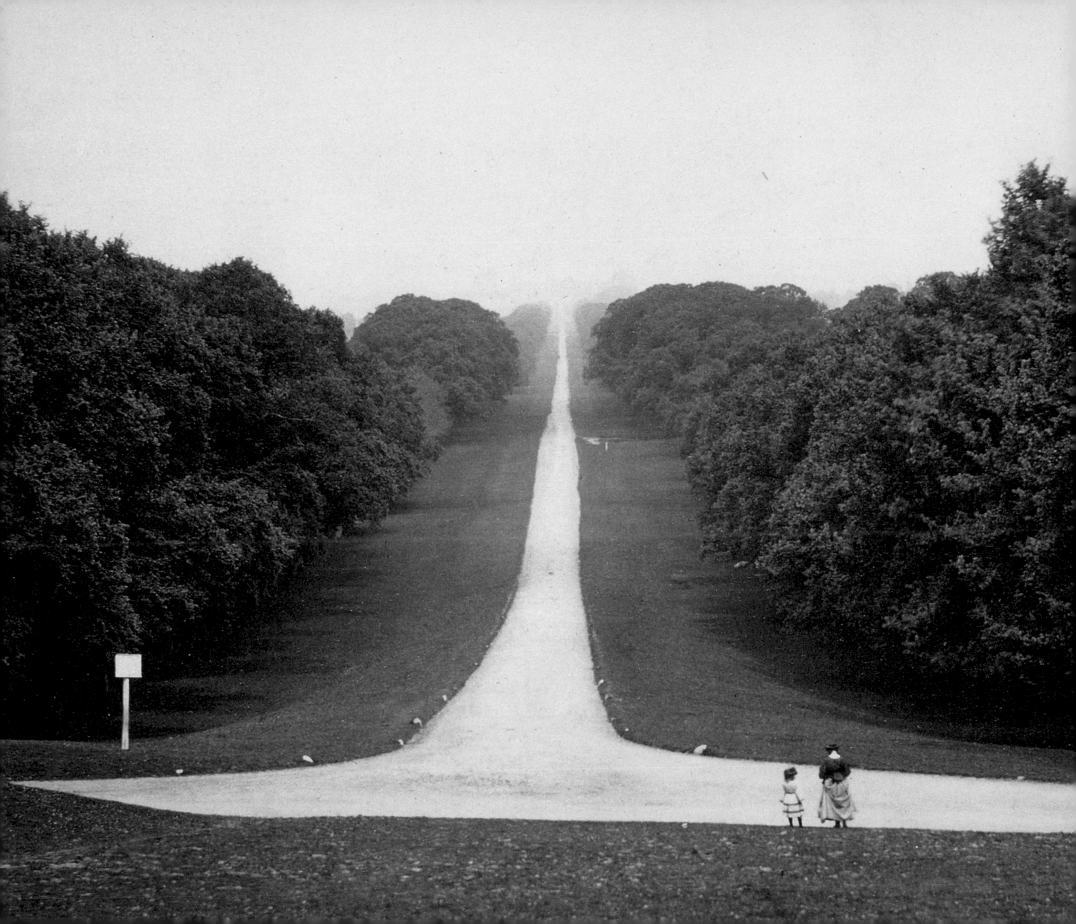

"A New Starting Point": Roger Fenton's Life

SARAH GREENOUGH

The eighty-third annual exhibition of the Royal Academy opened in London on May 2, 1851, with a private viewing of the more than thirteen hundred works on display.[1] The academy was especially proud of its new installation, in which paintings were hung in the more elegant and commodious of the rooms and architectural designs relegated to the decidedly unwelcoming "hall of torture."[2] Although the exhibition was hailed as "the best that has adorned these walls for many years," it was apparently not good enough for the fortunes of one young and struggling English painter, Roger Fenton.[3] In the previous two years Fenton's submissions had been entirely overlooked; this time his entry, *There's music in his very steps as he comes up the stairs*, was at least mentioned in one review.[4] But the critic, while acknowledging the head and petticoat of the figure to be "admirably painted," thought that the meticulous execution of the draperies and accessories overwhelmed the piece; criticized the "affected title"; and dismissed the work.[5]

Fenton's career up to this point had been checkered. Although in 1839 he had begun to prepare for a career in the law, he seems to have put this work aside to pursue painting in Paris and London. By 1851, however, Fenton was thirty-two years old, married, the father of two young girls, and plagued by professional indecision.[6] Perhaps in acknowledgment of his less-than-stellar abilities as a painter, he had earlier in the year resumed his law studies, and a week after the opening of the Royal Academy exhibition he was called to the bar, that is, admitted to the legal profession. Yet by the summer of 1852,

only twelve months later, Fenton had not only discovered a new profession—photography—and established himself as a leading figure in its growing community but had also awakened a passionate, ambitious commitment unknown in his earlier life.

The year 1851 was a pivotal one not only for Fenton but also for England as a whole. May 1, 1851, the day before the opening of the Royal Academy show, was proclaimed by Queen Victoria "one of the greatest and most glorious days of our lives."[7] On that day she and Prince Albert opened the celebrated and influential Great Exhibition of the Works of Industry of All Nations in the newly constructed Crystal Palace in Hyde Park. Although the previous few decades had brought violent upheavals on the Continent, England experienced only peaceful democratic changes, and at midcentury it was the most advanced nation on earth, with a military reach that extended around the world. Prince Albert, who had helped to shape the exhibition, hoped it would foster world peace by promoting friendly exchange between countries, but in reality it became a showplace for England's new technological prowess—its impressive new machines and its other wondrous inventions—as well as an implicit advertisement for the strength of its political system. Within the enormous structure, the newest, most powerful locomotives and blast furnaces, the fastest printing presses and carding machines, the strongest telescopes and microscopes, as well as the sensational American sewing machine and electric telegraph greeted the more than six million visitors who viewed the exhibition before its close in October of that year. The exhibition was "a new starting point," Prince Albert proclaimed, "from which all nations will be able to direct their further exertions."[8]

Opposite: Fig. 1. Roger Fenton, *The Long Walk* (detail), 1860; see pl. 82

But while this new starting point celebrated the triumph of both England and the machine age, it also highlighted the profound dilemma facing contemporary artists. The Industrial Revolution had transferred money from the aristocracy and gentry to the new industrialists of the north, in Manchester, Liverpool, Leeds, and elsewhere, who eagerly bought works of art. However, their tastes differed from those of earlier collectors: they sought not old master paintings but contemporary British art, not historical, allegorical, or mythological depictions but portraits, landscapes, rural studies, and especially scenes of everyday life. In unprecedented numbers this newly rich upper middle class amassed large collections of paintings, often buying directly from the artists themselves.[9] Moreover, with an increasing number of international fairs modeled after the Great Exhibition, a growing attendance at annual art exhibitions, and a rising middle class with disposable income, popular artists often reaped even greater financial rewards by also allowing their paintings to be reproduced as engravings.[10] However, this infusion of money into the art world brought with it significant self-scrutiny. If England in the 1850s was the age of the machine, if it was a materialistic culture enamored with science, technology, practical inventions, and verifiable facts, what, then, was the role of art? Aspiring to be more than merely decorative, how could it express the great ideas of its age? How could it compete, for example, with the Crystal Palace, Joseph Paxton's glass-and-iron monument to the industrial age, with its bold articulation and brazen "raw modernity"?[11]

The year 1851 was a new starting point for photography in England as well. The Great Exhibition, which was among other things the first large public display of photographs in England, highlighted the extraordinary appeal of the young medium, especially its seductive ability to record information about the world and simultaneously capture the spirit of the time. Equally apparent, though, was the poor quality of English photography. Although England won more awards in photography at the exhibition than any other country, this was probably an indication of the judges' partiality more than the true merit of the work. In their report issued the following year, the jurors themselves noted that France was "unrivalled" in the calotype (the negative/positive process invented by the Englishman William Henry Fox Talbot), while in the daguerreotype (the process invented by the Frenchman Louis-Jacques-Mandé Daguerre), "America stands prominently

forward." But English photography, the judges lamented, was noteworthy only for "distinct character."[12] The exhibition raised an obvious if difficult question: if an Englishman invented the calotype process and if other Englishmen were able to invent, design, and manufacture some of the most sophisticated machines and instruments ever created, why was the work of English photographers so lamentable? If English photographers were to keep pace with others around the world, the jurors concluded, they would have to do far more to explore the potential applications of the medium to art, science, and industry and demonstrate the ways in which photography benefited mankind.

Spurred by such sentiments as well as by the widely held conviction that the English patent system urgently needed reform, many prominent individuals pressured Talbot to relinquish the restrictive patents he had placed on his process, which required photographers to buy rights from him before making calotypes and thus severely inhibited exploration of the art. In 1852, Talbot agreed.[13] In addition, another new starting point for photography had surfaced at the Great Exhibition. There, among all the other inventions, Frederick Scott Archer presented publicly for the first time his newly discovered collodion process for making negatives. This technique, which combined the fine detail of Daguerre's daguerreotype with the reproducibility of Talbot's calotype, became the dominant method for making negatives in the 1850s. With these two developments, photography, after years of languishing in England, blossomed. New practitioners, both amateur and professional, flooded the field with their imagery, inventions, and aspirations for the medium. They opened photographic studios in unprecedented numbers and sold their works at seemingly ever cheaper prices; they founded photographic societies, first in London and then around the country; they organized annual exhibitions and traveling exchanges of their photographs; they published their work, improvements, and inventions in newly established journals dedicated to photography as well as in more general newspapers and publications; and they distributed their photographs, often through print or book dealers, both as individual prints and in albums and portfolios. Thus, in a way that it never had before, photography seeped into almost every aspect of middle-class English life.

But for many, this transformation sparked doubts as well as opportunities. Photography satisfied the growing materialism of the age and its seemingly insatiable appetite for the "facts, facts, facts" that Charles Dickens's character Thomas Gradgrind craved in *Hard Times* (1854), but to many minds it did so all too quickly, with little grounding in rigorous analysis or aesthetic scrutiny.[14] In the 1840s photography in England had been fairly rigidly divided between commercial practitioners, who usually made daguerreotype portraits, and gentleman amateurs, who usually made calotypes.[15] The former photographed purely for profit, the latter for private delectation. But by the 1850s, as most photographers adopted the collodion process, these divisions began to blur. Even more significantly, though, a new breed of photographer came to regard older practitioners of both types as obsolete and ill equipped to imagine a transformed role for photography. These emerging photographers sought both to professionalize the medium, enhancing its stature and providing it with institutional supporting structures, and to demonstrate that photography was a tool of social, political, even national significance. The struggle between the various factions—commercial practitioners, gentleman amateurs, and new professionals—was at the core of the photographic discourse in England in the 1850s.

Roger Fenton was not only a central figure in this dialogue but also frequently the catalyst for changes. One of the first and most forceful champions of the need for a learned society to support the efforts of photographers in England and abroad, he led in the formation of the Photographic Society and the establishment of its annual photography exhibitions. He was also one of the photographers who demonstrated to Queen Victoria and Prince Albert the power and potential of the new medium. The contemporary of such innovative and dynamic figures as the Frenchmen Gustave Le Gray (1820–1884) and Nadar (1820–1910) and the American Mathew Brady (1823–1896), Fenton was part of the second generation of photographers, who sought to propel the practice to a new level of maturity. Neither gentleman amateur nor commercial hack, he was determined to become the new kind of photographer: a professional educated in his craft, dedicated to its art and science, and committed to demonstrating how the medium could respond to the advances of the modern age. The range, accomplishment, and innovative vision of his photographs reveal his aspirations and establish him as one of the most important of all English photographers. Yet for all this, his career lasted only a little more than eleven years. Its brevity was perhaps as much a result of the changes Fenton himself fostered as of his own restless ambition.

1819–1851

The drive from Rochdale to Burnley is one of the grandest and most interesting things I ever did in my life . . . the cottages so old and various in form and position on the hills—the rocks so wild and dark—and the furnaces so vast and multitudinous, and foaming forth their black smoke like thunderclouds, mixed with the hill mist.
—John Ruskin, 1859[16]

Roger Fenton was born in 1819 into a world of intense contrasts. His birthplace, Crimble Hall, near Bury, was several miles north of Manchester in Lancashire, one of England's most beautiful areas. Its open countryside and expansive views, its hills, lowlands, and moors had captured the public imagination for many generations. But at the time of Fenton's birth, Lancashire and neighboring counties were being rocked by profound changes as the Industrial Revolution transformed cities like Manchester and nearby Liverpool, Leeds, Newcastle-upon-Tyne, and Sheffield into thriving hubs of manufacturing and commerce. A vast network of roads, railroads, and canals was built to transport both the raw materials consumed by numerous newly constructed steel and cotton mills and the products they generated. Thousands of poor, usually unskilled laborers, often from other parts of England or Ireland, flowed into the area, and all too soon, disease, overcrowding, poverty, and crime, accompanied by political unrest, plagued the cities.

Fenton was both removed from these changes and a part of them. His immediate world had been built, quite literally, by his paternal grandfather, Joseph Fenton. One of the storied generation of Manchester industrialists, merchants, and bankers, Joseph Fenton established a bank, Fenton, Eccles, Cunliffe & Roby, in the town of Rochdale, ten miles north of Manchester, in 1819—the year of his grandson's birth.[17] It prospered through most of the nineteenth century and endowed Joseph Fenton with more than enough capital to pursue other, even more lucrative business ventures. In 1826, taking advantage of the region's many canals and plentiful sources of power, he built a mill in Hooley Bridge, near the neighboring village of Heywood, for the spinning and weaving of cotton and fustian. While most nineteenth-century mills were places of desperate poverty and degradation—poor wages, long hours, dangerous working conditions, and unregulated child labor—such generalizations are perhaps more applicable to mills in large urban centers than to those in villages such as Hooley Bridge, Cheesden Valley, and Hurst

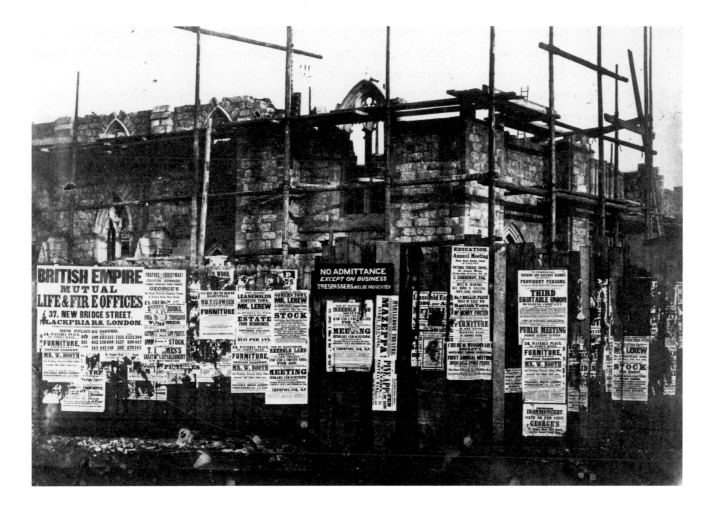

Fig. 8. Roger Fenton, *Billboards and Scaffolding, Saint Mark's Church, Albert Road,* 1852. Salted paper print from paper negative, 14.4 x 20.5 cm (5 ¹¹⁄₁₆ x 8 ¹⁄₁₆ in.). From the Paul Jeuffrain album, p. 22. Société Française de Photographie, Paris

new society. But an even greater challenge, as everyone knew, was posed by Talbot's rigorous pursuit of any infringements on his patent on the calotype. Hunt's communications with Talbot in the spring of 1852 became acrimonious. However, Sir Charles Eastlake—president of the Royal Academy, director of the National Gallery, and a member of the Society of Arts—stepped in and brokered an agreement.[52] In July, at Talbot's request, Eastlake and the noted astronomer Lord Rosse (William Parsons), "the acknowledged heads of the artistic and scientific world," petitioned Talbot to relax his patent so that the art he had "invented [might] flourish as much as possible."[53] At the first meeting of the Photographic Society several months later, on January 20, 1853, Eastlake was elected president (after Talbot declined the honor) and Fenton, in recognition of his critical work on behalf of the organization, honorary secretary. (For further discussion of Fenton's

involvement with the Photographic Society, see "The Exertions of Mr. Fenton" by Pam Roberts in this volume.)

Concurrently, Fenton was perfecting his own photography. While in Paris in October 1851 he had made collodion negatives and experimented with Le Gray's waxed paper process, but his first dated photographs are from February 18, 1852.[54] These salt prints from waxed paper negatives include views near his home in London (figs. 8, 20)—Regent's Park, Albert Road, Saint Mark's Church—and five rather stiff, hesitant portraits, perhaps including ones of his wife or a sister-in-law and a daughter, posed against simple drop cloths, as well as a self-portrait. In photographing the Zoological Gardens near his home in London later that summer, he used a stereoscopic camera that took two successive photographs from viewpoints several inches apart, which, when looked at in Wheatstone's reflecting stereoscope viewer, gave

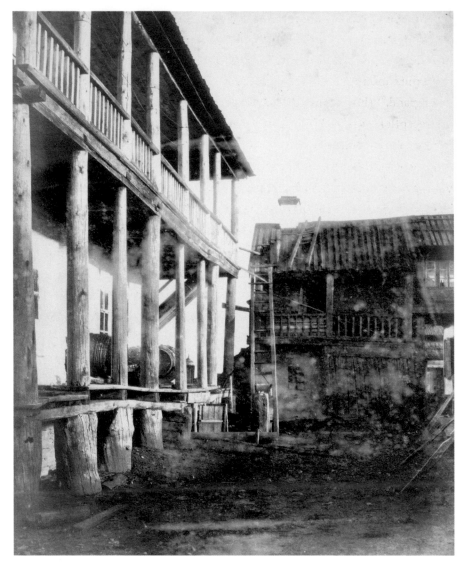

Fig. 9. Roger Fenton, *A Posthouse, Kiev*, 1852. Salted paper print, 36 x 28 cm (14⅛ x 11 in.). Collection Centre Canadien d'Architecture / Canadian Centre for Architecture, Montréal, PH1985.0693

the illusion of three-dimensional depth. Significantly, Fenton almost immediately circulated and published his photographs. He sent examples of his first dated works to a colleague in France, Paul Jeuffrain, and the following year sent photographs to Lacan in Paris, who exhibited them in his home.[55] In October and November of 1852, when he had been photographing for only a year, Fenton published six works in *The Photographic Album*, a two-part portfolio

issued by the London publisher David Bogue. Made in Gloucester and Cheltenham, they were of picturesque sites in the region and included *Tewkesbury Abbey*, *The Plough Inn at Prestbury*, and *The Village Stocks*. The press roundly criticized his efforts. Fenton had "much yet to learn," the *Illustrated London News* opined, while the *Athenaeum* said the "indistinctness of the objects in the foreground" in one print gave them the appearance of "being mildewed" and the *Art-Journal* lamented that Fenton had "aimed only at making the best of bad subjects" rather than selecting ones of "large—of national interest."[56]

These criticisms fell on deaf ears, however, for Fenton had already embarked on a bold photographic expedition. On September 24, 1852, he reached Kiev, arriving there a week after his friend Charles Blacker Vignoles (1793–1875), an engineer, to photograph the suspension bridge Vignoles was building over the Dnieper River for Czar Nicholas I. From the time work began on the bridge in 1848, the artist John Cooke Bourne had been employed to make sketches for the often-absent engineer and his demanding patron. Bourne also learned how to make daguerreotypes and calotypes—no doubt encouraged by Vignoles, an amateur photographer who understood the valuable role photography could play in the project.[57] Yet as the bridge neared completion, Vignoles clearly felt the need for more extensive photographic documentation of it. While the challenges Fenton encountered in making the photographs did not rival those Vignoles faced in constructing the bridge itself, they were formidable, especially for such a novice. With no prior experience in orchestrating such a complex undertaking or in making waxed paper negatives under adverse conditions, Fenton had to transport quantities of photographic equipment and chemicals and at least two cameras, including a large one used to make stereo views, over the hundreds of miles that separated Russia from England, and he had to cope with the dim light and often bitter cold of a Russian autumn.[58] That he was able to make any photographs at all is a testament to his perseverance and drive, coupled with what must have been fastidious planning; that he did so successfully is an indication of the remarkable progress he had made in only a few months, especially the lessons he had learned from using a stereo camera.[59]

The photographs Fenton made in Kiev, and later in Moscow and elsewhere, demonstrate a new level of competence and maturity. As their titles—among them, *Moscow, Domes of Churches in the Kremlin*; *Walls of the Kremlin, Moscow*; and *A Posthouse, Kiev* (pls. 2, 4, fig. 9)—make clear, he was now treating subjects of more than enough "national interest" and picturesque vitality to satisfy the *Art-Journal*. Far more comfortable with his cameras and more confident of his technique, Fenton now began to consider such issues as how camera vision differs from human vision and how to construct compositions of the many-colored world using only the monochromatic palette of a photographer. Displaying a newly sophisticated understanding of space, no doubt the result of his recent work with stereo photographs, he now employed dramatically receding diagonal lines to translate the illusion of three-dimensional depth onto a two-dimensional surface. Now understanding that his waxed paper negatives were not equally sensitive to all colors and that the monochromatic, matte surface of a salt print could further blur contours, he began to construct his images so that near and far objects echo each other in shape and pattern. And, now appreciating the power of empty space, he alternated voids with densely packed forms, thus energizing his compositions and giving them a sense of life. Only a few months after making the "mildewed" studies of Gloucester and Cheltenham, Fenton had come to recognize that a camera and photographic materials would not allow him to depict the world in the same way a painter does. Instead of struggling to make photography into something it was not, from this point forward he eagerly embraced it for all that it could become.

On his return to London that fall, Fenton showed some of his Russian work in the December exhibition of photographs at the Society of Arts. Comprising some four hundred photographs, the exhibition had been proposed by the book publisher and amateur photographer Joseph Cundall (1818–1875) and organized by Cundall, Fenton, and Philip Henry Delamotte (1820–1889), a photographer and illustrator. Although initially scheduled to be open for only a little more than two weeks, the show unexpectedly tapped into the public's fascination with both photography and exhibitions and because of its popularity was extended through the end of January 1853, while growing to include over eight hundred works.[60] This lesson in public taste was not lost on either the Society of Arts or the organizing photographers themselves.[61] In the months immediately thereafter, the Society of Arts circulated a smaller version of the exhibition, which included several of Fenton's photographs, to many similar societies around England. More daring was Cundall and Delamotte's opening of the Photographic Institution on New Bond Street, London, where they pre-

sented exhibitions of photographs that were for sale, with catalogues listing a price for each work. Fenton himself showed a number of photographs, including more than twenty views made in Russia, at the institution's opening exhibition in April 1853—the first commercial display of photographs in England.[62] (For further discussion of Fenton's exhibitions and their critical reception, see "A Most Enthusiastic Cultivator of His Art" by Roger Taylor in this volume.)

Cundall, Delamotte, and Fenton quickly discovered, however, that selling photographs was a tricky business. Since the early 1840s commercial portrait photographers had fulfilled the public's desire for cheap likenesses, but the sale of other kinds of photographs had been slow to catch on in Britain. By the early 1850s, however, members of the Victorian middle class, with far more disposable income than previous generations, were eager to own both reproductions of works of art and original prints. They purchased prints of all types, from cheap, crude woodcuts to more expensive engravings, etchings, and color lithographs (a newly invented, very popular medium). Hoping to tap into this burgeoning market, Delamotte and Fenton sought an audience for their work distinct from the clientele of the hack commercial portraitist. In an advertisement that appeared in the catalogue of the Photographic Institution's first exhibition, Delamotte described in detail the customers these new professional photographers envisioned for their work. They were people who wished to have portraits with "the appearance of beautiful mezzotint engravings"; artists who wanted a record of their paintings or statues or who needed depictions of live models or costume studies; engineers and architects who required records of buildings; nobility and gentry who desired depictions of country houses and of castles, ruins, or picturesque spots; and clergy who sought images of their churches or refectories.[63] To appeal to this discerning audience, the new professionals tried to make their photographs look like fine prints, mounting them on large sheets of thick paper with printed credits and plate marks. And like painters before them they adopted a hierarchy of subjects based on their perceived importance. For the Photographic Institution's 1853 exhibition, for example, Fenton priced almost all his photographs of cathedrals, churches, and monasteries significantly higher than his picturesque views of village streets or old barns.[64] Tellingly, he did not exhibit any portraits, nor did many other photographers.

While Delamotte and Fenton had defined the new audience they sought, reaching it proved more difficult. Exhibitions attracted some attention but never enough to generate substantial print sales. Arrangements made with established print dealers like Paul & Dominic Colnaghi or Thomas Agnew & Sons were more lucrative, but even these brought sporadic earnings at best. Fenton and others began to make photographs of picturesque or famous subjects on speculation, but the financial reward was meager in comparison to the expenditure. Moreover, the question of physical permanence plagued the practice. Even photographers themselves recognized that until they could vouch with greater certainty for the stability of their prints, there was little chance of selling their works at other than rock-bottom prices.

Government patronage, though, was absent and steady clients were rare. Thus, when the British Museum solicited proposals from both Fenton and Delamotte in the summer of 1853 to establish a photographic studio and record objects in the collection, it must have seemed as though an ideal patron had appeared.[65] Eager (as Fenton wrote), "to be connected with so useful an application of the photographic art" that would demonstrate how photography could help the museum catalogue, classify, and disseminate information about its burgeoning collection and prove photography's usefulness to the other arts, both men submitted bids.[66] Reflecting his grandfather's business acumen and the thoroughness and diligence of a man who had traveled to Russia to make photographs, Fenton's detailed proposal listed all the equipment, including various cameras, lenses, and darkroom materials, that would be necessary to photograph objects of varying size and texture. He even gave extensive instructions for the construction of a photographic studio on the roof of the museum, specifying the size of the building and describing blinds that could be employed to control the light.[67] Delamotte's brief letter, perhaps because of his own poor business skills, paled in comparison.[68] In October, after receiving a recommendation from Wheatstone, who described Fenton as "a good artist . . . very skillful . . . persevering and pain-staking, and at the same time expeditious," the trustees asked Fenton to perform some trials and spend up to 180 pounds on equipment, making him the first photographer to the British Museum and conferring institutional approbation on his new career.[69]

Fenton's work for the British Museum began in earnest in February 1854. While it may not have provided aesthetic rewards, it was technically and logistically challenging and once again put his organizational skills, as well

as willingness to adapt, to good use. For several months, dozens of rare Assyrian tablets—heavy, awkward, and fragile—were brought to the rooftop studio to be photographed, along with other recent acquisitions. With few precedents to follow, Fenton had to devise the best way to illuminate the objects, a difficult matter in the days before artificial light. It often entailed taking them out of the studio to the adjacent roof, where, to diminish the harsh contrasts caused by direct sunlight, he devised ingenious solutions, placing his camera in a box with curtains at the front that acted like a large lens hood, for example, and in later years even dusting sculptures with powder.[70] To avoid distortions he used five different cameras.[71] The complex undertaking was too much for one person; in his first year Fenton's business grew to include several assistants, employed at his own expense, who most likely helped him arrange and light the objects and prepared and developed his wet collodion negatives. The number of salt prints they made was astounding—more than two thousand in 1854 alone, and by May 1856 over eight thousand.[72] Although Fenton netted more than 350 pounds from this endeavor in the first year, he must have needed all his managerial skills to complete the work in a timely and profitable manner.[73] The trustees, fully satisfied with his work, late in 1854 directed that an additional one thousand pounds be allocated for continued photography of the museum's holdings.[74]

Another, ultimately far more important official recognition came to Fenton in 1854. On January 3 of that year his colleagues at the Photographic Society selected Eastlake and Fenton, the members most able to explain "the *artistic* and the *practical* sides of the art," to be the principal escorts for Queen Victoria and Prince Albert as they viewed the society's first exhibition.[75] During their lengthy tour, the royal couple, who had agreed to become patrons of the society the previous summer, expressed far more interest in the more than eight hundred works on exhibit "than is ordinarily displayed on the occasion of a royal visit."[76] They noted with "extreme satisfaction . . . the wonderful advance" photography had made in the last year and paid particular attention to Fenton's work, purchasing several of his photographs—including all of the more than twenty-five Russian views he exhibited.[77] "Mr. Fenton," the queen wrote later that day in her journal, "explained everything & there were many beautiful photographs done by him."[78]

Fenton's subsequent relationship with the royal family had a profound impact on his career. Both Queen Victoria and Prince Albert took a great

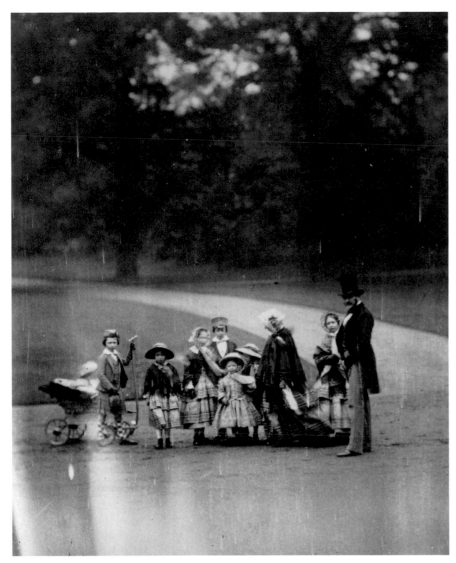

Fig. 10. Roger Fenton, *The Queen, the Prince, and Eight Royal Children in Buckingham Palace Garden, May 22, 1854.* Albumen silver print, 11.9 x 10 cm (4¹¹⁄₁₆ x 3¹⁵⁄₁₆ in.). The Royal Collection © 2004, Her Majesty Queen Elizabeth II, RPC.03/0002/91

and taught the young men photography. Also at that time Albert initiated an ambitious and innovative program to have the queen's entire art collection recorded photographically, and together Victoria and Albert began to build what would become a large and important collection of photographs.[79] Both personally and professionally, Fenton clearly impressed them more than any other photographer they had previously encountered, perhaps because he was an educated artist and from the upper levels of society. He was granted exceptional access to the royal family and invited to photograph them on many occasions. On January 23 and 25, February 1 and 10, April 10, five times in May, and several other times during 1854, Fenton appeared at Buckingham Palace or Windsor Castle to take pictures. Because his portraits were never intended to be seen by the public at large but were solely for the queen's own enjoyment, he was allowed to witness and record the daily life of the family, often in very private moments away from the trappings of the court and the constraints of its highly regimented life (see "Mr. Fenton Explained Everything" by Roger Taylor in this volume). Accustomed to wealth and privilege, Fenton was not intimidated by either his subjects or their surroundings and took full advantage of the exceptional opportunities given him, for example photographing the royal children in the costumes they had worn for a private family play, or the entire family—the queen, the prince, and their eight children—on the grounds of Buckingham Palace (fig. 10). Unaccompanied by attendants and without official accoutrements, they all wear simple day dress and look like just another upper-class family out for a Sunday stroll. Fenton's intensely personal records of an otherwise excessively public family obviously had special meaning for both their maker and their subjects, who provided him with even greater opportunities and an even more privileged vantage point in the months to come.

interest in advances in science and technology, and photography genuinely intrigued them. With his keen intellectual curiosity, Prince Albert wanted to understand all aspects of the medium: its science, practical applications, and artistic potential. In the early 1850s the royal couple's staff included Dr. Ernst Becker, librarian to Prince Albert and assistant tutor to the princes, who was an amateur photographer and member of the Photographic Society

1855

And who loves war for war's own sake / Is fool, or crazed, or worse; . . .

— Alfred, Lord Tennyson, 1882[80]

On Saturday, March 11, 1854, Queen Victoria, Prince Albert, and other members of the royal family boarded their yacht, *The Fairy,* and sailed through the First Division of the Baltic Fleet to salute the departure of the

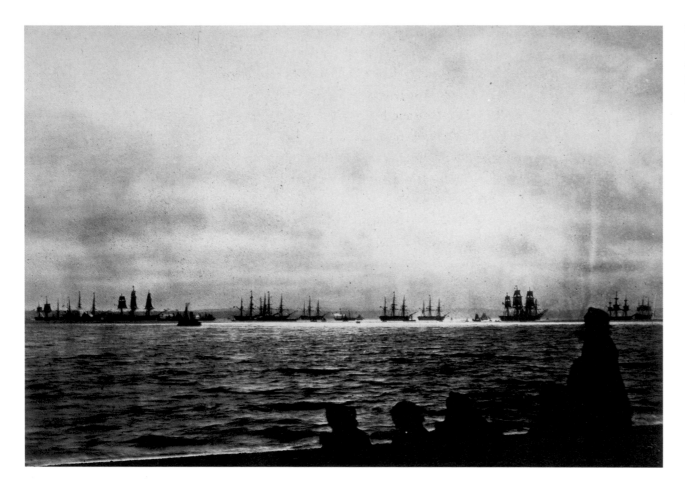

Fig. 11. Roger Fenton, *"The Fairy" Steaming through the Fleet, March 11, 1854.* Albumen silver print, 14.6 x 20.5 cm (5¾ x 8 1/16 in.). The Royal Collection © 2004, Her Majesty Queen Elizabeth II, RPC.03/0002/15

military forces for the impending war with Russia. As *The Fairy* glided out of Portsmouth harbor and passed each ship in turn—all with flags flying, yards manned, sailors on every inch of deck and still more hanging from the rigging—loud cheers rang out both from spectators lining the shores and from the men onboard because "Her Majesty [was] literally leading them out to sea."[81] When *The Fairy* reached the head of the fleet, guns on all the ships blazed in a deafening roar; then one by one the ships sailed past the queen to begin their long journey. Finally, as *The Fairy* headed off to Osborne, the royal residence on the Isle of Wight, a few sailors shimmied to the very tops of two of the masts of the *Duke of Wellington*, the flagship of Vice Admiral Sir Charles Napier and the last ship in the line, and waved so enthusiastically that they caught the queen's attention. Waving her handkerchief, she returned the cheer, as did the prince. Even as

the spectacle drew to a close, she was unable to tear her eyes away from the ships that towered so "majestically above the blue waters," she later recorded in her diary. "One gazed & gazed," the queen wrote, "till the noble ships could scarcely be discerned on the horizon."[82]

Roger Fenton also witnessed this grand display. Like his patron he was entranced by the spectacle and touched by its poignancy, and he too recorded the day, in an evocative photograph of a woman and children (possibly his own family) peering intently out to sea (fig. 11). For queen and commoner alike, rapt awe at the spectacle just witnessed was no doubt tinged with anxiety over the fate of the vessels, the sailors, and the nation. This day, portentous for both the queen and her photographer, would significantly affect the future course of their lives. In the days and weeks to come, England's alliance with France and Turkey against Russia would inexorably draw it deeper into a war that, while supposedly about "truth, integrity, honour,"[83] came to exemplify anything but those noble ideals. Eager to assert its power on the European stage, Russia had moved into Moldavia and Wallachia, principalities on the Danube then under Turkish control, and was threatening to make further incursions into the weakening Ottoman Empire. Allying themselves with the Ottoman sultan, England and France decided to teach the czar a lesson by capturing Russia's Black Sea naval base at Sebastopol, in the Crimea. Thus began a long, deadly siege, the centerpiece of one of the most disorganized and costly conflicts in all of English history. After forty years of relative peace, England was ill equipped to fight. Few commanders were younger than sixty and even fewer had actual field experience; a generation of officers had purchased their commissions; and neither they nor their troops had had much military training. Perhaps even more surprising, and ultimately devastating, was the woeful inadequacy of the infrastructure put in place to feed, clothe, and equip the troops once they arrived at the site of the war. The suffering of the common soldiers was horrific. The appalling casualties of battle were compounded, especially during the winter of 1854–55, by bitter cold, scant clothing and housing, nonexistent sanitary conveniences, and grossly inadequate nursing and hospital facilities. Troops had to scavenge fuel and provisions and cook their own meals. With so many people crowded into unsanitary living conditions, disease, especially cholera, became rampant. The soldiers were "overworked, badly fed with no fuel to cook with, only one blanket, many [with] no shoes," the head of the army medical unit in Constantinople, Dr. John Hall, abjectly recorded in his diary, and "dying by hundreds."[84] The agony of their families at home was made all the more excruciating by daily reports dispatched to the *Times* by William Howard Russell, who branded the conduct of both the English and the French leaders "recklessness verging on insanity."[85]

Like others, the queen and prince were genuinely appalled by these reports, but they were constitutional monarchs and it was not their role to question, much less criticize, the military's and the prime minister's handling of the war. They could, though, show concern for their troops in other ways. Queen Victoria regularly visited the hospitals filled with wounded soldiers sent back from the war and, despite feeling that her inadequate words "all stuck in my throat," endeavored to comfort the men.[86] She donated funds to provide artificial limbs for amputees and established the Victoria Cross for

acts of heroism and bravery, presenting it for the first time not to an officer but to an Irish mate on the *Hecla*, Charles Lucas. She also forged a close friendship with Florence Nightingale, who arrived in the Crimea in November 1854 and whose letters to the queen kept her abreast of the often dreadful conditions she and her nursing staff encountered. Victoria used her influence to have the commander in chief, Lord Raglan, appoint Nightingale sole supervisor of the nursing staff for the war.[87] When one of the queen's private letters expressing great worry about the soldiers' welfare and morale was published—an astonishing breach of protocol at the time—she did not criticize the disclosure but let her words stand as condemnation of the appalling debacle.[88]

Victoria and Albert also supported Fenton's photographic expedition to the Crimea in 1855. Since the inception of the war there had been speculation in the photographic press on whether the military authorities would appoint an official photographer, not just to record events but to describe the ports, fortresses, and disposition of fleets and even to copy maps and other important documents.[89] At the beginning of the conflict, in March 1854, a suggestion to the Photographic Society that it propose names of photographers to the military authorities elicited "a shower of letters," all addressed to Fenton as secretary of the organization, from hopeful volunteers who were no doubt motivated by both patriotism and the expectation that fame would accompany this appointment.[90] In April Captain Scott took an amateur photographer, Gilbert Elliott, on board his ship, the *Hecla*, to determine whether "instantaneous" photographs of sufficient clarity could be taken of the shoreline and fortifications from a moving ship; in May Fenton, not to be outdone, made photographs in Portsmouth of the fleet at anchor and under sail.[91] Soon, too, the *Times* began to print Russell's dispatches, and the *Illustrated London News* began to carry wood engravings copied from photographs made by James Robertson in Constantinople.[92] War as theater, as "spectator sport," had begun.[93]

We do not know who initiated Fenton's trip to the Crimea. Many scholars have suggested that the prince himself proposed it.[94] His deep interest in photography and understanding of its potential make this possible, but they do not tell us what his objective might have been. Was he motivated by sheer scholarly interest (possibly)? By a desire to produce propaganda (unlikely for a discreet, foreign-born prince) and if so, to benefit pro- or anti-war factions? Others, noting that Prime Minister Aberdeen's position was weakening in late 1854 and early 1855 as the debacle of the war grew ever worse and public morale plummeted, have theorized that he asked the Manchester printseller Thomas Agnew to send someone to the region to supply photographs that could refute the assertions of the liberal press.[95] This seems speculative at best, though, for the intense criticism of Aberdeen's administration did not begin in earnest until December 1854 and January 1855, when the Crimean winter caused extreme suffering; and we know that Fenton, in his usual organized manner, had begun preparing for the arduous journey a number of months before his February 1855 departure.[96] In the fall of 1854 he purchased a wine merchant's van and outfitted it as a traveling darkroom. He even traveled to Rievaulx Abbey and elsewhere to test it out, and subsequently made modifications.[97] We know for certain that Fenton was furnished with letters of introduction from Prince Albert; that Agnew financed the expedition; and that Fenton's passage on the *Hecla* was provided by the Duke of Newcastle, secretary of state for war, and Sir Samuel Morton Peto, a Manchester railway entrepreneur.[98] We can surmise, because both Agnew and Peto were from Manchester, that they knew Fenton, either personally or professionally. And since Agnew was not only a print seller but a publisher, perhaps eager to exploit the commercial potential of the public's interest in the conflict, we can also conjecture that he was the instigator of the mission. But what we indisputably have are the photographs themselves, as well as letters Fenton wrote to his family and to Agnew on his journey in 1855, all of which are rich with explicit and implicit information.

The tone of the letters is noteworthy. Although they were edited when published in 1954 and their more personal ruminations deleted, Fenton's sense of humor and his intrepid spirit are readily apparent.[99] Yet he also assumed the voice of an almost jaunty world traveler witnessing a spectacle that alternately amazed and amused him, that complicated but never confounded his efforts, and that, while it provoked periods of sadness, never aroused deep moral indignation. He described, for example, "the constant succession of startling novelties" he encountered within a few days of his arrival at Balaklava on March 8, 1855: the densely packed harbor crowded with more than 150 ships, and the dazzling mix of people and animals. "The emptying of Noah's Ark could not have been half so queer a sight," he wrote to his wife, for there was "an incessant stream of officers and men in all kinds of costumes, on foot and mounted on every variety of charger; Zouaves were

loitering about with baggy breeches, Turks with baggier."[100] He detailed his somewhat comical labors to get his van and thirty-six crates of materials and supplies off the *Hecla* and his persistent and ingenious efforts to outfit himself properly with adequate horses, saddle, and bridle. Even though he wrote of seeing dead bodies, he casually remarked that "life seems to be squandered here like everything else." Especially during the first few months, the war remained somewhat distant, "a picture of dreamy repose, which was only heightened by the contrast of a dashing Zouave clad in a garb of many colors."[101] Fenton's experience in the Crimea was far more positive than most in part because he did not arrive until the spring, when the devastating winter was over and some improvements had been made, but mostly because the letters of introduction he carried from Prince Albert guaranteed him exceptional access and privilege. While the journalist Russell was barely tolerated, everywhere Fenton turned he received "the assurance of assistance in every possible way" from the highest-ranking officers in the region, including Lord Raglan. The war Fenton experienced was one where officers had dinner parties with elaborate multicourse meals, wine, champagne, cognac, and cigars, and entertained visiting ladies; where he sat at a dinner "on Lord Raglan's right," near Lady George Paget, the "*belle* of the Crimea"; and where he quickly became a celebrity.[102] His hut was "the rendezvous of all the Colonels and Captains in the army," Fenton remarked to Agnew, "everybody drops in every day."[103]

Aided by two assistants, Marcus Sparling (a photographer, member of the Photographic Society, and former corporal in the Fourth Light Dragoons) and a handyman identified only as William, Fenton began to photograph within a few days of landing at Balaklava. Using a variety of cameras—he had brought five, including one specifically for portraits—he worked diligently for three months, making more than 350 negatives. Yet what he did not photograph is almost as revealing as what he did. In one of his early letters home he recounted that when in his van preparing or developing his wet collodion negatives he was repeatedly interrupted by soldiers, who, reading the words "Photographic Van" painted on its side, asked to have their pictures taken "to send home." But Fenton had no intention of becoming a hack portraitist of "all comers" who should happen to ask, even though he "might make a regular gold digging," as he told Agnew.[104] Nor did he have any interest in recording recent improvements that made life more bearable and

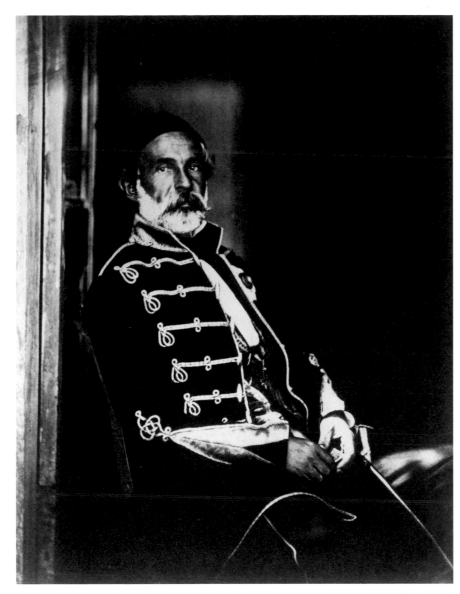

Fig. 12. Roger Fenton, *Omar Pasha*, 1855. Salted paper print, 17.9 x 13.4 cm (7⅟₁₆ x 5¼ in.). Gilman Paper Company Collection, New York, PH78.449

so.[105] He did not even record the extensive fortifications constructed by the allies, as the photographers James Robertson and Felice Beato did after his departure. For the purpose of his trip was not to produce propaganda, not to provide images that could be used as evidence either in support of or against the war itself; it was to create a commercially viable portfolio of photographs. The portfolio's high price—more than sixty pounds—makes clear that it was aimed at the upper levels of British society. This audience, many of whom had lost family and friends in the conflict, did not want to see photographs of death, suffering, chaos, and ineptitude, or images that would challenge their closely held belief in the necessity and correctness of the conflict. They wanted pictures to support the myth that their loved ones had died not ignominiously or in vain but with dignity, and in a noble cause.

To this end, Fenton tried to photograph the leading figures of all the allied armies. He depicted the commander of each: Lord Raglan—about whom "the soldiers have nothing but good words to say," he told Agnew; his French counterpart, Field Marshal Jean-Jacques Pélissier; and General Omar Pasha (fig. 12).[106] British officers he portrayed included General Sir James Scarlett, who had earlier commanded the heavy cavalry in the Battle of Balaklava; Lord George Paget, colonel of the Fourth Light Dragoons, who was in command of his regiment when it charged with the Light Brigade at Balaklava in October 1854; and General Sir John Lysaght Pennefather, who had led the Fourth Division at Inkerman in November, valiantly battling thirty-five thousand Russians with a force one-tenth the size. (Fenton was so intent on securing likenesses of all the key participants that he even made some after his return to England and incorporated them into his portfolio, *Photographic Pictures of the Seat of War in the Crimea*, with no explanation that they were later additions.)[107] He photographed notable officers such as Captain Adolphus Brown, Fifth Dragoon Guards, whose squadrons were hit hard by cholera, and Cornet John Wilkin of the Eleventh Hussars, who survived the charge of the Light Brigade (fig. 74). He also made "essays of camp life," which show officers, often attended by aides and surrounded by their regiments, relaxing near their tents (pl. 16). And he made studies of the picturesque and exotic individuals who populated this "Noah's Ark": the Highlanders in their colorful garb, the Grenadier Guards with a Nubian servant, a French *cantinière*, Russian children, the Zouaves, Croats (pl. 17), and Turkish soldiers.

viable in Balaklava in the spring of 1855, such as the newly built roads that he described in his letters. And, while battle scenes were beyond the technical capabilities of photography at the time, he also never violated Victorian taste by photographing the battle's aftermath, the dead bodies, or the chaos and clutter of the trenches, although he had plenty of opportunities to do

In 1861 he participated in two exhibitions but by August had stopped attending meetings of the Photographic Society Council. In December of that year, the family mill at Hooley Bridge, which had helped support his comfortable lifestyle, closed—a victim both of the American Civil War, which prevented cotton from reaching England, and of a family feud. Providing "the best illustration of Dickens' 'Bleak House,'" as one journalist wrote many years later, it never reopened, "swallowed up by that insatiable monster the law."[181] The death of Prince Albert on December 14, 1861, marked the end not only of the "new starting point" the prince had envisioned for English society, technology, and art but also of the new starting point Fenton had envisioned for photography.

In October 1862 Fenton announced his retirement from the profession of photography. To remove "all that might be a temptation to revert to past occupations," he sold all of his equipment and negatives.[182] Although the negatives were described as badly blistered, Francis Frith bought many of them and for the next several years made prints from them that were competent but cold and mechanical.[183] Fenton returned to the law and in 1863 was named counsel for the Northern Circuit, where he served as barrister for the courts in Manchester, Salford, and York counties.[184] After an illness of only six days he died at his home, Mount Grace, in Potter's Bar, north of London, on August 9, 1869, at the age of fifty.[185]

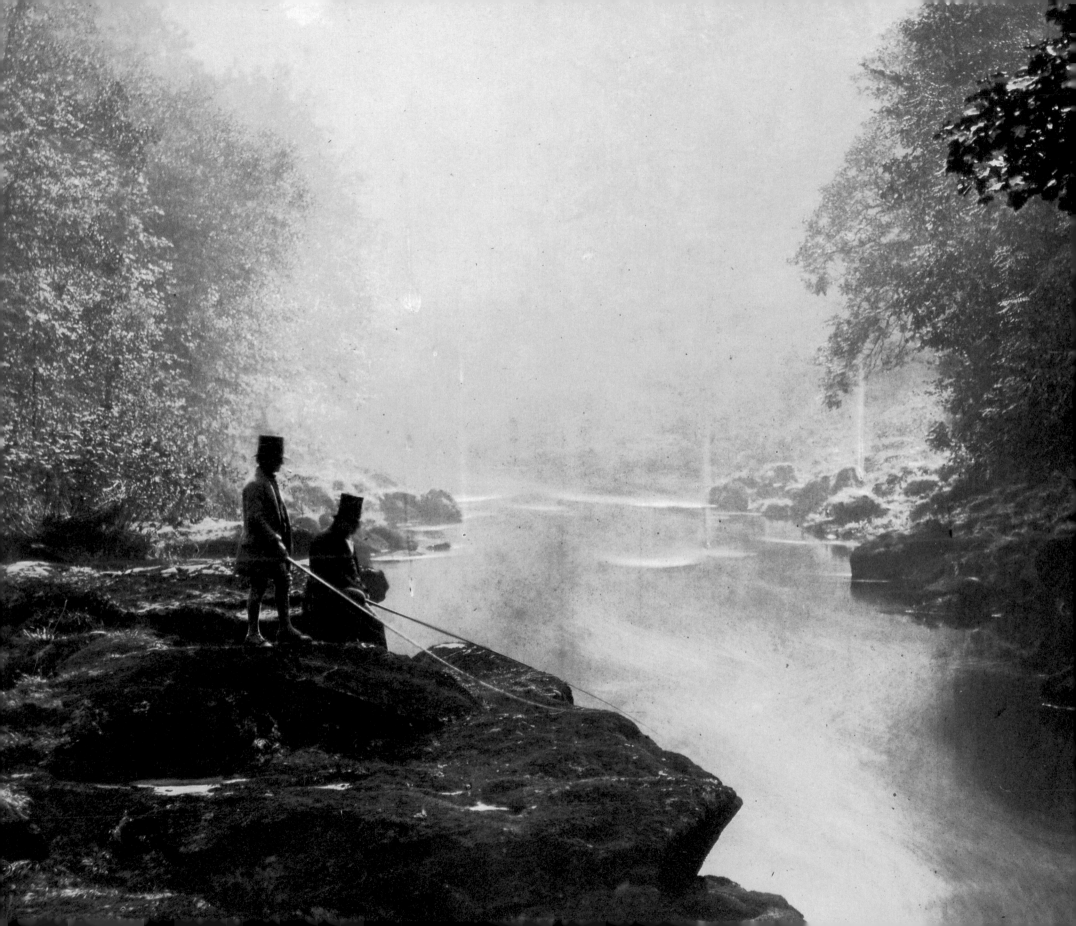

"On Nature's Invitation Do I Come": Roger Fenton's Landscapes

MALCOLM DANIEL

It is all one garden.—William Howitt, 1840[1]

That the English have a unique relationship with their land is evident to anyone who has walked the countryside. Footpaths worn into the terrain since ancient times were plotted on maps and detailed in walking guides long ago. Traversing public and private lands alike, they are guaranteed as public-access pathways by law and custom. "Every inch of English ground," wrote William Howitt in 1840, "is sanctified by noble deeds, and intellectual renown."[2] In America the great landscape photographers of the nineteenth century recorded a virgin landscape of immense proportion, a new Eden in Yosemite and a new Wilderness in the vast deserts of the Southwest. By contrast, every field, forest, lake, and moor in England had been managed, if not entirely transformed, by generation upon generation for farming, hunting and fishing, urban and industrial expansion, and even aesthetic delight. Still today, roads follow the course of those built by the Romans; fields are enclosed by seemingly endless stone walls built centuries ago or by hedgerows just as old; tracts of land continue to be assembled into vast estates and, often, parceled out once more; woods and streams are maintained as they have been since time immemorial by those who inherited or purchased the right to hunt or fish in them. In art and poetry, the very notions of the sublime and the picturesque are practically English inventions,[3] born, it would seem, from an innate understanding of the landscape as a player upon the emotions, a mirror of the soul, a stimulus to the intellect, and a delight to the eye.

It is not surprising that Roger Fenton, who excelled in every other genre of photography, turned his talent and his lens toward the landscape with equal success. Earlier in the nineteenth century, as the best French painters were tackling literary and historical themes, the greatest British artists took the observable world as their subject—the shape of the hills, the course of a stream, the rhythms of rural life, the changing effects of weather, the mutability of light and atmosphere.[4] Any British photographer seeking, as Fenton so explicitly did, to raise his craft to the level of art would have understood the position that landscape held in the hierarchy of artistic genres. No greater compliment could be paid than that bestowed on Fenton by the *Journal of the Photographic Society* in 1858: "He seems to be to photography what Turner was to painting—our greatest landscape photographer."[5]

It was partly the very lack of purpose aside from expression and visual delight, that set landscape so squarely in the artistic realm. This applies even to Fenton's first extended series of photographs, made in Russia in 1852. A few of his views along the banks of the Dnieper (pl. 7), for instance, in which distant architecture plays the most minor of roles, appear to be purely artistic essays. These contrast with the informative but relatively uninteresting views of the bridge construction that were the raison d'être for his trip to Russia[6] and also with the photographs of onion-domed churches, Kremlin walls, and town views of Kiev, which would have found a natural audience and marketability among armchair travelers (pls. 2–6).

Fenton, who seemed intent on exploring every aspect of the new medium's potential, pursued landscape throughout his career, without limiting

Opposite: Fig. 19. Roger Fenton, *Wharfe and Pool, Below the Strid* (detail), 1854; see pl. 13

himself to a single place or type of picture. His work in this genre was principally carried out in half a dozen major campaigns: in 1852 in and around Gloucestershire and South Wales, including Tewkesbury, Cheltenham, Tintern, and the Usk River valley;[7] in 1854 in Yorkshire, including the countryside near the ruined abbeys of Rievaulx, Fountains, and Bolton, particularly along the Wharfe River; in 1856 in northern England and Scotland during a trip to Balmoral, including views on the Dee, Feugh, and Clunie; in 1857 in North Wales, including the valleys of the Conway, Llugwy, Lledr, and Machno; in 1859 along the Ribble and Hodder rivers, near Stonyhurst in Lancashire; and in 1860 in the Lake District. Landscapes also constitute a small portion of campaigns the main purpose of which lay elsewhere: river scenes in Russia in the autumn of 1852; battlefield, camp, and harbor views in the Crimea in 1855; and contextual views of stately homes and castles such as Harewood, Wollaton, and Windsor.

The Great Exhibition of the Works of Industry of All Nations—the 1851 world's fair held in the Crystal Palace, London—provided the impetus for Fenton to take up the camera, as it did for numerous other British photographers. Its exhibition of French photographs, in particular, showed what paper photography was capable of when unencumbered by patent restrictions and practiced by talented and ambitious artists. In October of that year, Fenton traveled to Paris and visited the meeting rooms, gallery, and darkrooms of the Société Héliographique; tried his hand at collodion-on-glass negatives with the society's president, Baron Benito de Montfort; met with Gustave Le Gray and examined the several hundred photographs he and Auguste Mestral had just produced in the Loire Valley, Dordogne, and Auvergne; and learned the waxed-paper-negative process, a French variation on William Henry Fox Talbot's calotype.[8] Thus, as he set out to make his first photographs in early 1852, Fenton's technical formation (as, in part, his aesthetic formation as a painter) was French. His earliest pictures look to French examples at least as much as to English, few of which he would have had the opportunity to see. But he was quick to apply his newly learned skills to English subjects.

As with so many gentleman amateur photographers, Fenton began with what was closest at hand. His earliest extant firmly dated photographs, preserved in an album assembled by the French photographer Paul Jeuffrain and now in the collection of the Société Française de Photographie, Paris, include two views of Regent's Park, just steps from his Albert Terrace home,

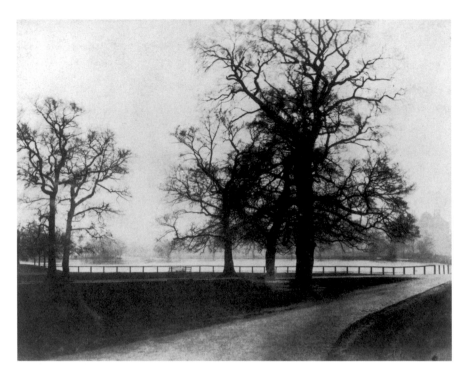

Fig. 20. Roger Fenton, *Regent's Park*, February 18, 1852. Salted paper print from paper negative, 16 x 20 cm (6⁵⁄₁₆ x 7⁷⁄₈ in.). From the Paul Jeuffrain album, p. 25. Société Française de Photographie, Paris

taken on Wednesday, February 18, 1852. As first trials they are extraordinary, using to fine advantage the tendency of paper negatives and salted paper prints to exaggerate contrasts of light and dark and to dissolve details in a fibrous web of photographic tone.[9] Although modest in scale (roughly 6½ x 8½ inches, closer to the size of Talbot's prints than Le Gray's), both are sophisticated in composition and admirable in technique. One is a view down a dark, tree-lined expanse of water, with a white suspension bridge reaching straight across the picture from edge to edge. In the other (fig. 20), a light patch of water stretches across the picture, much as the footbridge does in the first, and the bare branches of trees, silhouetted against the sky, spread out even beyond the picture's top edge.

Soon Fenton was searching farther afield for worthy subjects. Perhaps looking at French models to chart a parallel English course for his own work, he found a perfect counterpart to the Forest of Fontainebleau, south of Paris, where as early as 1849 his friend Le Gray had made some of his most compelling landscapes. The Burnham Beeches, an ancient stand of pollarded trees celebrated by artists and poets, lay northwest of Windsor, within easy reach of London. Although Fenton exhibited as many as a half-dozen different pictures entitled *Burnham Beeches* between 1853 and 1855, none can now be identified with certainty.[10]

Fenton's photographs of 1852–53 rarely exceeded 7 x 9 inches, and many—if not most—may have been made for viewing in a Wheatstone reflecting stereoscope. Designed by Charles Wheatstone in 1833 (i.e., even before photography), this device employed two nearly identical views made from slightly different positions in order to simulate binocular vision. A few of Fenton's photographs in the Regent's Park zoo and many of his Russian scenes were certainly intended to be viewed stereoscopically.[11] When they are, these early pictures shed their modest scale and take on a kind of virtual reality as the device blocks out all references to space and scale except those in the picture itself. The same powerful illusion of depth and three-dimensionality was later achieved with the smaller, classic stereoscopic cards, each of their paired images barely three inches square, meant for viewing in the handheld stereoscope first designed by Sir David Brewster. Thus, it is not surprising that Fenton would return to stereoscopy in the late 1850s, when it had reached the level of a fad, with contributions to the *Stereoscopic Magazine* and independently issued series on North Wales and Stonyhurst. Yet, despite the appeal of the viewing experience and the satisfaction that photographers must have felt at combining two remarkable new optical systems (photography and stereoscopy), the act of viewing photographs in a stereoscope effectively moved them from the realm of art into that of the optical toy or parlor entertainment. If Fenton intended to advocate a place for photographs alongside watercolors, prints, and paintings, his works would have to hold their own on the salon walls, and that is what he set out to do.

YORKSHIRE, 1854

It is just the sort of valley where one could live and die in peace with all men; thanking God from the beginning to the end of the chapter, that he made so beautiful a world for his dear creatures. The poet, the artist, the searcher-general after the picturesque could not hope for richer enjoyment than that which these woods and landscapes afford.
— *The Scenery of the Wharf*, 1855[12]

With his series of photographs made in Yorkshire in 1854, Fenton rose to a new level of ambition. Perhaps the relatively mundane (but lucrative) task of photographing objects at the British Museum, which he began in February of that year, gave Fenton the means, experience, and confidence to try working in the field with glass negatives and to employ a significantly larger camera than he had previously used when traveling. His work at the British Museum may also have instilled in him a new sense of professionalism that compelled him to leave behind the intimate scale, calotype negatives, and quaint subjects (in his words, "the peaceful village; the unassuming church")[13] favored by amateur photographers and move to the ambitious technique and artistically complex style that would characterize the remainder of his career.

Fenton's trip to the ruined abbeys and churches of Yorkshire was as much about landscape as about architecture. Remains such as those of the vast complexes at Rievaulx, Fountains, and Bolton were quintessential elements of picturesque Romantic landscapes, suggesting the inexorable passage of time and the power of nature to reclaim the most noble creations of humanity. Diderot expressed the idea eloquently: "The ideas ruins evoke in me are grand. Everything comes to nothing, everything perishes, everything passes, only the world remains, only time endures. . . . I walk between two eternities."[14]

Fenton was surely first drawn to Bolton Abbey by the ruins of the twelfth-century Augustinian priory nestled in a bend of the river, "one of the most delicious and paradisiacal scenes which the heart of England holds," according to a writer of the period, with "the gables and pinnacles of the Priory, appearing amongst a wilderness of trees in the open bosom of the valley."[15] But finding the surrounding scenery to be an essential element in his experience of the ruins, as well as a compelling subject in itself, he naturally integrated architectural and landscape compositions in a single series sharing a common spirit (fig. 21). Although we, as modern viewers, may make a division between landscape and architecture, for Fenton they formed a seamless continuum. One need only read the titles of his photographs to follow Fenton's footsteps and thought process down the wooded path along the river's edge: *Bolton Abbey; Bolton Abbey, Bridge on the Wharfe; Entrance to the Woods, Bolton Abbey; Valley of the Wharfe; Bend of the River; Opening in the Woods; Wharfe and Pool, Below the Strid; The Strid*. The Bolton countryside, "surpassed by that of few places for softness and beauty in the valley or grandeur and extent on the fells,"[16] was famed for its history and visual delight.

Mr. R. Fenton at the same time, and frequently from the same point of view, as those larger pictures which attracted so much attention in the Photographic Society's Exhibition. . . . I determined . . . to follow in Mr. Fenton's footsteps and examine for myself the spots he had selected for the subjects of his art."[52] Clearly, the venture relied upon Fenton's collaboration, and it is likely that the book's commentary reflects Fenton's own thoughts about the places visited (or at least those that were commonly held at the time) and thus provides as valuable a narrative as one might hope for, short of the artist's own words. Most of the descriptions accompanying the stereographs apply equally to their large-format cousins.

The old bridges of the area, where the time-honored tracks of man and nature cross, were among Fenton's most frequent subjects: not only the Pont-y-Pair but also the Pont-y-Lledr and Pont-y-Pant (pl. 36), both crossing the Lledr; the double bridge on the Machno (pl. 38); the bridge atop the Ogwen, or Benglog, Falls; and the Pont-y-Garth, near Capel Curig (pl. 32). It may seem curious at first that Fenton chose not to photograph Thomas Telford's Waterloo Bridge (1816), "an elegant structure of cast-iron, with an arch upwards of one hundred feet in the span, clasping the Conway from bank to bank,"[53] or Telford's equally innovative chain suspension bridge at Conway Castle (1822–26); both were engineering landmarks and trophies of the Industrial Revolution's early days. By contrast, the humble Pont-y-Pant and Pont-y-Garth, "rude wooden bridges, resting on piers of loose stones,"[54] may seem hardly worth celebrating. But Davidson describes Telford's bridges as "great engineering works, not especially connected with Wales itself,"[55] while these unassuming, picturesque structures were regarded as physical embodiments of the Welsh character. Like the inhabitants of North Wales, who were viewed by mid-nineteenth-century writers as emblematic of a disappearing, simpler, preindustrial country life free of the ills of modern urban existence,[56] structures such as Pont-y-Pant evoked a lost time and pastoral life that Londoners could only long for. "Whilst . . . the old national spirit of the Welsh people is being gradually, and of late years increasingly absorbed, under the influence of neighbouring countries," reads the commentary accompanying Fenton's view of Pont-y-Pant in the *Stereoscopic Magazine*, "the bold and picturesque scenery amidst which this valley holds a conspicuous place, must always remain unchanged. There the unusual forms and sounds of nature still retain their hold upon the imagination."[57]

Made of local stone and timber, Pont-y-Pant (Bridge of the Hollow) is ancient, solid, and functional. It lies along the route of the Sarn-Helen, the Roman road running north-south through the area, and the spot probably traces its origins as a crossing point over the Lledr to that time.[58] "The first sight of this extraordinary structure, standing in an unexpected position, arrests the eye in a way that cannot be forgotten," wrote Davidson.[59] Five miles from Bettws alongside the route to Dolwyddelan, the bridge was easily reached even with Fenton's cumbersome equipment. In *Pont-y-Pant, on the Lledr, from Below* (pl. 36), Fenton's new van, replacing the earlier mobile darkroom left behind in the Crimea, is visible at the edge of a road that Roscoe described as having a "primeval character . . . carried forward amidst natural features the most wild and savage."[60] And indeed the rigors of travel in such terrain—and of carrying out the manipulations required for large-format wet plate photography under such conditions—ought not to be forgotten. It is not surprising, then, to find that once arrived and set up at such a spot, Fenton found several possible pictures. In addition to the photographs of the bridge itself from both upstream and downstream, each giving a good sense of the rude construction spanning the rocky torrent, he made several views from the bridge, looking down the gorge into the wide, fertile Lledr Valley (pl. 35).[61] In each, figures are present to give a sense of scale[62] and to tie the historic sites and structures to present-day experience.

Such scenes would also have provoked in Fenton's viewers a deeper, geological sense of time. Davidson repeatedly commented on the strata visible in Fenton's photographs of the rocky landscapes of Wales, and at Pont-y-Pant, despite the relatively low water at the time, he found that "the empty channel spoke of the presence, at former periods, of its active and irresistible forces."[63] To survey the landscape (or, by extension, Fenton's photographs) and imagine the volcanic eruptions that had formed the granite; the earthquakes, glaciers, and torrents that had scattered boulders like children's blocks; and the eons that had since passed—all this was a relatively new and heady experience. Only in the late eighteenth and early nineteenth centuries did modern geological theories based on observation of the natural world gradually replace a religious cosmology that had imagined the world to be a mere few thousand years old.[64] The rise of geology as a science did not negate the spiritual element of the landscape, however. By invoking the visible evidence of geological formation, Davidson surely hoped also to evoke thoughts of the sublime—of the

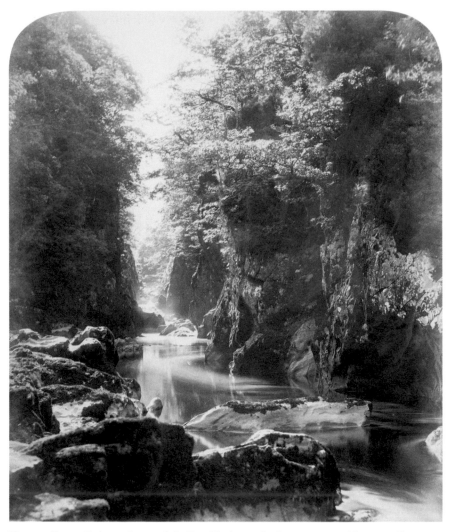

Fig. 27. Roger Fenton, *Gorge of the Foss Nevin, on the Conway*, 1857. Albumen silver print, 40.9 x 33.7 cm (16 1/16 x 13 1/4 in.). The RPS Collection at the National Museum of Photography, Film & Television, Bradford, 2003-5000/3203

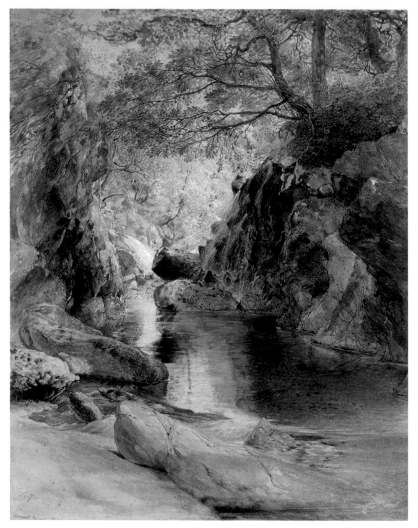

Fig. 28. Samuel Palmer (English, 1805–1881), *A Cascade in Shadow, Drawn on the Spot, near the Junction of the Machno and Conway, North Wales*, 1835 or 1836. Watercolor over graphite and brown ink, 46.4 x 37.5 cm (18 1/4 x 14 3/4 in.). Collection of Malcolm Wiener

immeasurable scale and incomparable power of nature. Likewise, one cannot know whether Fenton took any interest in, or tried to illustrate some aspect of, the geological discussions of the period, or whether—more likely—he responded to the dramatic natural environment in a more directly aesthetic way, like the youthful Wordsworth, for whom the rocks, rivers, and woods of South Wales were "An appetite: a feeling and a love, / That had no need of a remoter charm, / By thought supplied, or any interest / Unborrowed from the eye."[65]

At Foss Nevin, for instance, a spot popularly known then and now as the Fairy Glen, Davidson again wrote of nature's power.[66] But Fenton's photograph, *Gorge of the Foss Nevin, on the Conway* (fig. 27), is an irresistibly romantic composition depicting a spot frequented by artists before and after Fenton (fig. 28).[67] Unlike the roadside Pont-y-Pant, this narrow gorge is accessed with difficulty, and transporting his bulky photographic equipment must have presented Fenton with a far greater challenge than that faced by

44

watercolorists and sketchers. But the rewards were obvious. Here, as in many of his Welsh pictures, he explored the seductive potential of light and air, the "*plus* Turnerian atmospheres" praised in the *Athenaeum*.[68] Davidson, perhaps prompted by the photographer himself, pointed out that "an hour has been chosen when the sun was shining directly down the chasm, illuminating its recesses and perpetuating their outlines imperishably in the camera" and took special note of the "dreamy effect of these warm, soft, intermingled and half absorbed lights, occupying every degree in a scale of which the dark hollows form the base, and the flashing water, grey rocks, and glancing oak-leaves are the high points."[69]

Similarly, "tender gradations of sky" and "delicate *nuances* of shade"[70] were praised in Fenton's more sweeping views of Moel Siabod rising in the distance above Dolwyddelan and the Lledr Valley (pl. 37) and in his dramatic vistas of the Nant Ffrancon Valley from the Ogwen Falls (pl. 31, fig. 29). Nant Ffrancon, in particular, presented a different type of landscape from the narrow, wooded gorges of the area around Bettws; here the deep green valley and rugged, barren crags—"beauty sleeping in the lap of horror"[71]—showed the majestic scale of nature. Roscoe found the Nant Ffrancon glen "savage and romantic" and sketched for the artist a scene that combined in one place all three principal concepts of landscape aesthetics. "The view presented itself full of picturesque grandeur and beauty . . . the narrow patch of green meadow overhung by lofty mountains; the bright river meandering towards the sea" (the beautiful and picturesque); "the waters of the lakes rushing down the steeps, with the distant prospect, and the gloomy horrors of the mountains far around me"[72] (the sublime).

Again, Fenton made several images from essentially the same spot: at least three views looking down the valley (one vertical, two horizontal), two of the mountains above Llyn Ogwen, and one of the Ogwen Falls, though no stereoscopic images of this locale are known. The spot is a particularly pivotal one, where a large lake, towering mountains, precipitous falls, an ancient road, and an expansive valley pinwheel in every direction. Fenton may even have felt some frustration at trying to encompass all the elements within his frame.[73] *View from Ogwen Falls into Nant Ffrancon* (pl. 31) effectively conveys the rushing water at the viewer's feet, the sheer cliffs and plunging drop to the valley floor, and the soaring peaks in the distance; the horizontal variants (fig. 29) naturally emphasize the winding course of the Ogwen River, the

diminishing scale and aerial perspective of the receding hills, and the gradual descent of the roadway toward the valley floor.[74]

What is nowhere seen in these photographs, and with one exception nowhere in the entirety of his Welsh series, is the reality of contemporary life. Interwoven with the picturesque and sublime scenes that Fenton experienced and captured was another Wales. At the far end of the Ogwen Valley, for example, two hundred tons of slate were extracted daily from the Cae Braich y Cafn quarries and sent by rail to Port Penrhyn, just north near Bangor.[75] Roscoe, delighted by the employment that the slate trade brought to a relatively impoverished region, reported happily that "the startling blasts which occur every four or five minutes . . . carrying their sound like the voice of thunder into the deepest mountain recesses,—altogether make up a picture that seems raised by enchantment, especially when contrasted with the grim solitude around."[76] Fenton's sole view of modern Wales shows the small pier at Trefriw (pl. 39), the southernmost navigable point on the Conway,[77] where slate, hone-stones, and mineral

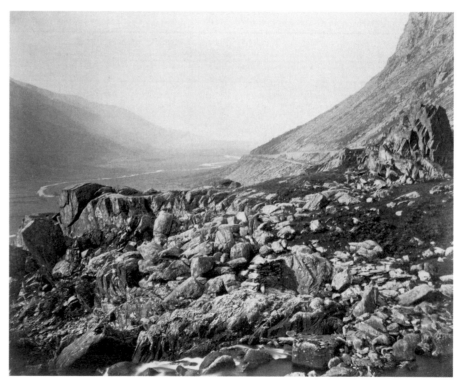

Fig. 29. Roger Fenton, *Rocks at the Head of Glyn Ffrancon*, 1857. Albumen silver print, 36 x 43.3 cm (14³⁄₁₆ x 17¹⁄₁₆ in.). The J. Paul Getty Museum, Los Angeles, 85.XM.169.19

ores were shipped out and coal and limestone brought to the region.[78] Rarely does Fenton so carefully craft a pastoral scene—here with winding river, gravel bank, rail fence, and receding mountains—and then let modern industry take up a foreground position.

If Fenton sought with his trip to Wales to reassert his reputation as the premier landscapist, he could not have hoped for more positive reviews. At the 1858 exhibition of the Photographic Society, he displayed twenty-two photographs from the Welsh series,[79] and they were universally praised: "No one can touch Fenton in landscape," wrote the *Journal of the Photographic Society*, ". . . There is such an artistic feeling about the whole of these pictures . . . that they cannot fail to strike the beholder as being something more than mere photographs."[80] The *Athenaeum* praised "Mr. Fenton's Welsh scenes, with tender, loving distances, with miles of fading and brightening light. . . . The aerial perspective in some of these scenes is delicious, because true."[81] The *Literary Gazette* found that the medium's most marked and decisive progress was being achieved in landscape photography and judged that "here the palm must be unquestionably assigned to Mr. Roger Fenton."[82] And *Photographic News* declared flatly, "Nobody will be inclined to dispute Mr. Fenton's unrivalled claim to be the best English landscape photographer. He has succeeded in giving such breadth to his landscape pictures, that one is at first almost inclined to look upon them as copies of pictures." The views of Wales, the writer hoped, were but "the foreshadowings of still greater efforts" on Fenton's part.[83]

VALLEYS OF THE RIBBLE AND THE HODDER, 1859

Of the hundreds . . . who have been to Paris, and Switzerland, and the Rhine, how few have gone up their own river a few miles, to a spot, which, were it a hundred and fifty miles away, and a "cheap trip" were advertised thither now and then, would attract thousands! —William Dobson, 1877[84]

The majority of Fenton's efforts in 1858 were directed toward architectural subjects and his series of Orientalist tableaux; his submissions to the exhibition of the Photographic Society in 1859 included only a meager selection of landscapes made along the Wye and the Dove and at the Cheddar Gorge. Again the comparison with Bedford tilted away from Fenton, with the

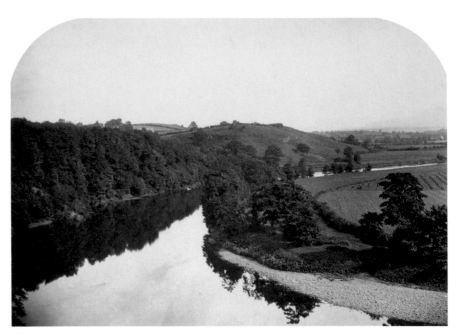

Fig. 30. Roger Fenton, *The Raid Deep, River Ribble*, 1859. Albumen silver print, 28.5 x 40 cm (11 3/16 x 15 3/4 in.). The RPS Collection at the National Museum of Photography, Film & Television, Bradford, 2003-5000/2973

Photographic News obviously disappointed by the follow-up to the spectacular Welsh views. "Fenton we have always regarded as the leading English landscape and architectural photographer," the reviewer declared. "Now, however, Bedford seems likely to take the lead. In the productions of the former we see scarcely any progress, on the contrary, rather retrogression, while in the latter gentleman's pictures . . . there is great and decided improvement." Fenton's landscapes in particular were, the critic regretfully found, "far below the average merit of his pieces."[85]

Perhaps feeling the sting of criticism or the spur of competition, he again turned his lens to the landscape in 1859, this time to a softer, more civilized, and more familiar terrain—that corner of his native Lancashire where the rivers Hodder and Calder join the river Ribble. Fenton photographed the buildings and surrounding landscape of Stonyhurst College on at least two visits, in June or July and again in late December, when the yews were covered with frost and students ice-skated on the ornamental lakes flanking the entrance drive. This Jesuit school was established in 1593 in Saint-Omer, France, as a place where well-to-do English families could send their sons

In Pursuit of Architecture

GORDON BALDWIN

For the late Valerie Lloyd, who imparted her enthusiasm for the work of Fenton,
and for the late Kelly Edey, whose architectural library remains an inspiration.

The best-known and most widely exhibited photographer of the 1850s, Roger Fenton had begun to attract the attention of the press even before the Crimean work of 1855 that made his reputation.[1] In the years that followed, the variety of his subject matter, coupled with the consistently high quality of his work, guaranteed the continuation of that interest. Fenton went on photographic expeditions in Britain in the late summer and early autumn of every year from 1852 to 1860, except for 1855, when he was in the Crimea, and each time he made both landscapes and studies of architecture—of time-wracked abbeys, weathered cathedrals, or country houses. (While reviewers of the later 1850s often thought of Fenton's ruined abbey views as landscapes[2] and distinguished them from his other architectural studies, here they will all be treated as part of the same innovative enterprise.)[3] The following winters, at exhibitions in London, he showed his trophies. From 1854 until 1861 he placed work in every annual exhibition of the Photographic Society in London as well as at other venues in London and elsewhere. Records indicate that his landscapes were sometimes mixed with his purely architectural studies, but it is unclear how much control he had over the placement of his pictures.[4] He made at least 450 images of buildings, more than of any other class of subject except the pictures made between early 1854 and 1860 to record objects in the collections of the British Museum.[5] When he was free to choose his subject, most often he photographed architecture.

Opposite: Fig. 35. Roger Fenton, *Roslin Chapel, South Porch* (detail), 1856; see pl. 26

While an intrepid voyager, Fenton blazed no trails in selecting architectural sites. Nearly invariably he went to celebrated places, the exceptions being locations to which he had ties of kinship.[6] During the first half of the nineteenth century there were numerous publications devoted to prints of ruined abbeys, cathedrals, and other noteworthy British edifices. These engravings or lithographs were usually accompanied by texts ranging in content from the historical to the descriptive and in tone from the reverent to the chatty. As James Ackerman has pointed out, the illustrations for these books "established conventions of architectural representation that were adopted, no doubt unconsciously, by photographers: the positions from which to shoot the facades and apsidal ends of churches, the interiors, the choice of details."[7] Indeed, the formal geometric configurations of buildings like cathedrals in and of themselves dictate certain logical viewpoints to both the graphic artist and the photographer. Views aimed straight at a principal front or a side of these buildings are as inevitable as they are informative and particularly reveal the structure's formal planar geometry. Views made at an angle offer a more volumetric description. In his mature practice Fenton's usual method was to employ both types, varying their proportions in response to the particularities of the site, and occasionally incorporating a narrative element. His interest was always pictorial, not didactic.

FIRST FORAYS, 1852

Fenton's first depictions of buildings are salt prints from paper negatives that he made at Cheltenham, Tewkesbury, Gloucester, and Tintern in 1852,

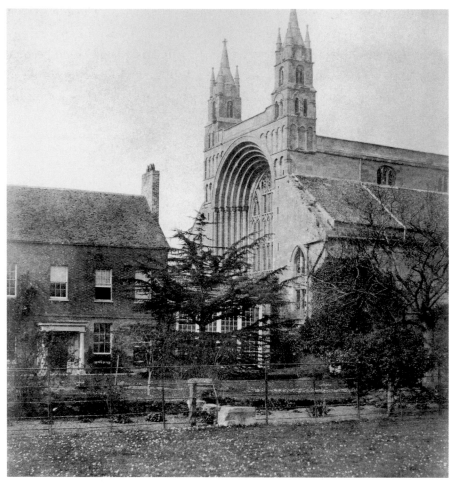

Fig. 36. Roger Fenton, *Tewkesbury Abbey*, 1852. Salted paper print from waxed paper negative, 21.3 x 18.1 cm (8⅜ x 7⅛ in.). From *The Photographic Album*, part 1 (London, 1852). Photographic History Collection, Smithsonian American Art Museum, Washington, D.C., 319,886

at the beginning of his photographic career. They were presumably accomplished during a single trip from his home in London, as the four locations lie relatively close to one another in southern England and nearby Wales. The subjects included a spa and its surrounds, parish churches, a ruined abbey (fig. 36), and a cathedral; he made several views of most of these buildings. A few were published at the end of the year[8] but were not much liked by the *Illustrated London News*, although acknowledged therein as the product of an artist's eye.[9] Another trip in 1852 took him to Crimble, near Bury, in Lancashire, where he visited his father and stepmother and

their children and made a photograph of the house in which he was born.[10] In short, when Fenton left for Russia in September of 1852 he had some experience in photographing architecture but had not yet arrived at a specific approach.

His nominal commission in Russia was to document the construction of a four-span suspension bridge across the Dnieper at Kiev that an acquaintance, the sometimes difficult engineer Charles Vignoles, had undertaken for Czar Nicholas I. Oddly, almost no photographs of Vignoles's bridge by Fenton seem to have survived;[11] however, in Russia he seized the opportunity to create his first substantial body of work on architecture or, for that matter, any class of subject, and the pictures still exist, often in multiple examples.[12] Made using Gustave Le Gray's process for waxed paper negatives, which, advantageously for a traveler, could be prepared in advance, these are quite possibly the earliest surviving photographic images of Russia.[13] They were taken in Kiev, Moscow, and Saint Petersburg; most are distant views of the walls of the Kremlin in Moscow, with churches and palaces ranged behind the fortifications (pl. 4). Fenton's overall view from what he called "the old bridge" across the Moskva River encompasses the slender water tower, beyond it the then-new great palace of the Kremlin, the early-sixteenth-century octagonal bell tower of Ivan the Great, and the Cathedral of the Archangel (pl. 3). Towers and walls recede into the distance in a fleeing perspective enhanced by the sweep of barges angling away from the bridge and down the river.[14]

Fenton partially circumnavigated the great walls enclosing the Kremlin complex and made several views of it from across the river, but if he also took views from its landward sides, they have not survived. There are gaps in his series of negative numbers, so perhaps some negatives proved impossible to print on his return to England.

A more dynamic image, taken from the riverside rampart, looks along foreground merlon crenellations past a series of towers that jostle to be seen, then zigzags to the distant water tower at the end of the rampart, with the river below and an immense construction project in the far distance (pl. 5). Because of the spectral imbalances in his photographic materials, the green slope at the right appears far darker than it was in actuality, a deeply shadowed void that dramatically counterbalances the whites of the towers and the profusion of riverine detail. While the Kremlin, a famous, large, and sprawling subject, was hard to encompass, Fenton realized that he had entered nearly virgin photographic territory and intended to produce several summary overviews of it. His compositional abilities raised these images above conventionally descriptive touristic views.

A quietly spectacular image of the domes of the Cathedral of the Assumption was taken, as John Hannavy discovered and recounted, from a ledge halfway up the tower of Ivan the Great (pl. 2)[15]—a perch that took considerable effort for Fenton to reach with his bulky camera and supplies. The burnished foreground domes, which almost seem imbued with personalities, are echoed by their huddled fellows in the middle ground; the city of Moscow lies beyond. Light on a variety of surfaces—gilded metal, rough roof tile, white plaster, stone—is gently conveyed in the soft tones that a paper negative yields. One wonders what kind of permissions Fenton obtained to gain access to these ramparts and the tower staircase, since these parts of the Kremlin were effectively private property belonging to the imperial family.

A construction site, in this case that of the Church of the Redeemer, was an unusual subject choice for the period. The unfinished cathedral seems to have been adopted for purely pictorial reasons, unless perhaps Fenton's companion Vignoles wished to document the mammoth scale of this project (pl. 6). Undertaken to commemorate the epochal events of 1812, including Napoleon's burning of Moscow and the subsequent decimation of the French army, the church took from 1839 until 1883 to complete. The serried stacks of tree trunks that fill the foreground were raw material for future scaffolding; they provide a nearly abstract foil for the workers' barracks in the middle ground and the sheathing on the rising behemoth beyond. The dense overall patterning of the image, made up of repeated small-scale components that include the range of dormer windows, is relieved by the emptiness of the sky. Having lugged his equipment to this spot, Fenton also turned around and used the same battalions of wood as foreground for a long-range view of the Kremlin.

Russia provided Fenton with a variety of opportunities to develop his skill in photographing architecture, which, except for a few portraits of Russian individuals, constituted nearly his sole subject matter there. Because the Russian pictures were usually made at some distance from their subjects and have the softness that a paper negative produces, they offer general impres-

sions of the appearances of buildings and their contexts. These were not studies of architecture per se, as would later be the case with Fenton's pictures of types of buildings more familiar to him. His vision would become more expansive, his images more powerful, with time (and a change of medium and scale); but the Russian photographs were the foundation for what followed.

IN SEARCH OF THE PICTURESQUE, 1854

Having been trained as a painter in the 1840s, Fenton could hardly escape the preoccupation with the picturesque—amounting almost to a cult—that was an essential component of British art in the first half of the nineteenth century. It is true that his own eclectic, if not particularly distinguished, collection of engravings, watercolors, and paintings was made up largely of history paintings and genre scenes, with a sprinkling of portraits, still lifes, and watercolors made in Wales.[16] On the evidence of their titles, the three paintings of his own that he placed in exhibitions in 1849, 1850, and 1851 were also genre scenes.[17] But if it cannot be said that an idea of the picturesque was fundamental to Fenton's artistic vision before he took up photography, it became so soon afterward. Describing his experiences in the Crimea in a speech given to the Photographic Society,[18] he mentioned a preliminary trial expedition with his photographic van in 1854 in which he set out for the ruins of Rievaulx Abbey "in search of the picturesque." He used the word without irony and expected that his audience would fully understand what was by the 1850s a thoroughly established artistic canon.[19]

When Fenton chose to go to Rievaulx in northern Yorkshire in the early autumn of 1854 to photograph the remnants of the great twelfth-century Cistercian abbey, he was displaying no great ingenuity, since the site, although isolated, was well known and much appreciated. As early as the 1750s a local landowner, Thomas Duncombe, built terraces into his landscaped grounds to afford distant views of the remains of the buildings. John Sell Cotman painted watercolors on the site in 1803, as did Joseph Mallord William Turner in 1812. Fenton may have seen these paintings and would certainly have had a general knowledge of these artists' works. William Westall (1781–1850) made and published a drawing of the distant ruin seen from Duncombe's terrace in 1820,[20] and William Richardson (1822–1877)

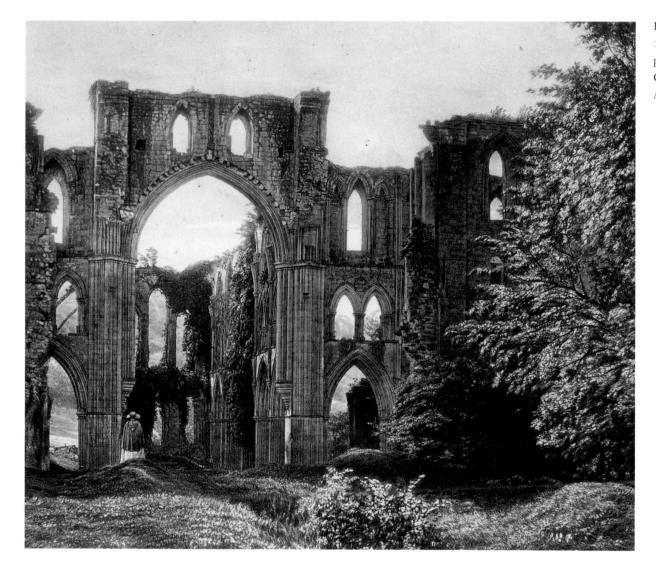

Fig. 37. Roger Fenton, *Rievaulx Abbey, the Transepts*, 1857. Photogalvanograph of original 1854 salted paper print, 18.6 x 22.4 cm (7 5/16 x 8 13/16 in.). Collection Centre Canadien d'Architecture / Canadian Centre for Architecture, Montréal, PH1980:0018

produced a series of precise, delicately colored Romantic views of Rievaulx. These and his other paintings of decrepit ecclesiastical buildings in the region were published as lithographs starting in 1843.[21] The photographer Benjamin Brecknell Turner exhibited a single talbotype of Rievaulx at the annual exhibition of the Photographic Society in London in January of 1854; it was presumably made the previous year and was surely seen by Fenton. In the same show Fenton himself exhibited a number of architectural studies, including a single salted paper print of Gloucester Cathedral, two albumen prints each of Raglan Castle and Tintern Abbey, and five of Gawthorpe Hall, all made in 1853; and a small host of salt prints of ramparts, cathedrals, and

palaces in Russia from his 1852 trip.[22] (Fenton's photographic output in 1853 was smaller than usual, perhaps because he was too busy launching the Photographic Society, mastering the wet-collodion-on-glass process, and seeking employment with the British Museum.)

Nor was Fenton the last photographer to work at Rievaulx. His greatest contemporary rival in the field of architectural photography, Francis Bedford (1816–1894), was there during the same summer.[23] Philip Henry Delamotte (1820–1889) and Joseph Cundall (1818–1875) published their albumen prints of Rievaulx in *A Photographic Tour among the Abbeys of Yorkshire* in 1856. The peripatetic Francis Frith, the architectural specialist

William Russell Sedgfield, and both the now-obscure Reverend Dr. Henry Holden (active late 1850s) and the even more obscure J. Beldon (active early 1860s) all exhibited their photographs of Rievaulx in London. In other words, the site, although remote, was famous. What Fenton accomplished there, however, was uniquely his own.

The evocative remains of Rievaulx are cupped in a serene, verdant, steeply wooded valley less than ten miles from Harlsey Hall, the house in which Fenton's wife, Grace Elizabeth Maynard, had grown up. If he had not already fixed on these lovely ruins as a destination after seeing earlier works of art made there, perhaps she suggested them as a subject. In either case, his extensive photographic expedition to Yorkshire in the summer of 1854 was undoubtedly combined with visits to her extensive family, many of whom were scattered through the county. (In 1856 he would again visit East Harlsey, this time on his way to Scotland.)

At Rievaulx Fenton used photography both to picture an extraordinary place (unspoiled to this day) and to construct a narrative, or rather, two contrasting narratives. In his transverse view across the presbytery, an extension of the nave—the nave itself had completely disappeared by the time of his visit—Fenton placed a single female figure, in all probability his wife, kneeling at the deeply shadowed site of what was once the high altar (pl. 11). In doing so he was invoking English religious history and the original use of these precincts (although not by women). If ruins represent the surrender of art to nature, here the overzealous agents of the picturesque were Henry VIII's commissioners, who had carried out the destruction of this and other monastic communities. The overt Romanticism of this image of a woman in prayer is reinforced by its predominantly dark tones, with her cloaked form nearly lost in the gloom. To achieve this composition the photographer was required to hoist his camera up onto adjacent fallen masonry.

On the other hand, in Fenton's long view back down the presbytery to the single remaining arch where transepts and nave once crossed, a solitary woman sits reading in the late afternoon sunlight, enacting a contemporary, secular use of the premises for leisure, rather than devotion (pl. 12). Within the vertical composition her diminutive figure emphasizes the tremendous size of the soaring crossing arch that spans and frames the distant landscape—which itself continues the recession into space and then closes it. To obtain a high vantage point Fenton placed his camera in a window frame

above and behind the high altar. Therefore the perspectival lines formed by the column bases, capitals, and springings of the arches converge well above the grassy floor. For draftsmen and watercolorists of the period, a classic single-point perspective of this kind down the long axis of a church was possible even in ill-lit interiors, and indeed, predictable. But because of the limitations of his photographic materials and the dimness within medieval buildings, Fenton was generally able to produce this kind of axial view only in roofless ruins,[24] as he did at Rievaulx and also at Fountains and Furness abbeys.

While it is close to certain that the same person appears in both views, the first of these two photographs represents the past, the second the present. Fenton's diversity of mood from one photograph to another speaks to his complex intentions at Rievaulx and hints at his own church attendance and underlying belief.[25] These two principal scenarios are also enacted in two other photographs of the seven that he made at Rievaulx. In the first, which seems in equal parts picturesque and religious, the woman, again wearing a cloak but with the addition of a wide-brimmed hat, stands in the middle distance, her back to the camera (fig. 37). She is nearly lost among the humps of luxuriant greenery that cover the fallen stones of the nave and is dwarfed by the foliage-tufted walls of the ruined transepts and the crossing arch, now seen from the opposite direction. The camera is placed low, seeming to follow in the woman's footsteps. Her stance, as if contemplating the ruin before her, and her garb, which resembles a pilgrim's, make the photograph into a melancholy invocation of a vanished past.

In another image the same woman sits reading in the foreground outside the church, in the shelter of a small pointed arch, while a girl, presumably Fenton's eight-year-old daughter, Annie Grace, poses as if climbing a rustic fence (pl. 10). This is a representation of a relaxed and pleasant outing. Like another photograph of the same two people, in which nothing of the abbey is visible,[26] it suggests to the viewer how the site is to be enjoyed in the present. Watercolorists were free to interpolate figures of any sort into their compositions and occasionally they depicted persons in medieval dress, but Fenton seems to have been the only photographer who used actual people to evoke the past. Neither when playing roles from the past nor as themselves in the present can these figures be considered to embody orthodox picturesque taste, which preferred the gypsy or beggar to the priest or tourist.[27] The pictures that Fenton made at Rievaulx not long after he had begun seriously to photograph monastic architecture reflect a certain spontaneity, a personal response to the buildings not always found in his later work.[28] Perhaps the presence of his wife and daughter provided inspiration.

From 1854 on Fenton employed collodion-coated glass negatives. For this process chemical manipulations had to be carried out both immediately before and immediately after the exposure of the negative in the camera, and thus a portable darkroom was a necessity. To house and transport his darkroom and numerous requisite photographic chemicals and supplies, Fenton purchased a carriage in 1854 from a Canterbury wine merchant and had it elaborately refitted to his purposes.[29] Following its baptismal expedition to Rievaulx the carriage was shipped to the Crimea in 1855, where, after hard usage, Fenton sold it. He had another built when he returned to England. In all probability he most often used the railroads to transport his vehicle to the station nearest the site he wished to visit, rather than having his assistant, Marcus Sparling, drive it all the way from London to distant counties along what were still rather rudimentary roads.[30] Fenton and his companions, whether his wife and family or Sparling or other assistants, then also traveled by train to these rendezvous, although several changes may have been required; there was not yet a united rail system, only many small lines.

INTO SCOTLAND, 1856

At the beginning of his photographic expedition to Scotland in 1856, off the windy coast of Northumberland, Fenton visited the stark ruin of Lindisfarne Priory, on a tidal island that had been revered as a holy site since the seventh century. Who accompanied him is not known, but in one photograph the informal dress and nonchalant pose of the shirtsleeved figure with his back to the camera suggest that he is the invaluable Sparling (pl. 24).[31] Out of the disorderly components of the ruined eleventh-century Norman priory Fenton wrested a roughly symmetrical composition centered on the one remaining diagonal crossing arch, which had spanned the space where nave and transepts once met. To do so he placed his camera at a forty-five-degree angle to the axis of the nave so that its direction was perpendicular to the span, a view that would have been wholly impossible inside the building when it was intact. In fact, the blocky ends of the gaunt arch connecting the west side of one transept with the east side of the other lie in two different planes, but the flattening effect of the lens makes them appear to be at equal distances from the picture plane. Fenton managed to torque the Romanesque masonry into place on the surface of the paper and use the great arch, now sometimes called the rainbow arch, to frame the tidal flats and coastline in the distance.[32] While on the Holy Island he also made separate views of the adjacent salt flats. His work in this isolated place, which even today can be reached only at low tide, was an auspicious prologue to the series of photographs he made at the ruins of Kelso, Jedburgh, and Melrose abbeys in the Scottish Borders as he gradually moved north that autumn, switching from landscape to architectural study as the opportunity presented itself.

He made five studies of the ravaged but still substantial remains of the abbey at Melrose, moving his camera around the tilting tombstones in the churchyard cemetery. In a vertical study of the south transept, an enormous window filled with an elegant filigree of flamboyant Gothic tracery soars above the tiny figure of a woman in white, posing on the threshold of the porch (pl. 25).[33] Closer to Edinburgh, Fenton stopped at Roslin to photograph a disused fifteenth-century chapel that after a turbulent history had been reroofed, repaved, and reglazed in the eighteenth century. While the ostensible subjects of his study of the south porch are the foliate-patterned window frames (filled with comparatively modern glass) and the porch with its heavy arch and empty niches flanking the door, the photograph is primarily an exercise in depicting depth (pl. 26, fig. 35). The view, taken from outside the building, looks through the doorframe into the chapel and across its width, then out a door on the north side that opens onto the churchyard, through a doorway in the boundary wall, and past a crude fence of pointed sticks, coming to rest on a postage-stamp-sized landscape of distant fields. By opening three doors each more distant from the camera, Fenton obtained a series of frames of diminishing dimensions and turned the chapel into a telescopic tunnel of stone leading the eye through successive shifts between light and dark. His ability to recognize that an ordinary architectural study could be transformed into a sophisticated composition of varying planes is an aspect of the highly sensitive perception that distinguishes Fenton's photographs from the work of his contemporaries.[34]

After stopping in Edinburgh, the Scottish expedition moved north and terminated in September in the Highlands, where Fenton photographed, at Queen Victoria's request, her newly completed castle of Balmoral and made

to the sky at right angles to the long horizontal run of the linked church and palace. The exposure must have been short, since the outline of the steam vessel crossing the river is distinct and clouds are visible. The muddy tidal flat on which the tripod sat would soon disappear with the construction in the middle 1860s of the Albert Embankment on the south side of the river.

To make his most distant and atmospheric view of Parliament, Fenton stood on Waterloo Bridge facing upstream (pl. 60). He used the long arc of the chains of the Hungerford suspension bridge (built by Isambard Kingdom Brunel in 1845), which bore pedestrians, not vehicles, to frame his view of Westminster.[81] By rounding the upper corners of the print he eliminated areas of inadequate plate coverage while echoing, in reverse, the curving chains. The dark form of the bridge stands out against the progressively lighter gray tones of buildings receding along the shoreline to the west. These delicately modulated tones are complemented by the striated clouds overhead. This is one of numerous works that demonstrate Fenton's ability to carry the eye into the depths of an image— his mastery of aerial perspective. The composition also makes evident how completely the towers of Parliament and Westminster Abbey dominated this part of London in the mid-nineteenth century and how central the river remained to the life of the city, acting as both an artery and a barrier.

In addition to surveying Parliament from Lambeth and from Waterloo Bridge, Fenton took at least two views along Victoria Street as he approached the west facade of Westminster Abbey, flanked by the parliamentary clock tower on the left and Victoria Tower on the right (fig. 78). There were also at least three studies of the exterior of the new House of Lords: one shows its flank and that of the adjacent, ancient Westminster Hall, and two others concentrate on the Peers' Entrance, both with and without a hansom cab drawn up at the door.[82] There were three if not four views of the main front of Buckingham Palace, inside which Fenton had frequently portrayed the royal family.[83]

Involved since 1854 in a project to document parts of the British Museum's collections and some of its galleries, Fenton also made two studies of the building's front exterior (pl. 40). To establish a fleeing perspective, he placed his camera so that the sharply raking lines of the entablature of Sir Robert Smirke's Neoclassical facade begin in the upper left corner of the photograph and, with all the other perspectival lines, continue to a vanishing point at the right beyond the frame of the image. The heavy Ionic colonnades encasing the blocky volumes of the museum's two wings and central pavilion pivot around the stubby, black iron lamppost with which his camera was aligned. The scale of these elements and of the forecourt itself wholly dwarfs the woman and two children who bring life to what would otherwise be an empty, even ominous scene. The only persons who stayed still long enough to register clearly on the negative, they are altogether likely to be Mrs. Fenton and two of her young daughters. Fenton's other view of the museum's exterior, taken straight on and thus more static, is a study of its central pedimented portico.[84] As previously noted, when studying buildings Fenton had always been concerned with establishing them in their context, whether woods, street, lawn, or waterside, but as he continued to make images of city structures he became increasingly interested in depicting urban space for its own sake. For example, when photographing the buildings along each side of Trafalgar Square he took pains to include the square itself, even though that meant diminishing the scale and visibility of the surrounding museum, church, hotel, and office buildings. This interest in space as shaped by architecture would continue to develop in his later work, particularly that done at Harewood in 1859 and at Windsor Castle in 1860.

HAREWOOD, MENTMORE, STONYHURST, AND OXFORD, 1859

Fenton had far greater access to the magnificent eighteenth-century Harewood House in West Yorkshire than had been the case at Haddon, Hardwick, and Chatsworth. When he went to Harewood in 1859 his brother-in-law Charles Septimus Maynard was the estate manager.[85] This connection, and a commission from the Lascelles family to document at least some aspects of their house, made it possible for Fenton not only to survey it from a distance and photograph its terraces but also to make group portraits of its inhabitants on the terraces. His most distant view of Harewood, taken from the south, is more landscape than architectural study (pl. 66). Within an oval format, an irregular dark wreath of foliage opens just enough to show one wing of a building on a slope above a lake that returns barely discernible reflections of house, hillside, and trees. This can be thought of as a view of a Neoclassical house in the picturesque style.

To encompass the whole of the house rather than just a wing, Fenton moved out of the trees and to the right for a view across a meadow and the

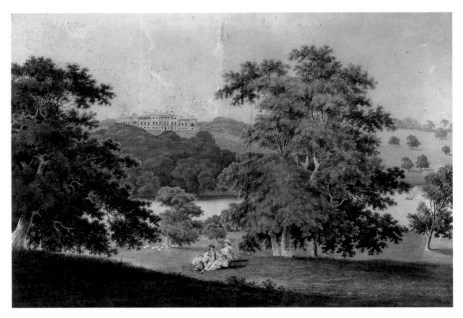

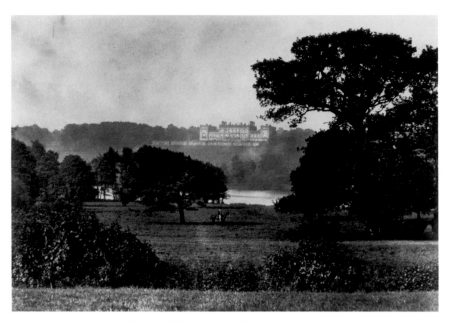

Fig. 43. Paul Sandby (English, 1731–1809), *Harewood House*, ca. 1785. Watercolor, 61.5 x 87 cm (24¼ x 34¼ in.). Reproduced by the kind permission of the Earl and Countess of Harewood and the Harewood House Trust Ltd., HHTP:2001.2.47

Fig. 44. Roger Fenton, *Harewood House*, 1859. Albumen silver print, 28.5 x 43.5 cm (11⁵⁄₁₆ x 17⅛ in.). Reproduced by the kind permission of the Earl and Countess of Harewood and the Harewood House Trust Ltd., HHTPH:2001.1.5

lake and up the slope to the house. The photograph was made near the spot from which Turner depicted the same subject for its owners in 1798, but it more closely resembles a watercolor of the same view by Paul Sandby (figs. 43, 44). The picnicking figures in Sandby's meadow are replaced in the photograph by a stout figure on horseback, Fenton's father-in-law, John Charles Maynard, who evidently accompanied Fenton in order to visit his son.[86] Whether or not Fenton had seen the works by Sandby and Turner or engravings after them, in this photograph and a variant made nearby he chose to adopt what seems to be the established vantage point from which to show Harewood's graceful integration into the surrounding landscape.[87]

Then moving to the house itself, he made five studies of the great terrace on its south front that overlooks the lake. The documentation of this recently completed construction, designed by Sir Charles Barry for Louisa, Lady Harewood, wife of the 3rd Earl of Harewood, must have been Fenton's principal commission.[88] From the central door of the south front, which Barry had extensively remodeled, a few steps descend to a landing where stairs branching left and right lead to an upper terrace, and from there two more flights go down to a broad lower terrace. It has a large central fountain and

symmetrical box-bordered flower beds filled with arabesques of greenery and pointed topiary. At the edge farthest from the house is a balustrade that bows out in two places to hold benches.

Fenton placed his camera on the upper landing to make two views over this lower terrace and lawn, past a group of shoreline trees, and across the lake to the park from which he had taken his distant views of the house (pl. 68). The highly ordered parterre in the foreground gives way by stages to the comparatively wild woodland in the distance. These views of the lower terrace taken from above differ only in the groupings of various members of the Lascelles family ranged along the balustrade, standing, sitting, or lounging on a bench.[89] (How much Fenton directed their poses can only be speculated, but we know that he posed groups in the Crimea, and he may have done so here.) They present a relaxed and charming picture of an aristocratic family at leisure in an expansive setting, in "the perfect middle of a splendid summer afternoon."[90] Their forms are echoed by those of the sculpted figures on the fountain, just as its still surface is mirrored by that of the distant lake. Fenton made the people and fountain into visual centers of interest to punctuate his depiction of the terrace rather than relying on the geometry of the garden alone to structure his composition. It is a wholly satisfying synthesis of natural and shaped landscape.

Fenton's view along the length of the upper terrace is at such an acute angle to the facade of the house that the structure's lateral proportions are indecipherable (pl. 67). The architectural elements include end pavilions with Palladian windows and short connecting wings containing trios of arched windows, flanking a central block where giant Corinthian pilasters alternate with windows in two stories. The central entablature is topped by a balustrade with finial-topped urns that march down toward the horizon. This lavish array of stonework is played against the nearly empty quadrant of sky and the plain expanse of white gravel that floors the terrace. The converging edges of the gravel walk reach a dead end in a dark mass of trees. The face of a man who leans against the terrace balustrade looking out into the distance is averted, but a nearby stone sphinx stares blindly at the camera. One might imagine the man a stand-in for the architect, although his stance seems more ruminative than proprietary. Individually and collectively, the photographs from Harewood represent some of Fenton's finest works in architecture.[91]

We know more about how Fenton came to be at Harewood than about the origins of his work at any other country house (unless Windsor Castle can be counted as a country house). It is tantalizing to conjecture that his work at Chatsworth, Wollaton, or Mentmore was also commissioned and that groups of photographs of these places, perhaps in albums, have yet to be discovered. This is particularly the case with Mentmore, the great Rothschild house in Buckinghamshire constructed to Sir Joseph Paxton's designs in the middle 1850s, because the fact that Fenton had access to its interior implies some specific connection to the Rothschild family. Two photographs inside the billiard room are known, one in which Fenton poses alone, leaning over the large billiard table with cue stick in hand, and another made at a slightly different time in which a group of people are posed around the table (pl. 72). The first image was perhaps a test study for the second.[92] In the second, six people, all of unknown identity, act out a scene of indoor domestic amusement. (Are the women who wear hats planning to go outside or are they guests? Is the man at the right an instructor advising the young woman at the table on the pocket to which she should direct her next shot or just a helpful friend or relation? Why is she the only one holding a cue stick?) Although it is rare to find any photographic depiction of people at leisure in an interior or of a domestic interior during this period, it is the dramatic light, with shadows slashing across the floor and onto the tabletops, that makes the photograph astonishing. The plethora of detail contained is also remarkable; for instance, while the woman standing in the doorway at the end of the room appears to be wearing a white cap, it is in fact the top of a marble bust on a mantelpiece in the next room and the reflection of the bust in a mirror behind it. Fenton was able to capture the particularities of all of these objects because, unlike most Victorian interiors, the room was abundantly lit. Originally designed as a conservatory, it had been converted into a billiard room shortly after the completion of the house, without any alteration to the ample window at the far end of the room and those along one side. The photograph seems likely to have been a commission, but whatever the answer to the question why Fenton was given such liberty in an aristocratic household, the result is a work of considerable sophistication and great visual brilliance.

Fenton made another significant interior study during one of his two visits (in summer 1859 or at Christmas in 1859) to Stonyhurst College, a Jesuit institution in his native Lancashire that was housed principally in a sixteenth-century manor house. In the refectory, another room that had large windows running along one side, he photographed students seated at a midday meal, with servants and a priest standing among the tables (pl. 73).[93] This photograph lacks the overall luminescence of the one from Mentmore, however, probably because the impossibility of making dozens of boys sit still for long limited the time of the exposure. His preliminary studies without the students had longer exposures and are more evenly lit. Fenton did not show pictures from Stonyhurst until January of 1860, at which time he exhibited thirteen selected from his two visits,[94] a few less than three weeks old, together with a few Lancashire landscapes made on land belonging to the Fenton family that was adjacent to the school.

At the same 1860 Photographic Society exhibition Fenton also showed a series of views of Oxford from the late summer of 1859. He seems to have summarily surveyed many of its colleges, making at least one image each at Wadham, New, University, Merton, Christ Church, and Brasenose. With the exception of a view through a gateway and a streetside study, they are all, predictably, of quadrangles, the most accessible areas of the colleges. For unknown reasons he was granted liberal access at Magdalen and made nine photographs there in two different size formats, showing quads, gardens, gates, and most memorably the great tower. There are also five views of Oxford's not-quite-finished museum of natural history.[95]

AN ABBEY AND A CASTLE, 1860

If Fenton chose his destinations with upcoming exhibitions in mind, it would have been in anticipation of the Architectural Photographic Association's fourth exhibition in 1861 that he journeyed the previous summer to Furness, on the west coast of England in Cumbria, where the impressive remains of a once-powerful Cistercian abbey stood. Since travel to Furness had been quite difficult until the arrival of the railroad in 1846,[96] few prototypes existed in the graphic arts. Fenton completed at least twenty-two different views of the majestic ruins in much the same vein as those he had made at Rievaulx and Fountains, including two backlit studies of two different young girls (possibly two of his daughters) in an archway at the top of a flight of steps.[97] He showed seventeen of these photographs from Furness at the Architectural Photographic Association in January of 1861 and three others at the nearly simultaneous exhibition of the Photographic Society in London.

When Fenton went to Windsor Castle in the summer of 1860 he apparently did so on his own, not in response to a royal commission.[98] He was highly productive there, creating at least thirty-one images of the residence at varying distances, often from the surrounding parks, a project that must have required several days. Taken from a wide assortment of directions, the views are mostly of the early-nineteenth-century exterior of the upper castle. The most distant and comprehensive view of the castle complex is that made from the town park (pl. 81). As with his view of Ely Cathedral from the park (pl. 50), Fenton played the dark density of middle-ground foliage against lighter stonework in the distance. Here, however, he used a wide foreground expanse of lawn to emphasize the scale of the castle stretched out along the horizon. (Had he moved closer he could still have encompassed the entire building, but the tree would have loomed larger, interrupting the castle's skyline and making it appear smaller.) Of the tiny figures sprinkled across the middle distance, only the two dark-clothed men in the center, backs to the camera, are likely to have been asked to pose. A minor turret of the

overly regularized facade (by Sir Jeffry Wyatville) falls at the center of the picture; the greater bulk of the building, on the left, is roughly balanced by the masses of the round tower and tree to the right. In an elegant, subtly modulated composition, Fenton summarized this quintessential British monument.

Within the lower precinct at Windsor, Fenton made four views. Two look uphill along the side of Saint George's Chapel toward the ancient round tower that dominates the castle complex; one shows the chapel alone; and another looks back downhill from the foot of the tower (pl. 83). At first glance this last image seems empty of people except for a ghost figure at the right, but a closer examination discovers a whole troop of soldiers lined up as if for inspection in the distance near the perimeter wall. Beyond the wall are the rooftops of the town, and even farther away lies a hazy line of low hills. It is no wonder that contemporary reviewers commended Fenton's mastery of aerial perspective.[99] The foreground clarity gradually dissolves, diminishing in delicate shades of gray into the farthest distance. Well exemplified in this image is the way Fenton's considerable experience photographing landscape informed and influenced his treatment of buildings and their relation to their settings. Although stonework frames the picture at right, left, and bottom, the principal subject is as much the shaping of external space by architecture as the architecture itself.

Both views looking back uphill to the round tower are so animated with figures deployed on the slope that the architecture and the contours of the space became somewhat subordinated to them (pl. 84). This effect is enhanced by the anomalies of the photographic materials, which make the spectators in their dark clothing appear more substantial than the buildings around them. Four Grenadier guards, two other soldiers, and eighteen men, women, and children are scattered up the roadway, along a path that veers to the left, and at the entrance to Saint George's Chapel; all of them face the camera.[100] Fenton's ability to elicit the cooperation of two dozen people (only one of whom visibly moved) depended to some extent on the fact that by 1860 exposure times in broad daylight were short, and to a considerable extent on his possession of persuasive powers even outside the courtrooms in which he appeared when intermittently practicing law. Still, why he asked them all to turn toward the camera is a puzzle. A great deal of detail is conveyed in the image; it even is possible to see, although very dimly, swaths in the grass that appear to show the direction in which it had been mowed. While the recession of planes is less than perfectly balanced, the photograph is nonetheless one of Fenton's best.

Although his thirty-one Windsor pictures would seem to have represented considerable potential for sales, Fenton entered none of them in the Architectural Photographic Association show in January of 1861 and displayed only two in the concurrent exhibition of the Photographic Society.[101] He had been instrumental in founding that organization and for seven years had made steady contributions to its shows, but this was the last in which he placed his work. In the International Exhibition of 1862 he showed examples of his landscapes, a work for the British Museum, an Orientalist image, and some architectural studies, including one Windsor picture. It was the last time he ever exhibited.[102]

Fenton's architectural work took considerable sustained effort to accomplish, not least the planning and carrying out of extensive travel at a time when such was far from smooth. Discernment in choosing desirable buildings to photograph, judgment in assessing specific sites immediately on arrival, and ingenuity in fixing on appropriate vantage points and camera placements were all necessary for achievement of his compositional intentions. Agility was occasionally required for hoisting his cumbersome equipment into place, and from 1853 forward, after he had adopted the wet-collodion-on-glass process, speed was a necessity. Above all Fenton needed patience, much patience, when waiting for the sun to arrive—if it arrived at all, given the exigencies of the British climate—at the place where it best illuminated his subject. Once safely home with his fragile glass negatives he employed his considerable technical skill to produce prints of great finesse, with rich tonal values and subtle gradations of gray.

Fenton's great steadiness of purpose, as resolute as that of his Lancashire forebears, produced a formidable body of architectural work diverse in subject, effect, and mood: from bold to contemplative, from pastoral to urban. Collectively these pictures celebrate the accomplishments of generations of British architects and builders. His gaunt arches and tumbled stones of ruined abbeys, his scarred and weathered cathedrals bear witness to enduring faith, passing history, and devouring time. Fenton depicted English prosperity and pride, as embodied in country houses, and patriotism, as reflected in the urban monuments of London, capital of the mid-nineteenth-century world. The figures that animate these images filled with stone, sky, and vegetation insinuate a modest narrative that softens the pictures and makes them more approachable. Fenton's photographs of architecture form the most important component of his extraordinary photographic career. A man of acute visual intelligence and perseverance, he truthfully and with great sensitivity translated the three-dimensional solidity of architecture onto the surface of the page.

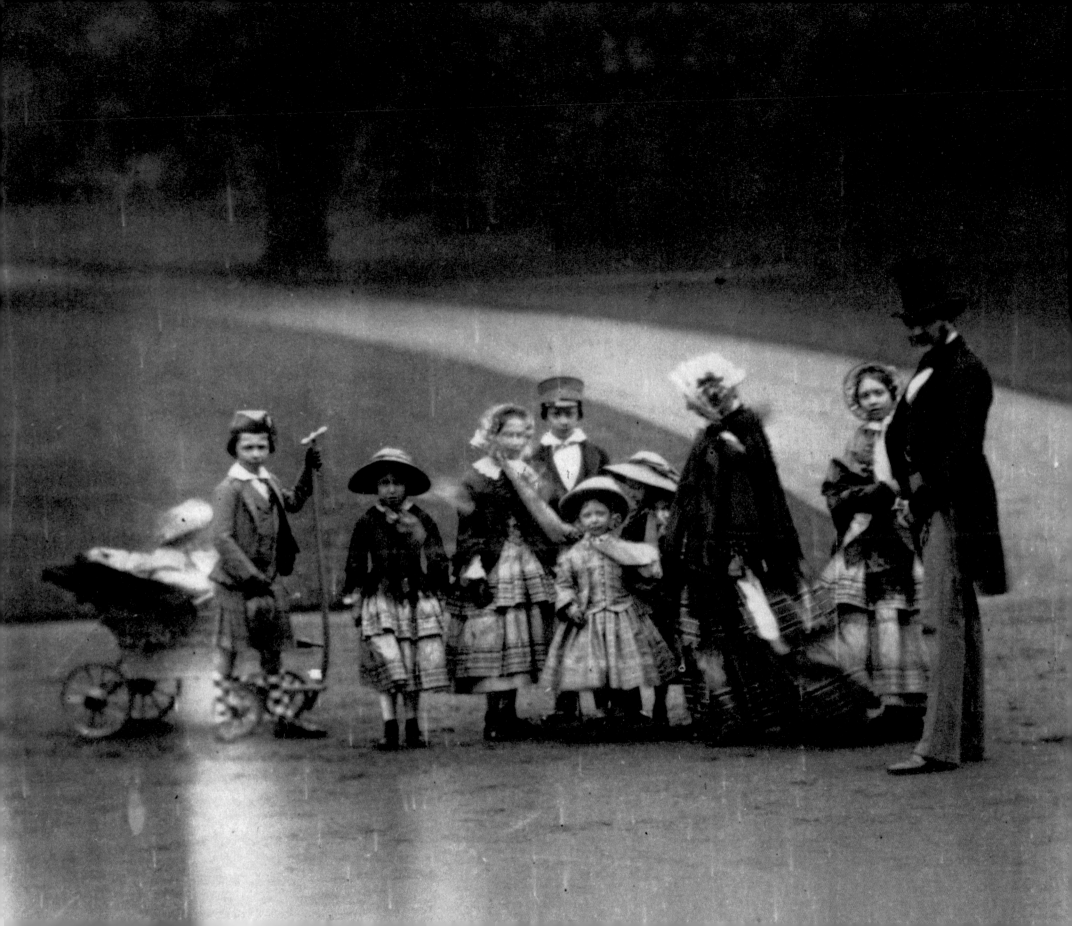

"Mr. Fenton Explained Everything": Queen Victoria and Roger Fenton

ROGER TAYLOR

The first few days of 1854 opened memorably, with heavy snowstorms and some of the coldest weather in living memory. In London the entire city gradually fell silent as deepening snow brought traffic to a halt. The adventurous braved the weather and went skating in Regent's Park, but during the nights it became so cold that two constables from the metropolitan police force froze to death while on duty.[1] Some twenty miles to the west, Queen Victoria and Prince Albert awoke on January 3 to find the windows of Windsor Castle covered with icicles following a night that brought "twenty one degrees of frost." Despite the weather and the hazardous state of the roads, they "wrapped up well in furs" and left for London, driving "at once to Suffolk Street to visit the Photographic Exhibition." They were met by a small party including Sir Charles Eastlake, president of the Photographic Society, and Roger Fenton, the honorary secretary, who, as the queen remarked, "explained everything."[2] The two men had been nominated by the society as the most suitable members to elucidate "the *artistic* and the *practical* sides of the art." During the course of the visit, which lasted more than an hour, Fenton drew upon examples of his own work and that of others to illustrate the latest advances.[3]

In June 1853 Queen Victoria and Prince Albert had agreed to become patrons of the newly formed Photographic Society, and their support proved crucial in making photography socially acceptable.[4] Their visit to the inaugural exhibition, especially under such hazardous conditions,[5] demonstrated that they were committed to the society and that they would continue their active patronage. Most likely a key figure in the planning and organization of

the visit was Dr. Ernst Becker, an accomplished amateur photographer himself, a founding member of the Photographic Society, librarian to Prince Albert, and assistant tutor to the young princes.[6] Fenton and Becker would have known each other, perhaps well, through the Council of the Photographic Society, on which both had served from the outset. At a time when all official communications with the royal family were ruled by etiquette and protocol, Becker's role as an informal link between the court and the society should not be underestimated.

Fenton's debut performance for the royal family undoubtedly gained their confidence, for within a month he began a series of photographic portrait commissions, chiefly at Buckingham Palace and Windsor Castle. His appointment was one of the first in a wider program of photographic activity begun in 1854 by Queen Victoria and Prince Albert. From that year on, prints were regularly purchased for the Royal Collections, either directly from photographic exhibitions or through established London print dealers, who were then adding the work of British and Continental photographers to their inventory. With photography becoming acceptable as an ideal "rational recreation" for young gentlemen, Becker made the subject part of the curriculum of Edward, Prince of Wales, and Prince Alfred, ordering regular supplies of chemicals, glass, and paper for their lessons.[7] Such was the newfound enthusiasm for photography that a portable darkroom and photographic portrait room were installed in both Buckingham Palace and Windsor Castle. A camera was even mounted on the superstructure of the royal yacht *Victoria & Albert*.[8] This new interest received frequent coverage in the popular press.[9] Given the rapid development of photography in Britain during the early 1850s, it is easy to see why Queen Victoria and Prince Albert were attracted to the medium. What it offered could be used

Opposite: Fig. 45. Roger Fenton, *The Queen, the Prince, and Eight Royal Children in Buckingham Palace Garden, May 22, 1854* (detail); see fig. 10

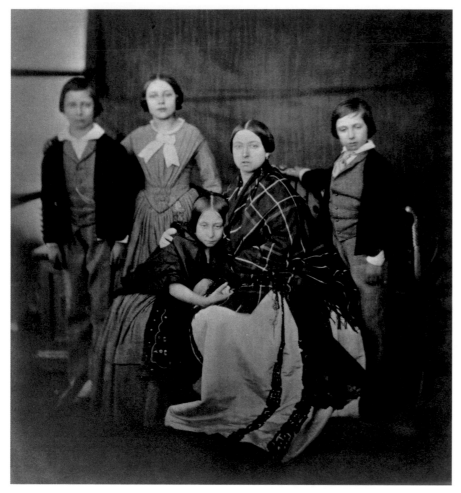

Fig. 46. Roger Fenton, *The Prince of Wales, Princess Royal, Princess Alice, the Queen, and Prince Alfred, February 8, 1854.* Carbon print copy of original albumen print, 21.9 x 19.7 cm (8⅝ x 7¾ in.). The Royal Collection © 2004, Her Majesty Queen Elizabeth II, RCIN 2900013

for many desirable purposes: art, science, recreation, documentation, family records, and the efficient distribution of their portraits to the four corners of Europe. In return the royal family offered photography their patronage, giving it a status and authority that led to its speedy acceptance in fashionable circles. It was the perfect symbiotic relationship.

In 1854 Fenton received no less than a dozen separate photographic commissions from the royal couple, some of them complex and others involving just a single sitting. It was by far his most productive year in this regard, for although he continued to photograph for the royal family in 1855 and through

1857, his output during those years was significantly less. His first commission was prompted by a performance of *Les deux petits Savoyards* given by the royal children on January 16.[10] The young actors were dressed in eighteenth-century costume, and although the Prince of Wales had been "painted" by his father "to look quite hideous," everyone involved was "very happy" with the outcome.[11] A week later, on January 23, this picturesque performance was restaged for the camera, as the queen noted in her diary: "Mr. Fenton photographed the children in their costumes."[12] It was undoubtedly a tricky undertaking, since the portraits had to be made in an improvised studio indoors, in such light as was available. In midwinter these circumstances invariably meant long exposure times that went against the natural inclinations of very young children unfamiliar with striking a pose and keeping still. But somehow Fenton succeeded, although Princess Helena, aged seven, had to be placed on a plinth to bring her up to the height of the camera.[13] This series of portraits is among the earliest to commemorate an event in the life of the royal children. For the remainder of their married life Queen Victoria and Prince Albert regularly engaged photographers to document such noteworthy moments and even extended the custom to include portraits of Highland servants, favorite pets, and farm animals.[14]

In a life crowded with historic events and significant moments, it may seem surprising to find Queen Victoria laying such emphasis on the anniversaries and birthdays that marked the passage of her own life. These were never overlooked and were invariably celebrated with some small occasion to mark the day. This fondness for family celebrations is actually quite understandable, however, for the queen's own upbringing had been lonely and occasionally difficult, and the immorality of her immediate forebears had brought little but disgrace to the monarchy. Rejecting her unhappy past, she chose to build her life on a foundation of idealized love and family values. Throughout her long reign she held fast to these ideals, becoming a principled role model for the nation and in the process reforming the way in which the monarchy was perceived by its subjects.

The anniversary of the queen's marriage to Prince Albert, that "ever blessed day,"[15] was so important to her that she always celebrated it twice, first on February 8, the day he had arrived at Buckingham Palace from Germany, and again on February 10, the day of the wedding itself. To commemorate the fourteenth anniversary of Albert's arrival Fenton was commissioned to make a series of portraits of the royal couple and seven of their eight children, the exception being Prince Leopold, who was then just nine months old. Although the photographs were taken at Windsor Castle on January 25, 1854, the entire series of fourteen portraits is dated February 8. The most telling portrait, one that reveals how she wanted to be remembered by her family, shows the queen surrounded by her four eldest children (fig. 46). Dressed simply, without ornament or embellishment, and with a plaid shawl around her shoulders, she has shed the aura and trappings of monarchy to appear as a conventional wife and mother.

On February 10 the royal couple's fourteenth wedding anniversary was "ushered in with music and the never failing tender love of my beloved Albert." Later that morning, after the exchange of presents, they read through their marriage service together, and the queen was reminded of her promise "to love, cherish, honour, *serve & obey*." In the late afternoon the couple went to the Rubens Room, "where the Children had kindly arranged a charming surprise,"[16] a complex series of tableaux vivants that relied upon the combined skills of Edward Henry Corbould, historical painter and court artist; Mr. Gibbs, the principal tutor; and Miss Hildyard, the children's governess. The first four tableaux were freely based on James Thomson's celebrated

poem *The Seasons*, which had remained popular with the public for well over a hundred years. For the fifth tableau, the grand finale, additional verses were specially commissioned from Martin Tupper, author of *Proverbial Philosophy*, a sugary book of homespun truths and homely beliefs. To the relief of all, the royal children recited their verses clearly and without faltering, and everything was carried off to perfection.

Some time later, Fenton photographed the children reenacting the tableaux complete with costumes, props, and telling theatrical gestures. But the scenery of the original performance was replaced by rumpled backdrops and draped sheets that make the photographs look amateurish and incomplete. This mattered little, however, since the photographs were never intended to be seen in that form: much grander things had been planned for them. For the queen's birthday on May 24, Prince Albert proposed to give his wife a "crimson velvet portfolio" containing five watercolors by Carl Haag that would reproduce scenes from the tableaux with extracts from the relevant poems elegantly inscribed beneath.[17] Because Haag had not seen the performance, Fenton's photographs were to be used as figure studies for his watercolors. In this way the artist could re-create the sense of the original tableaux and people them with recognizable portraits rather than mere

Fig. 47. Roger Fenton, *The Princess Alice as "Spring" in the Tableaux Represented February 10, 1854*, winter or spring 1854. Salted paper print, 18.6 x 14.5 cm (7⁵⁄₁₆ x 5¹¹⁄₁₆ in.). The Royal Collection © 2004, Her Majesty Queen Elizabeth II, RCIN 2900024

Fig. 48. Carl Haag (German-born, active in Britain, 1820–1915), *The Princess Alice as "Spring,"* winter or spring 1854. Illustration for James Thomson, *The Seasons*. Watercolor painted over Roger Fenton's salted paper print of figure, 36 x 45 cm (14³⁄₁₆ x 17¹¹⁄₁₆ in.). The Royal Collection © 2004, Her Majesty Queen Elizabeth II, RCIN RL 31944

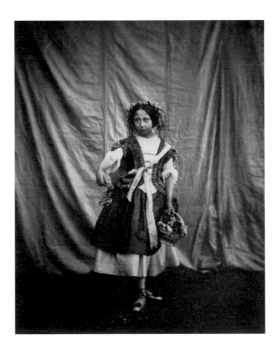

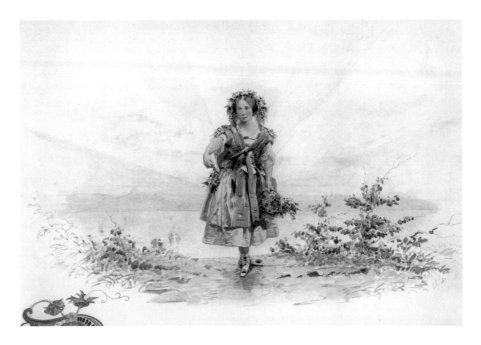

"Trying His Hand upon Some Oriental Figure Subjects"

GORDON BALDWIN

Fenton's continual quest to raise photography to the status of a fine art led him to appropriate the subject matter of painting: most notably and consistently landscape, but also, briefly, both still lifes and genre scenes. His interest in making photographs that had storytelling content or elements of masquerade was perfectly aligned with the Victorian passion for staging tableaux, dressing in costume, and otherwise attempting to escape the constraints of the ordinary. Flight from the mundane was one of the motives underlying the phenomenon known as Orientalism, which in the visual arts was essentially the depiction of scenes of life in a Near Eastern world far more imaginary than actual. Fenton was familiar with the work of a number of French and British artists—most notably Eugène Delacroix, David Roberts, and John Frederick Lewis—who in paintings of the 1840s and 1850s pictured a life in the Near East characterized by visual splendor, indolence, luxury, sensuality, exotic ritual, and barbarism.[1] Fenton's foray into this collective fantasy of Oriental life is one more instance of his adaptation of the subject matter of painting to photography.

DRESS REHEARSALS

Well before he carried out his suite of about fifty Orientalist pictures in his London studio in mid-1858,[2] Fenton made pictures of himself and members of his family assuming identities other than their own. The earliest example is the appearance of his wife, Grace Elizabeth, as a stand-in for a medieval pilgrim in two photographs taken at Rievaulx in 1854 (see above, p. 59).

Opposite: Fig. 51. Roger Fenton, *Orientalist Group* (detail), 1858; see pl. 63

Another kind of make-believe, although uncostumed, takes place in a set of four photographs of his sister-in-law Sarah Jefferson Maynard and Jack Stayplton Sutton, arranged to illustrate the happy progression of a courtship.[3] When exhibited in 1855 the series was called A Romance, with individual titles like *Popping the Question*; but since the models were in fact engaged or perhaps even already married, the degree of playacting was minimal. More notable examples of masquerade are Fenton's self-portraits in the uniform of a French Zouave, which he made in 1855 while in the Crimea. In an improvised studio with a fur rug on the floor he posed in a borrowed uniform, seated on the sheepskin-lined overcoat of a captured Russian officer (fig. 52). In the several images he used various masculine props—tankard, wine bottle, rifle, pipe.[4] Since Fenton had surmounted great obstacles to document the activities of the troops and had shared their considerable hardships, his wish to identify with them was not surprising. When he exhibited any of these self-portraits as part of his Crimean oeuvre he simply titled it *Zouave, 2nd Division*, leaving it up to the initiated to recognize him. It is only when the viewer knows Fenton to be the sitter that the playful nature of the poses becomes evident.

In an enigmatic photograph, Fenton posed members of his family to enact a narrative in his London studio. One of his daughters gazes pensively over the cradle of a sleeping infant while another buries her face in her mother's lap (fig. 53). The work's traditional title is *La Faute*; does this refer to a mistake or to a moral fault?[5] In one possible interpretation, consistent with one meaning of *faute*, the infant is a child born out of wedlock to the apparently grief-stricken girl who hides her face. But this would make Fenton a more daring storyteller than seems to accord with his generally conventional character, and is it likely that he would have cast one of his daughters as an unwed mother? We lack the key to the picture's meaning. Whatever the story, clearly the intention was to make a photograph with narrative content, like genre paintings of the period.

THE CAST

Of the nearly fifty images that make up Fenton's Orientalist suite, he appears in only two (perhaps because he was usually too busy behind the camera to appear before it). In one of these, *Pasha and Bayadère* (pl. 62), he appropriately cast himself as the most powerful figure, the pasha. But any pasha has retainers or companions; uncovering the identities of the other members of the cast will help us determine what they contributed to their roles.

The discovery that a group of Fenton's Orientalist photographs once belonged to the English landscape painter Frank Dillon (1823–1909) led to the realization that Dillon frequently figures in the photographs. In *Pasha and Bayadère* he plays the musician to Fenton's pasha, and he appears as one of the actors in at least ten other images (pls. 63, 64).[6] He is also seen alone in two costume studies and two other solo poses (figs. 54, 55).[7] Four years younger than Fenton, Dillon began exhibiting at the Royal Academy at the same time Fenton did. Both showed there in 1849 and 1850, and these may have been the events that first brought them together. Most relevant for the making of Fenton's Orientalist suite is that Dillon, an inveterate traveler, spent the winter of 1854–55 sailing up the Nile and during that time made numerous watercolors at Thebes, Luxor, Karnak, Aswan, and elsewhere.[8] Although he is better known for his landscapes, titles like *Arabs Resting at Asouan, Figures on the Outskirts of Asouan,* and *A Group of Arabs at Luxor* make it clear that he closely studied the appearance—including postures and body language—of people in the Islamic world.[9] In 1856, 1857, and 1858 he exhibited paintings drawing on his first Egyptian expedition at the Royal Academy, where Fenton no doubt saw them. When Fenton enlisted Dillon in the making of the Orientalist suite in 1858, Dillon brought with him considerably more knowledge of the Near East and the behavior of its people than Fenton possessed.[10] There is even a possibility that the project was suggested by Dillon, but whatever its genesis, the painter's experience undoubtedly informed the posing of figures for the photographs.

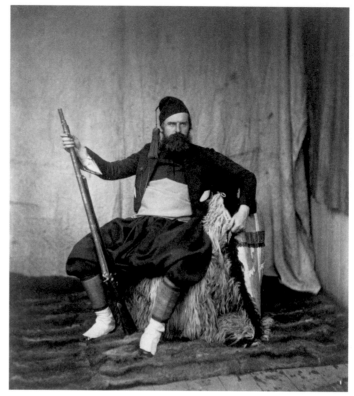

Fig. 52. Roger Fenton, *Self-Portrait as Zouave, 2nd Division,* 1855. Salted paper print, 19.2 x 15.9 cm (7 9/16 x 6 1/4 in.). Wilson Centre for Photography, 97:5626

Another person who may appear in a few of these photographs is the photographer Gabriel de Rumine (1841–1871), a Russian whose aristocratic family had settled in Lausanne. In an album that includes six of Fenton's Orientalist photographs, one of them has inscribed below it the title *Coffee Making* and written next to it in the same hand, "The Slave Gabriel de Rumine."[11] One problem with this identification is that the figure in the photograph (visible only obliquely) seems to have a beard heavier than likely for a man of seventeen. De Rumine was certainly precocious in his activities, if not his physiognomy, since in 1858 he became a member of the Société Française de Photographie and set off in October with Grand Duke Constantine, a brother of Czar Alexander II and the head of the Russian navy, on a nine-month Mediterranean cruise carried out by a squadron of five ships—photographing sites that included Nice, Naples, Pompeii, Sicily, Athens, and Jerusalem.[12] It is tempting to speculate that de Rumine was in London in 1858 to learn photography from Fenton, but it is perhaps more probable that he was taught by a Frenchman.

In 1962 a photograph from the collection of the Bavarian-born watercolorist Carl Haag (1820–1915) appeared on the market, and it was suggested in the auction catalogue that Haag is the heavily bearded, turbaned man who is seen with a veiled woman (fig. 56). The print was offered with another image of the woman standing alone; neither was described as the work of Fenton.[13] In the early 1980s three other photographs using the same two models appeared at auction.[14] In the same period, other prints of all five images that came from albums closely associated with Fenton and likely belonging to him or his family appeared on the market.[15] In this way the five images came to be known as Fenton works. They are, however, something of an anomaly among his Orientalist photographs. This man and woman are dressed in full regalia far more elaborate and authentically Near Eastern than the garments worn by Fenton's other sitters. The couple did not pose with the people in the larger series (although the man may appear in one of the group pictures in that series). Also, the setting cannot be clearly identified as Fenton's studio.[16]

There are documented connections between Haag and Fenton. In 1854 Haag had applied color to a series of salt prints by Fenton showing Queen Victoria's children dressed for a pageant celebrating her wedding anniversary. These are the first images Fenton made of tableaux. (See also figs. 47, 48.) Additionally, two watercolors by Haag were included in the sale of Fenton's collection in 1870.[17] Therefore it can be presumed that the photographer and the watercolorist knew each other. Was it coincidental that soon after Fenton completed his Orientalist series Haag left England for an extended sojourn in Egypt and Palestine?[18] Still, Haag's appearance in Fenton's photographs remains a matter of conjecture. The four other men who figure in the series can be assumed to be friends of Fenton's rather than models, but their identities—and whether they too were artists—are wholly unknown.[19] The nexus in Fenton's studio of photographers and artists, most of whom had or would develop interests in the Islamic world, suggests that an air of collegiality as well as high jinks may have prevailed.

The woman who appears again and again in the photographs was surely a professional model because some of the poses reveal her anatomy to an extent that would have been unthinkable for a "respectable" woman. The

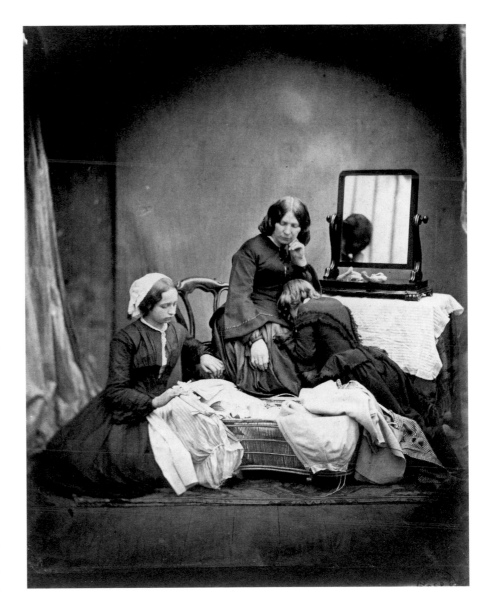

Fig. 53. Roger Fenton, *La Faute*, ca. 1855. Albumen silver print, 36 x 27 cm (14⅜ x 10⅝ in.). Société Française de Photographie, Paris, 140/8

Orientalist fantasy of western Europeans of course included the idea of women as both subservient and sexually available. Around the woman's presence and these attendant attitudes the whole of the series can be said to pivot. If the photographs discussed in connection with Dillon, de Rumine, and Haag are excluded, there are only seven pictures for which she did not

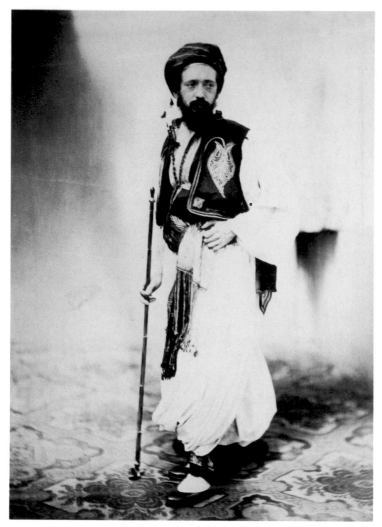

Fig. 54. Roger Fenton, *Frank Dillon in Near Eastern Dress*, 1858. Albumen silver print, 25.8 x 18.1 cm (10 3/16 x 7 1/8 in.). The J. Paul Getty Museum, Los Angeles, 84.XP.219.34

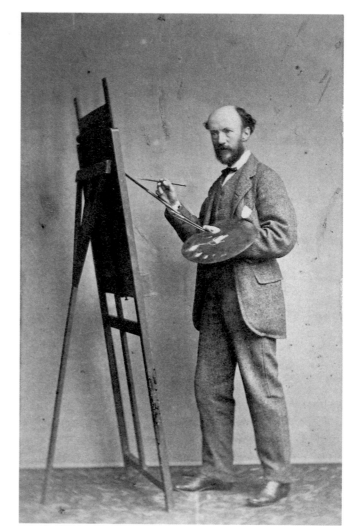

Fig. 55. Unknown photographer, *Frank Dillon at His Easel*, ca. 1865. Albumen silver print. Private collection, England

pose; she figures in thirteen photographs with other people and fourteen by herself. In the latter group she bears a large clay pot meant to represent a water vessel (pl. 65) or sits on a low divan, in three variant poses wearily propping her head on her wrist, meditatively cradling a goblet drum in her lap, or mimicking playing a lute.[20] When she is posed with men she entertains them by dancing or playing an instrument (pl. 62), keeps them company (pl. 63), serves them by carrying burdens, or cowers before them (pl. 64). In the

photograph that most epitomizes the sensual allure of the world of Orientalist fantasy, she reclines at full length on a low divan, her upper clothing loosened, her feet bare, and her heavy-lidded eyes gazing unfocused in what seems a dreamy trance (pl. 61).[21] Fenton exhibited it under the title *The Reverie*. The woman was evidently both patient and pliant, although judging by her facial expressions she was occasionally bored or uncertain about what she was being asked to portray, if in fact she was given specific cues.

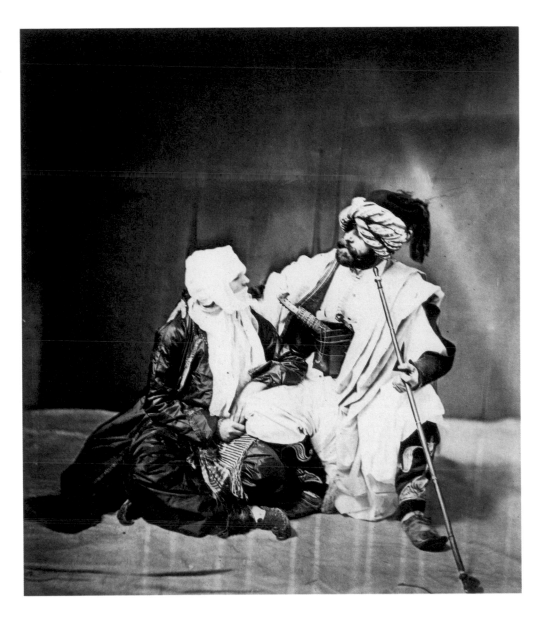

Fig. 56. Roger Fenton, *Couple in Fancy Dress*, 1858. Albumen silver print, 23.6 x 20.4 cm (9⁵⁄₁₆ x 8¹⁄₁₆ in.). The J. Paul Getty Museum, Los Angeles, 84.XM.922.2

SET, COSTUMES, PROPS

All of the photographs were made in Fenton's London studio, which was at his home in Albert Terrace, most likely in a building behind the house itself. The studio skylight is visible at the top of the untrimmed print of *Pasha and Bayadère* (pl. 62), as are the wires that made it possible for the model to hold her arms motionless above her head throughout the exposure.[22] An Anatolian rug conceals nearly all of the European carpet on the studio floor. In this image a miscellany of Near Eastern objects, including a spiked fiddle, an octagonal table with mother-of-pearl inlay, an inlaid tambourine, a goblet drum, a hammered brass coffeepot, and a water pipe have been used to dress the set. They will be rearranged for other photographs, as will the brocade cushions and draperies. Rather makeshift costumes, partly authentically Near Eastern but from various regions and partly improvised, are worn by the players.[23] Some of the props and garments may have been souvenirs from Dillon's Egyptian journey of three years earlier. An inlaid table of exactly

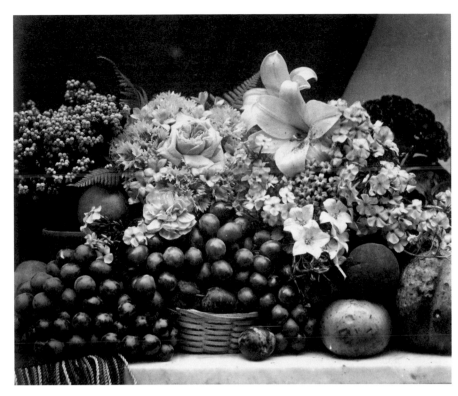

Fig. 63. Roger Fenton, *Flowers and Fruit*, 1860. Albumen silver print, 28.1 x 28.8 cm (11¹⁄₁₆ x 11⁵⁄₁₆ in.). The RPS Collection at the National Museum of Photography, Film & Television, Bradford, Gift of Fenton descendants, 1934, 2003-5000/3105

compared directly to Lance: "Mr. Roger Fenton has come out in an entirely new character, and may now be regarded in the photographic world in the same light as Lance amongst painters. . . . 'How delighted Lance would be with these!'"[43] Reviewers encouraged buying: "We congratulate collectors of photographs upon the new pleasure that is in store for them in acquiring some of this novel class of productions." Prints were for sale at ten shillings and sixpence apiece.[44]

One reviewer raised the issue of color for the still-life studies. "It is true that to acquire all possible beauty they do require the application of colour. We remember to have seen some specimens of flowers, on a smaller scale, that had been well tinted, exhibited at one of the meetings of the North London Photographic Association, and are convinced from what we then saw that a profitable field is open in this direction to any artist having the requisite skill, as such productions, well got up, would meet with eager

purchasers."[45] It is not clear whether the hand-colored flower studies mentioned were also by Fenton; if they were, they have not survived. Nor indeed have many Fenton still-life photographs, suggesting that these works did not sell as well as the reviewers, and perhaps Fenton, expected.

Fenton's still lifes reflect the interests and material resources of the wealthy Victorian middle classes: Chinamania, exotic products of the British Empire both edible and decorative, the new greenhouse technology, the coded language of flowers. But it is the reality of these images, the three-dimensional density of their compositions of fruit piled upon fruit, that is most startling. And because they are so abundantly real, these displays are transmuted into something lush, sensuous, and ultimately bound to decay—true *nature morte*.

Fenton often observes the classical traditions of still-life composition that can be seen in the paintings of Lance and Ladell: peaches always seem to come in twos, translucent white currants must always hang over the edge of the tabletop, baskets must always be wicker, the fruit must be arranged on a pedestaled tazza. But, employing the skills of his particular art, he infuses the still life with something quite his own.

The three cameras are set up—the six-lens stereo and the 15 x 15-inch- and 20 x 16-inch-plate cameras. It is often possible to see a suggestion of camera reflections in the polished surfaces of grapes and cherries; but reflections of at least two cameras and tripods are very clearly visible, one assumes purposely, in the silver goblet used in several photographs (fig. 57). Typically, the stereo view pulls away from the arranged still life, which occupies perhaps 60 percent of the image, to show it isolated in an outdoor setting against a bare brick wall draped with cloth (fig. 62). The 15 x 15-inch format comes closer, showing the same dents in the foreground apple, the same mold on the melon, the same wizened grape near the bottom of the bunch; but now the composition is tighter, cropping out the brick wall and most of the drape so that the still life occupies 75 percent of the image (fig. 63). Finally, the 20 x 16-inch image moves right to the heart of the subject (pl. 86). The composition has been slightly rearranged, with the flowers at the right replaced by a vase for better balance, but the fruits, complete with dents and misty bloom, are intact. The image is tight and fills 90 percent of the photograph. The print's top has been arched to even more fully immerse the viewer in this most stunning of Fenton's still lifes.

The bad spring and summer of 1860 may be what allowed Fenton to achieve the impossible and photograph together fruit that in the British climate would normally reach maturity over a four-month period, from gooseberries in early June to grapes in late September. That year the early outdoor-grown fruit ripened late in the inclement weather, while the late fruit ripened early in the greenhouse. Imported exotic fruits had also become relatively common. In 1853 the *Illustrated London News* mentioned the first large twenty-four-day cargo of pineapples, imported from Eleuthera in the Bahamas.[46] In the Crimea in 1855, Fenton had "stock" with him from Fortnum & Mason, grocers to the royal family, and later he may have bought his still-life supplies from them.[47]

Grapes, white, black, and red currants, plums, peaches, melons, pineapples, strawberries; pinks, China asters, Hoya, lilacs, lilies and roses (flowers associated with the Virgin Mary and the Annunciation), fuchsia, chrysanthemums; cherries, gooseberries, raspberries, apples, ferns, sweet william, laurel, cucumbers, pansies, and Canterbury bells are just some of the items of produce that jostle for position in these heady photographs. Each also has a time-honored symbolic meaning. The carved ivory caskets, the richly wrought hunting cup carved with the legend of Saint Hubert and decorated with silver fox heads, the ornate silver mirror and chased silver goblet—all exquisite, intricately hand-crafted items of value—represent taste, trade, wealth, and possessions.

Fenton obviously intended this series of still lifes to express homage to the grape. Grapes are everywhere, figuring in thirty-three of his thirty-nine still lifes in the Royal Photographic Society Collection. And these grapes, still white with bloom, will ferment and make wine. To emphasize the point further, Fenton introduces wine-related objects: three different decanters, two chased silver goblets, a glass beaker, a Parian ware vase dripping with grapes and vine leaves in relief, a silver-and-ivory tankard carved with grape-picking cherubs.[48] Close observation reveals that one particular bunch of grapes in a wicker basket, recognizable from a wrinkled specimen at its bottom and the shape of the bloom on two adjoining grapes, played a part in seven different still lifes before the wrinkled grape, perhaps too wizened for beauty, was removed (and eaten?). Marks that look suspiciously like teeth indentations appear on one of the peaches.

Fenton continued to receive admiring reviews for his still lifes and—ironically, given all the glories of his photography that had gone before—a medal at the International Exhibition of 1862 "For great excellence in fruit and flower pieces, and good general photography."[49] But the relative scarcity of these still-life images now—fewer than fifty-five worldwide—suggests that the Victorian public did not purchase them in great numbers. In February 1863 the *Stereoscopic Magazine*, announcing Fenton's retirement from photography, featured one last still life and stated gloomily, "Neither fruit nor flowers are good subjects for photography. It has long been deemed hopeless to be able to apply the art to the purposes of botanical illustration. This and one or two other pictures already given in our magazine are equal to any that have been produced; and it is not likely that any further use will be made of photography for the delineation of such subjects."[50]

After the deaths of Hunt and Lance in 1864 and of Ladell in 1886, still-life painting ceased to be a genre that on its own could afford an artist in Britain a healthy living. Nor did British photographers strive to emulate Fenton's glorious example, perhaps quite rightly assuming that his still-life photographs could not be bettered. While photography, it later proved, never did "destroy all necessity of men wasting their time in painting still-life" as the *Athenaeum* predicted in January 1859, British photographers did not choose to assume the temporarily discarded mantle.[51]

PLATES

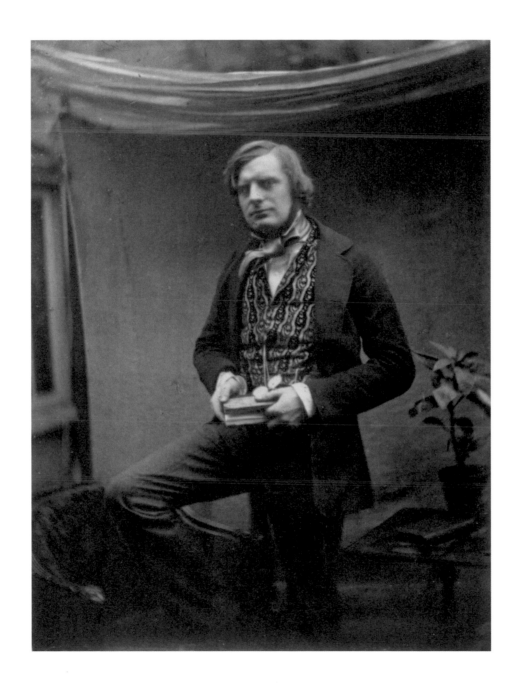

1. Self-Portrait, February 1852

RUSSIA, 1852

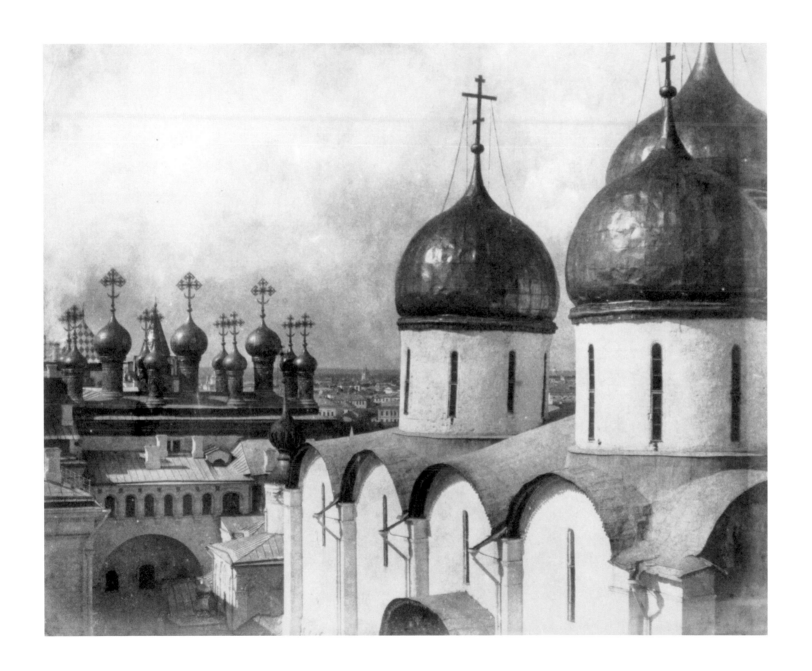

2. *Moscow, Domes of Churches in the Kremlin, 1852*

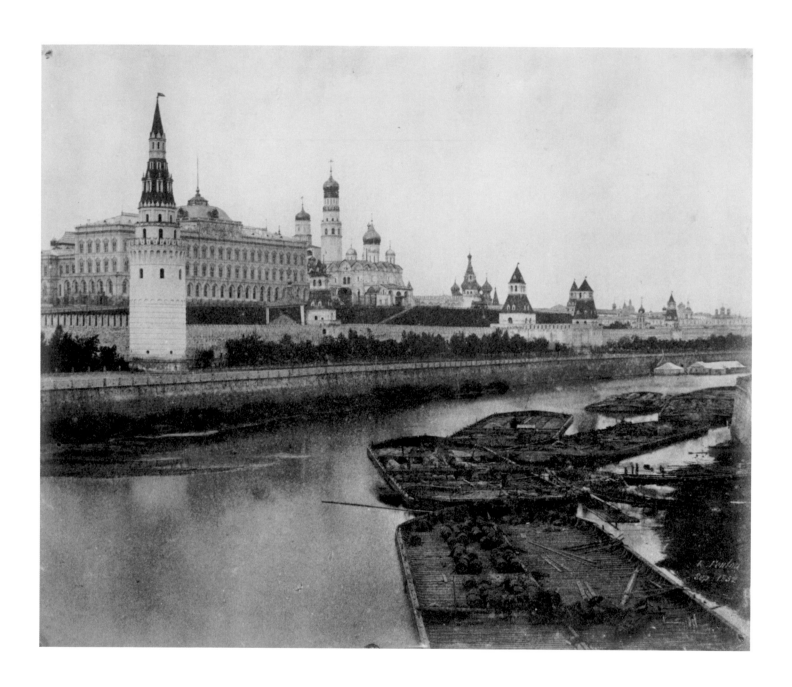

3. *South Front of the Kremlin from the Old Bridge*, 1852

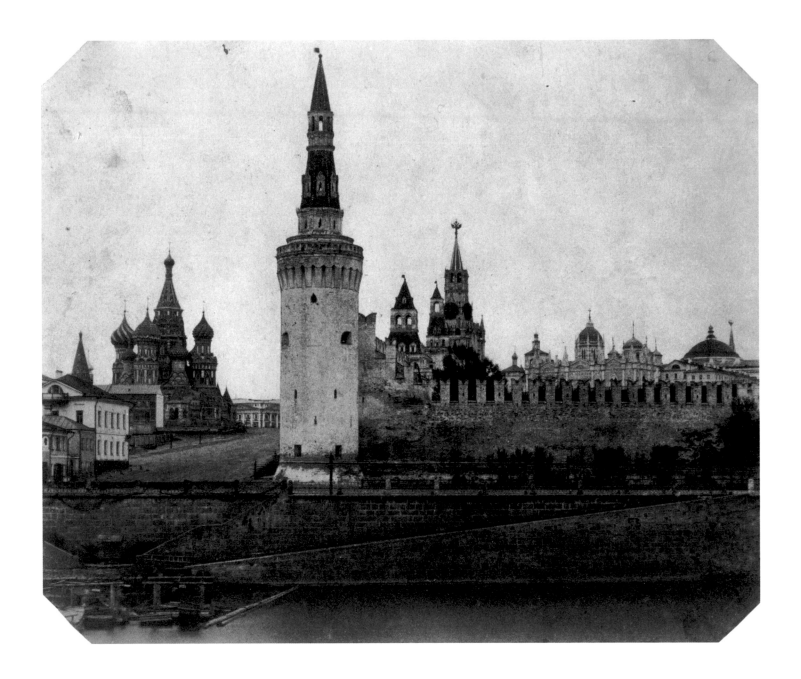

4. Walls of the Kremlin, Moscow, 1852

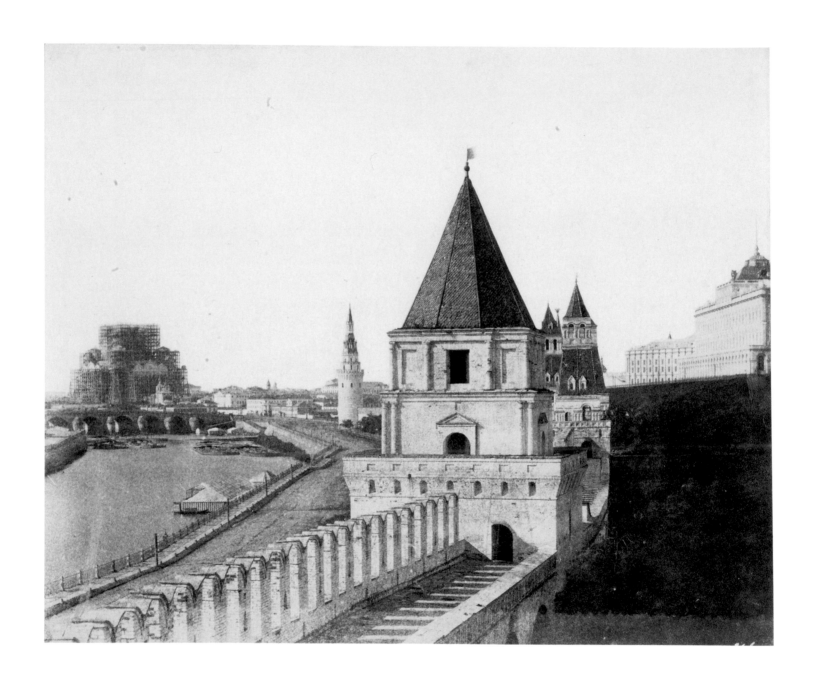

5. Walls of the Kremlin, Moscow, 1852

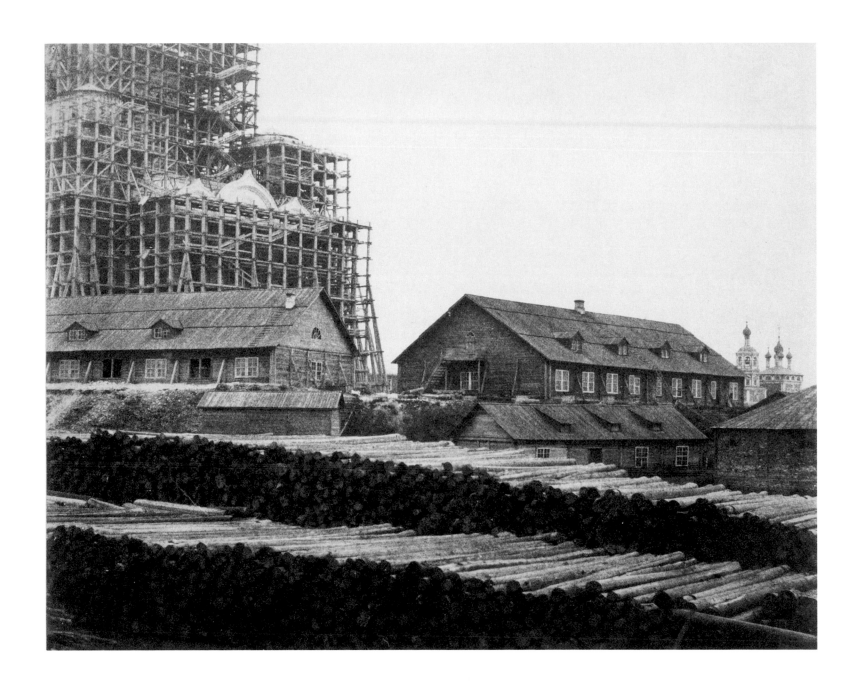

6. The Church of the Redeemer, Moscow, under Construction, 1852

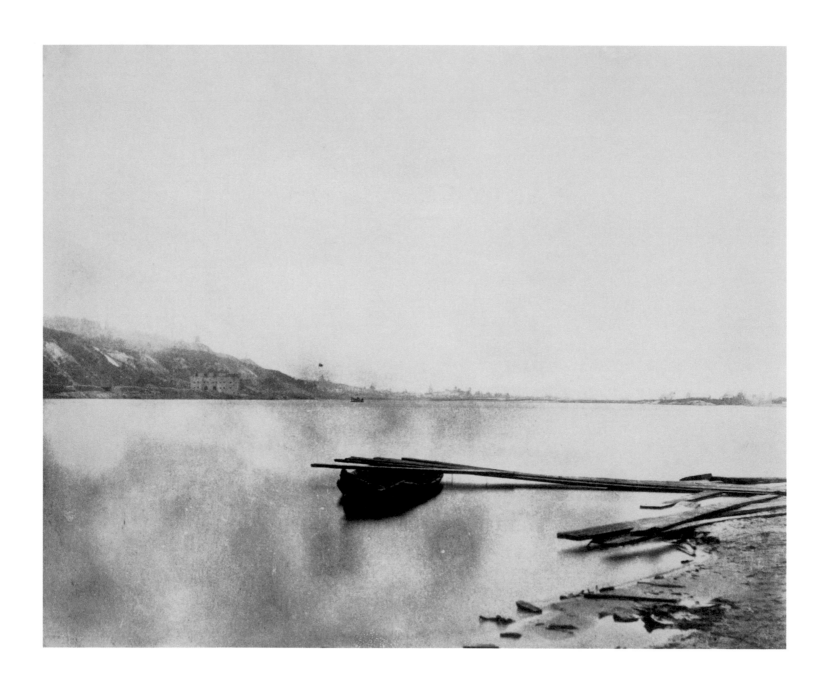

7. *Banks of the Dnieper; Distant View of the Forts and Low Town of Kief,* 1852

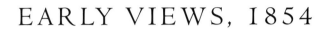

EARLY VIEWS, 1854

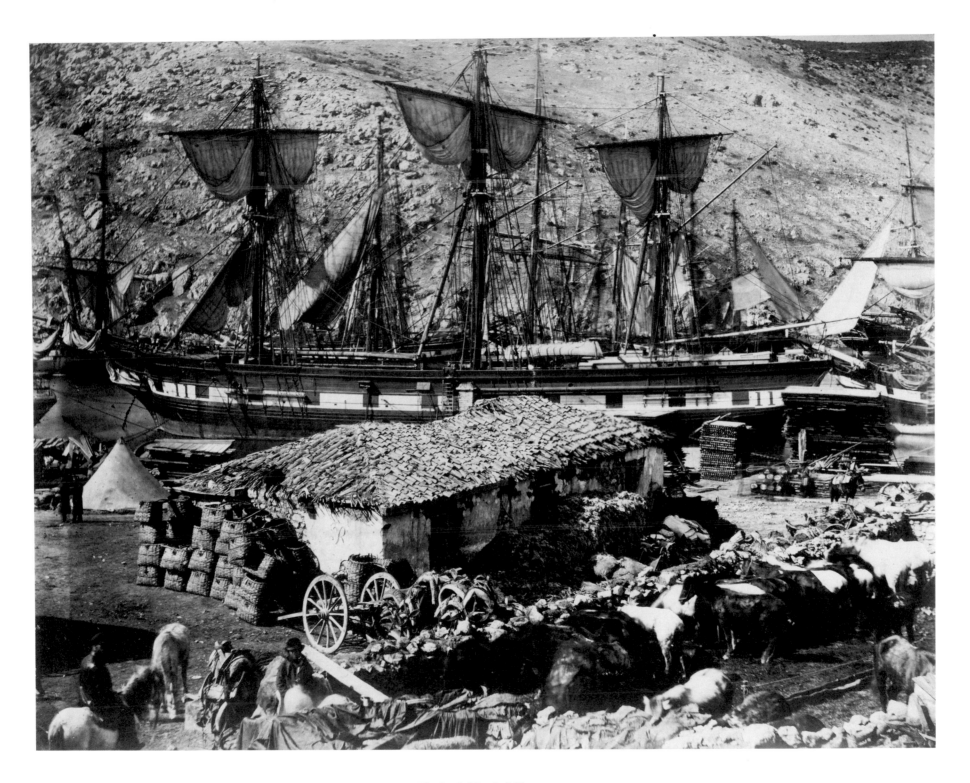

14. *The Cattle Pier, Balaklava*, 1855

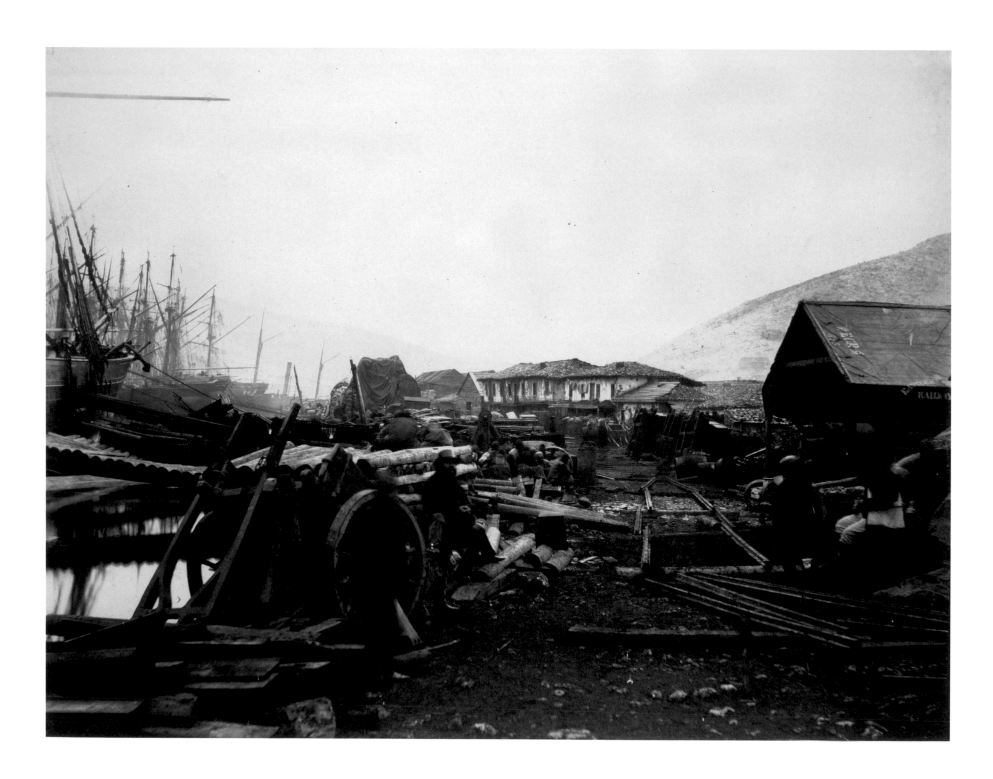

15. *Landing Place, Railway Stores, Balaklava,* 1855

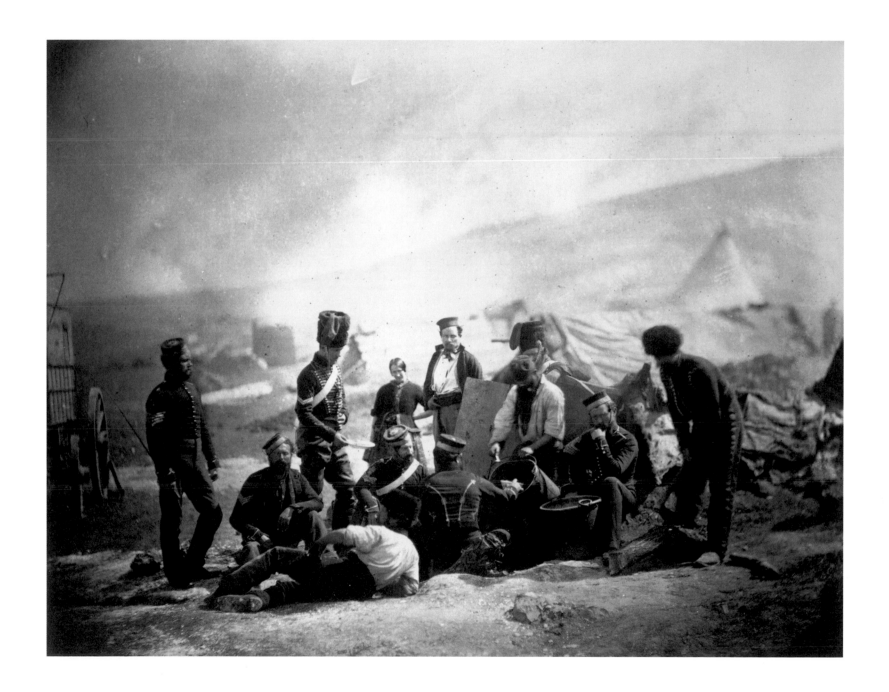

16. *Cookhouse of the 8th Hussars*, 1855

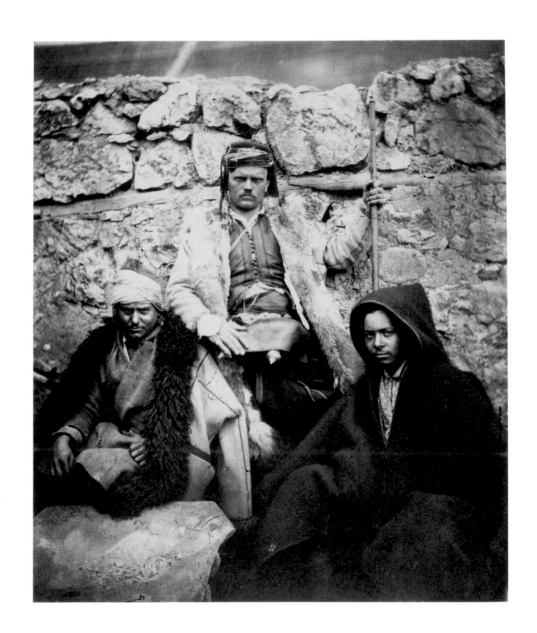

17. *Group of Croat Chiefs,* 1855

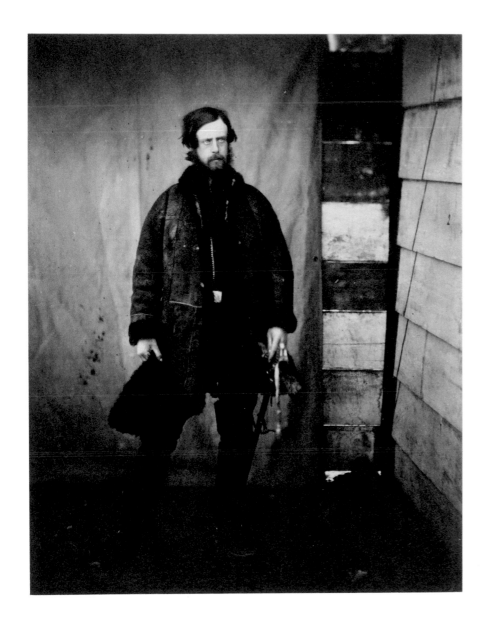

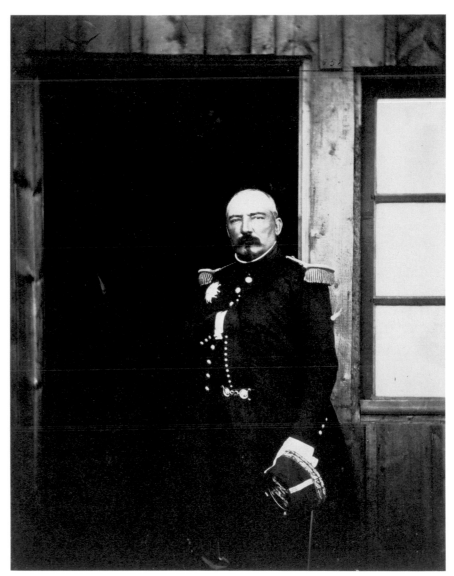

18. *Captain Lord Balgonie, Grenadier Guards,* 1855

19. *General Bosquet,* 1855

20. *Sebastopol from Cathcart's Hill,* 1855

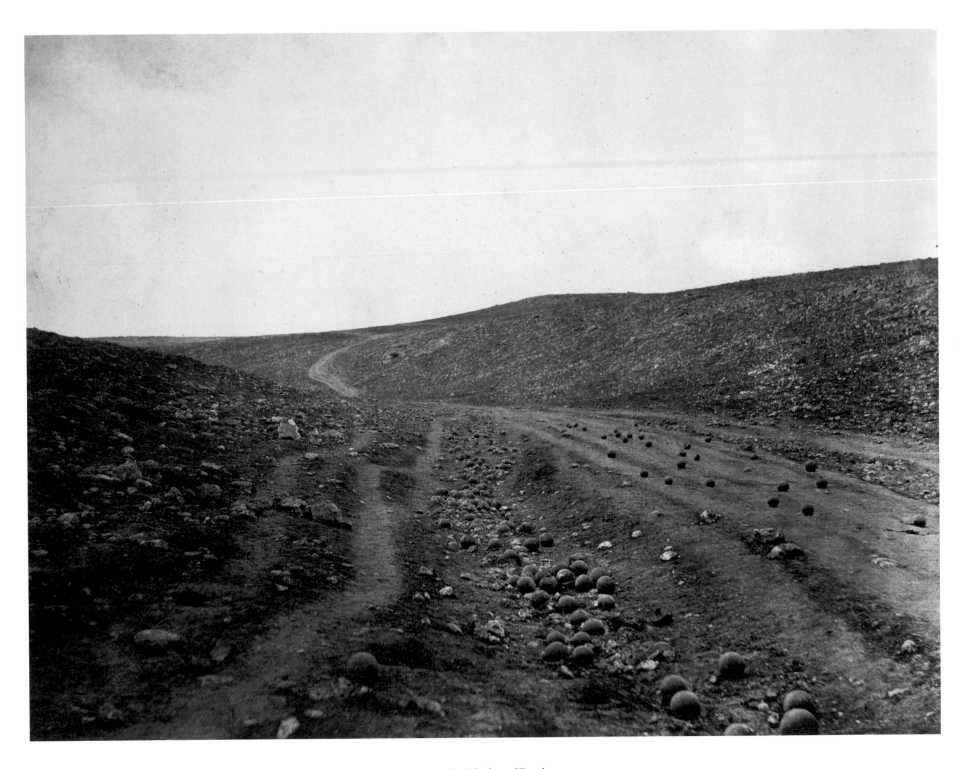

21. *Valley of the Shadow of Death*, 1855

EXCURSIONS TO SCOTLAND AND WALES, 1856 AND 1857

22. Landscape with Clouds, [1856]

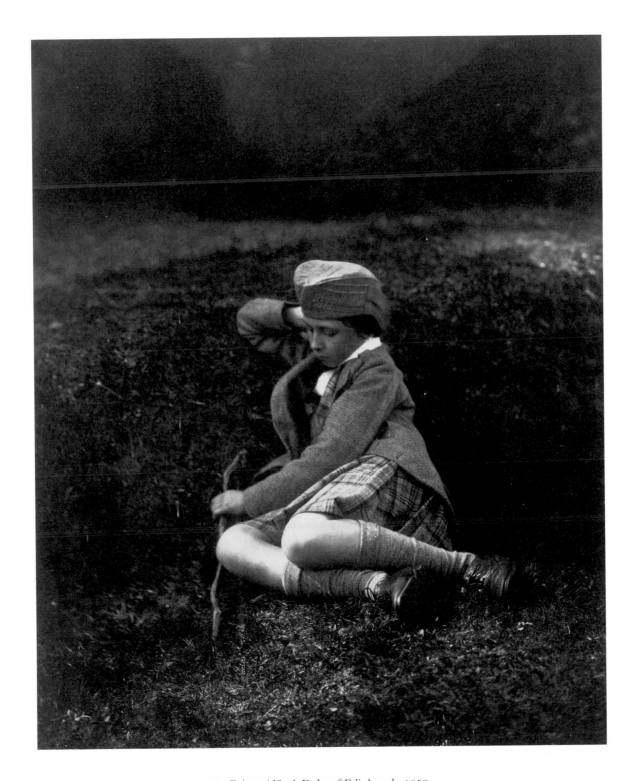

30. Prince Alfred, Duke of Edinburgh, 1856

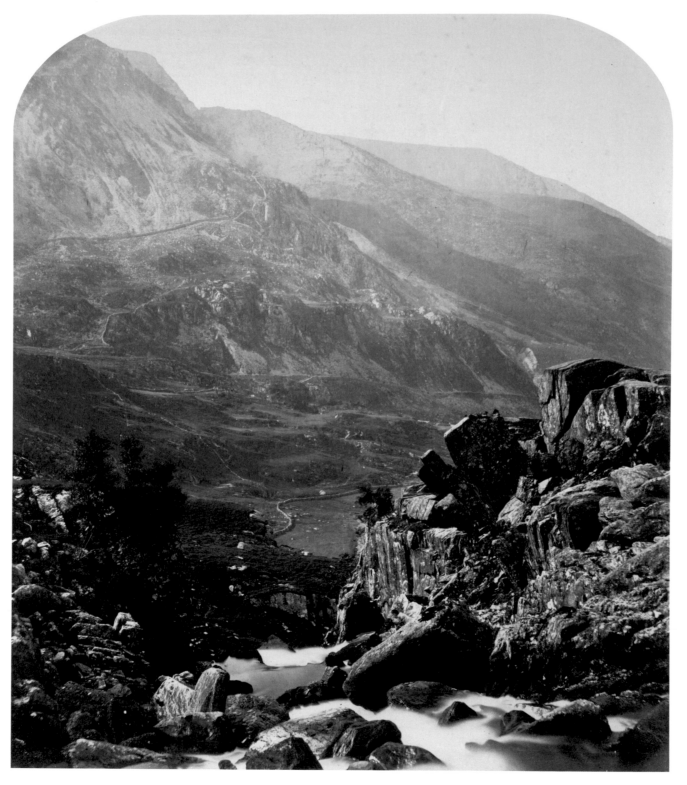

31. *View from Ogwen Falls into Nant Ffrancon,* 1857

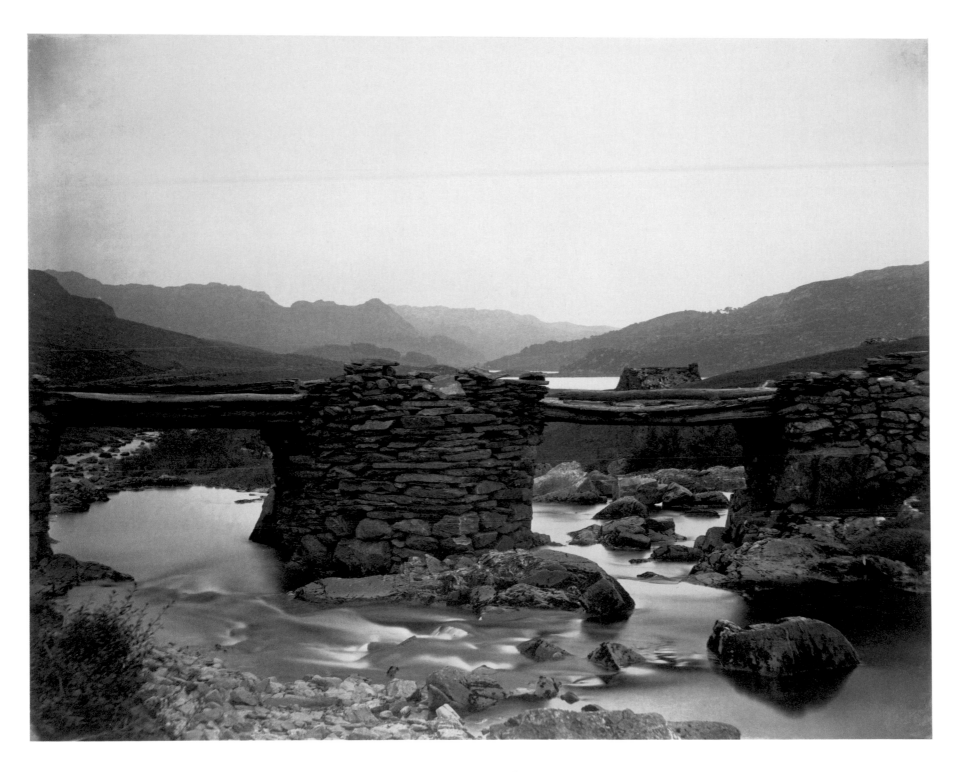

32. *Pont-y-Garth, near Capel Curig,* 1857

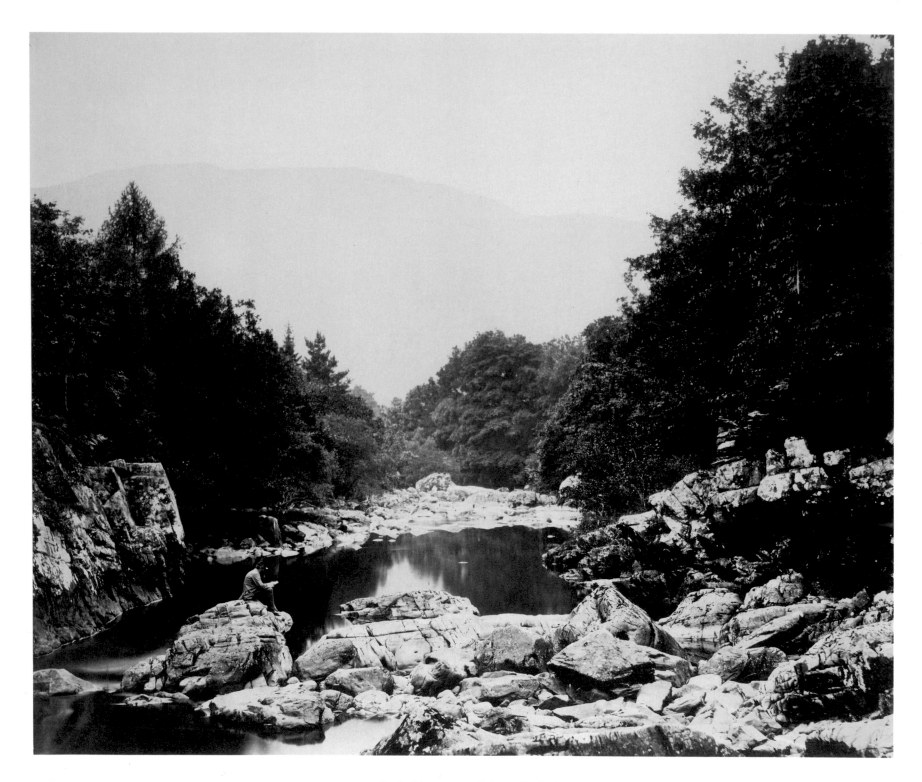

33. *On the Llugwy, near Bettws-y-Coed*, 1857

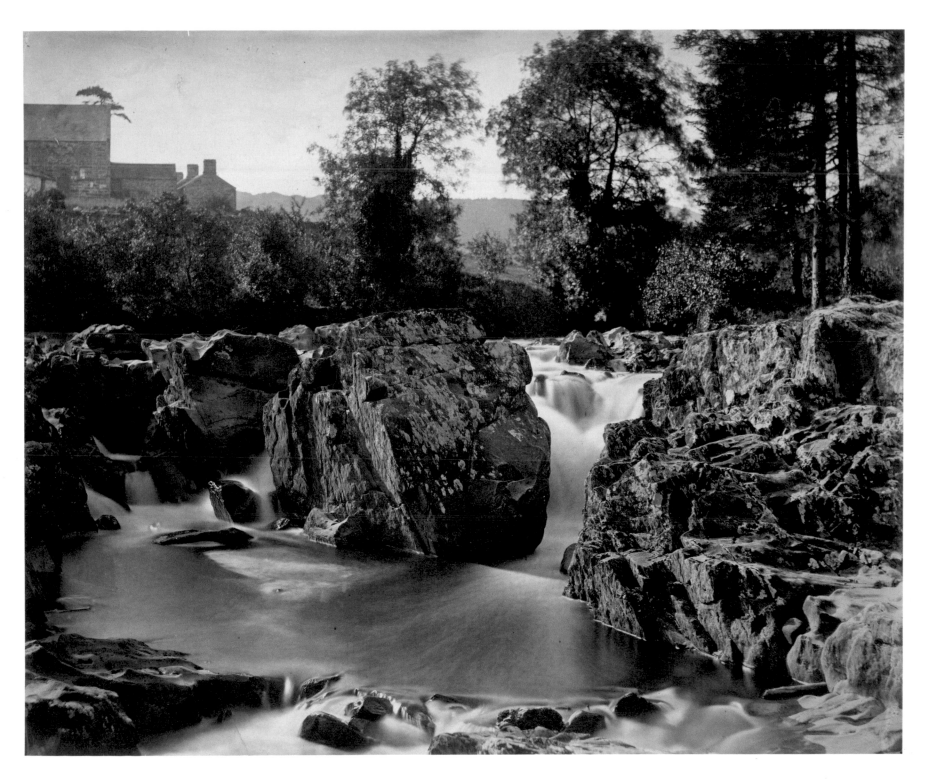

34. *Falls of the Llugwy, at Pont-y-Pair*, 1857

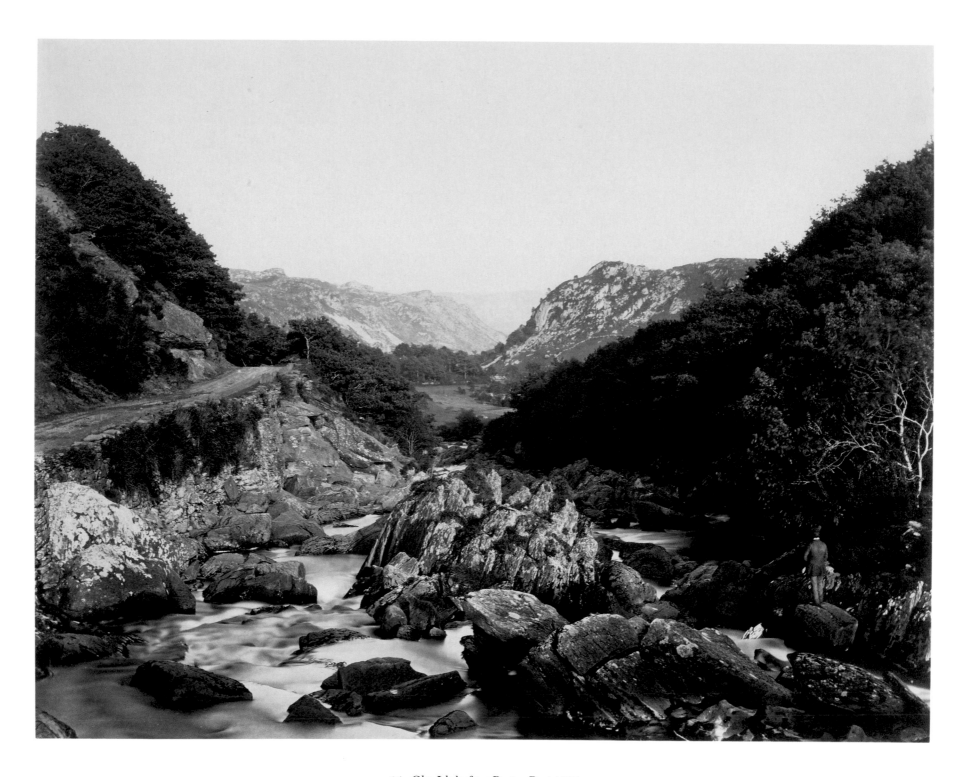

35. *Glyn Lledr, from Pont-y-Pant*, 1857

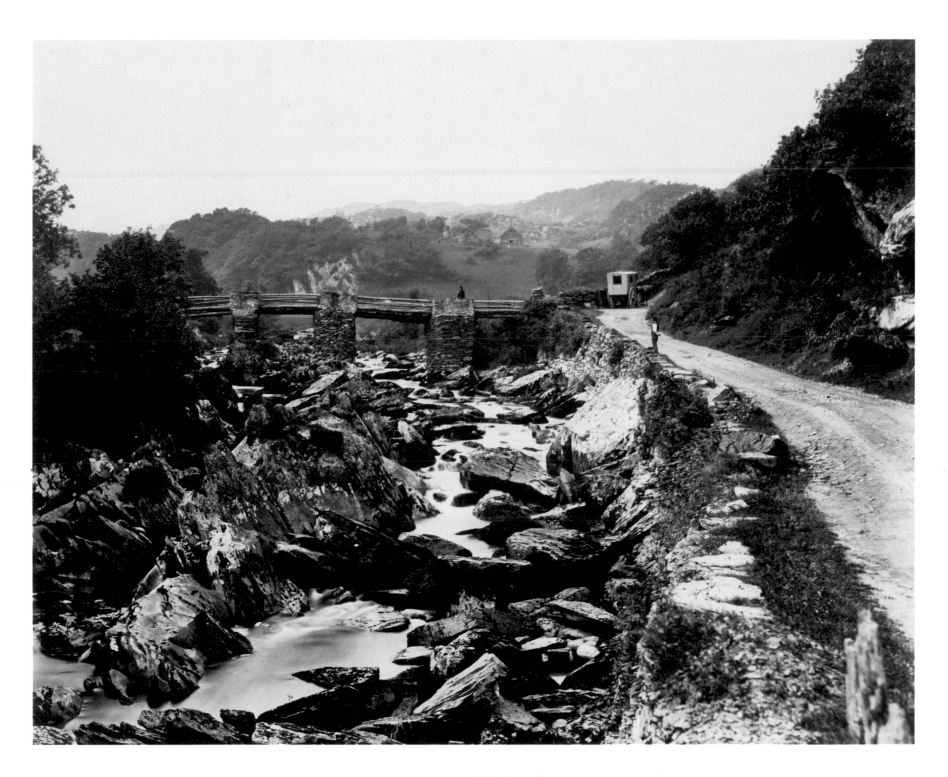

36. *Pont-y-Pant, on the Lledr, from Below,* 1857

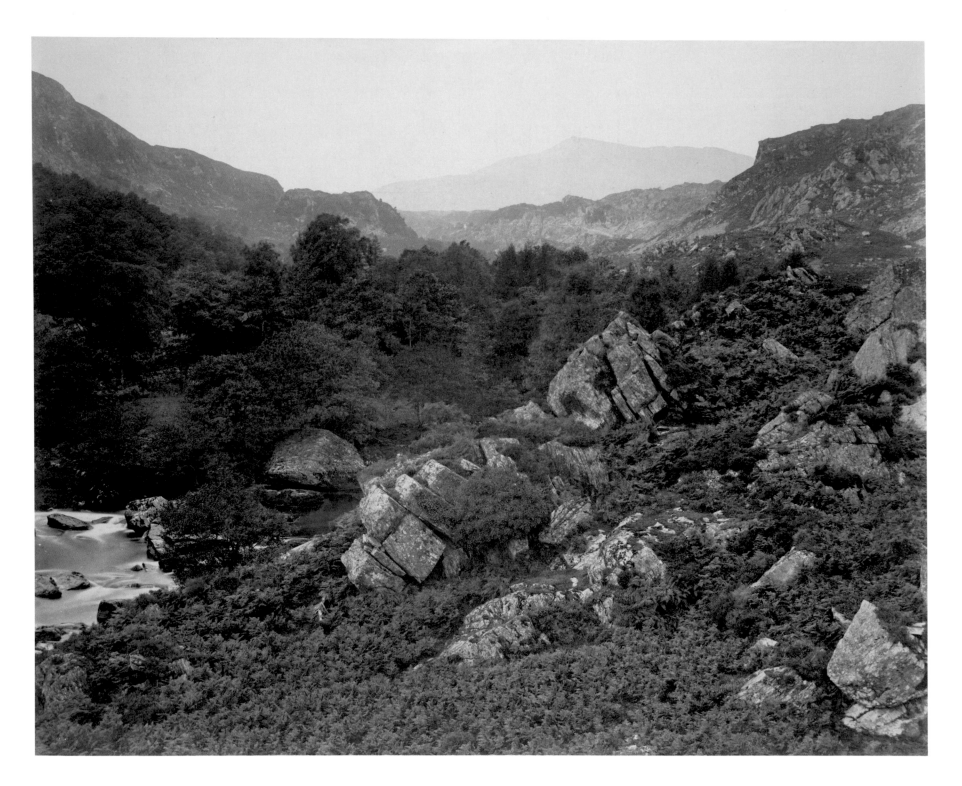

37. *Moel Seabod, from the Lledr Valley*, 1857

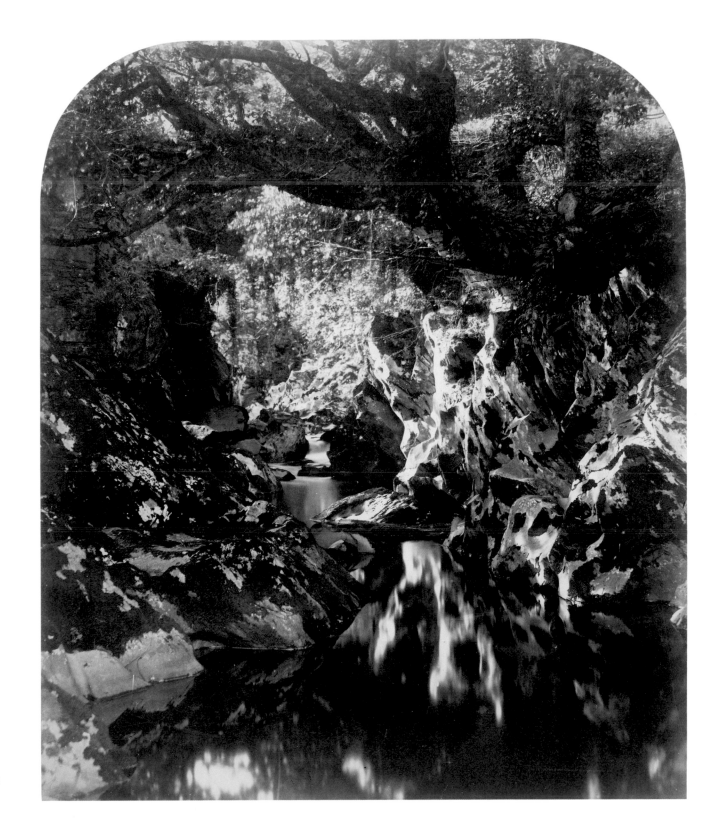

38. *The Double Bridge on the Machno*, 1857

SACRED AND SECULAR ARCHITECTURE, 1857–1858

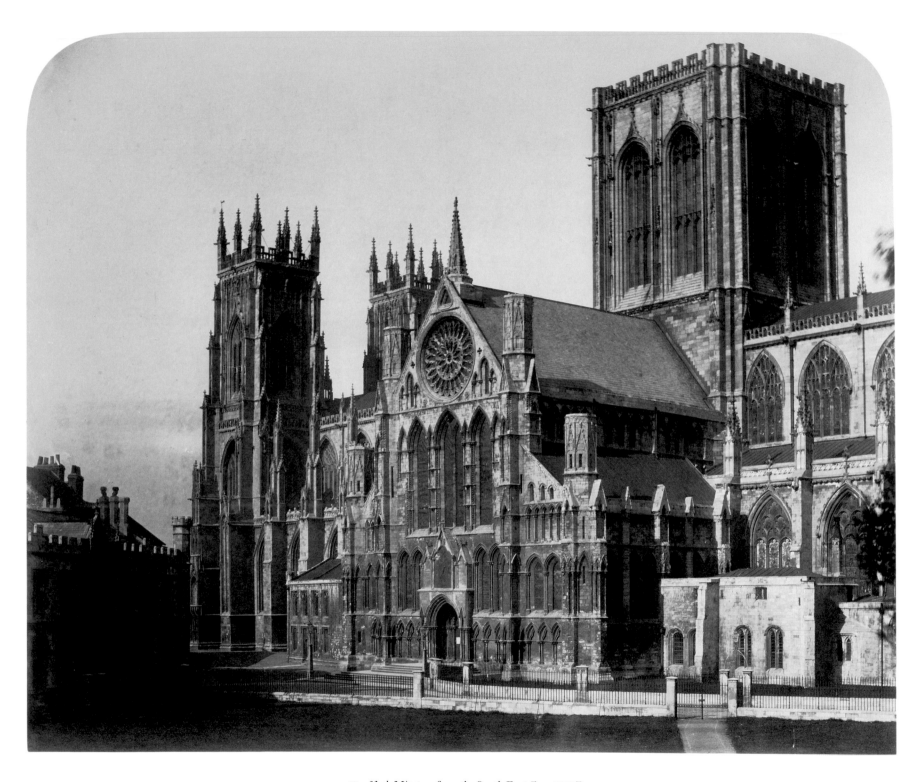

47. *York Minster, from the South East,* [ca. 1856]

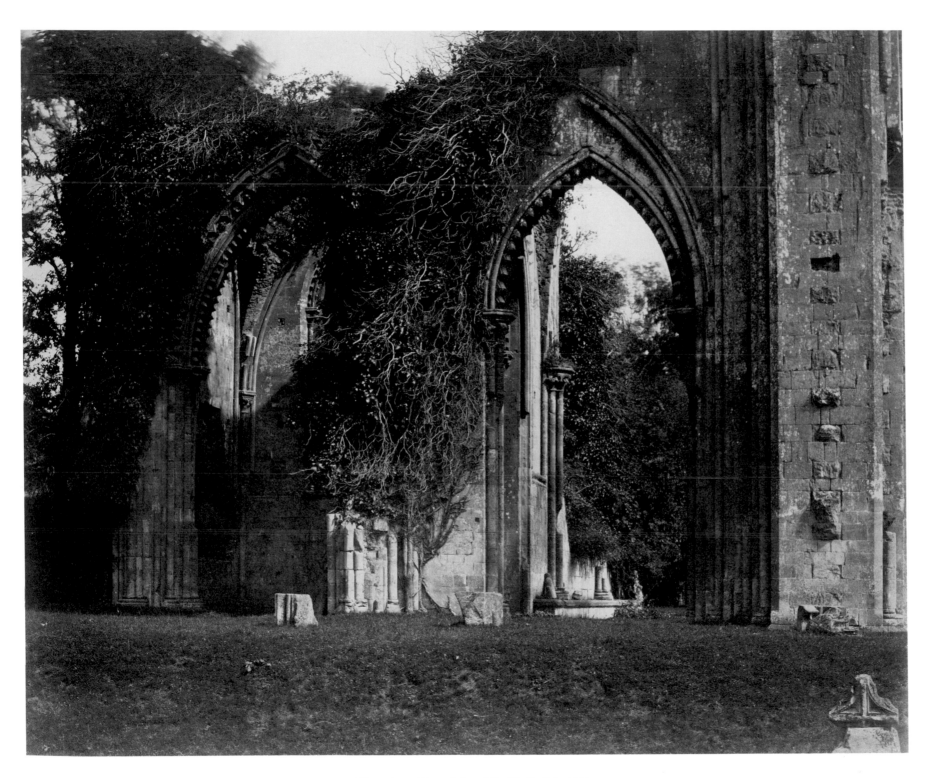

48. *Glastonbury Abbey, Arches of the North Aisle*, 1858

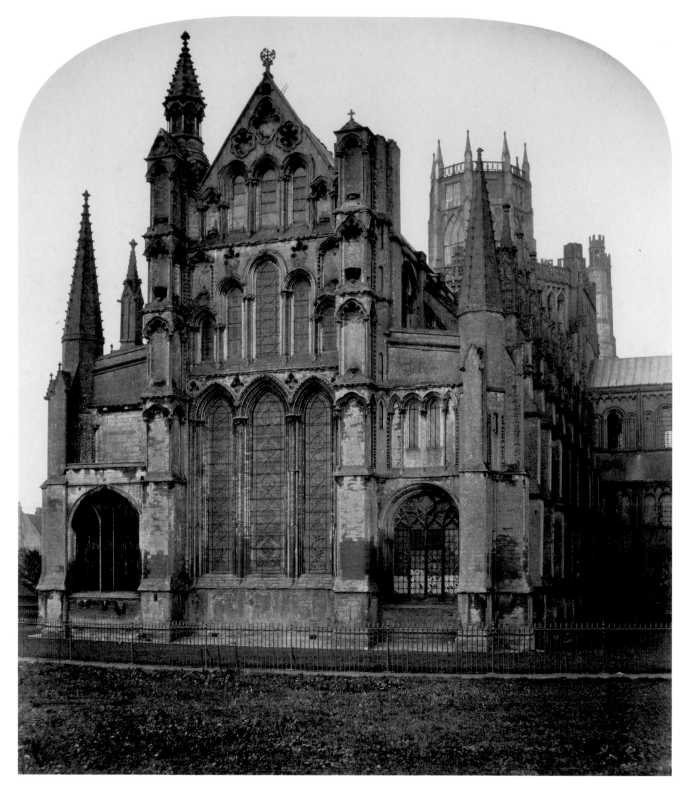

49. *Ely Cathedral, East End*, 1857

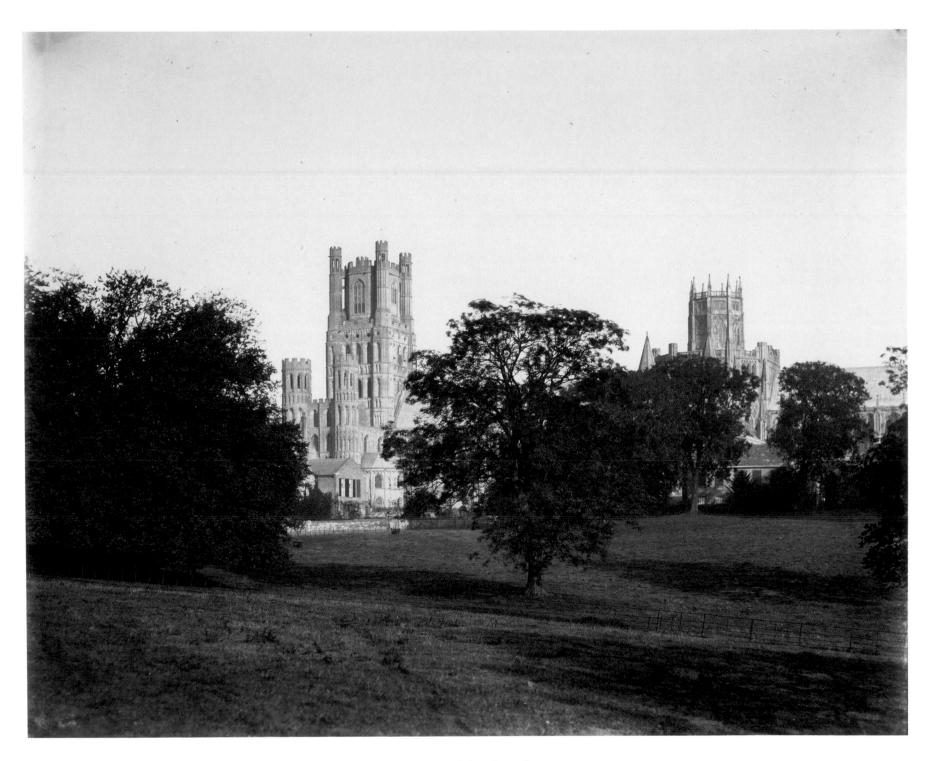

50. *Ely Cathedral, from the Park*, 1857

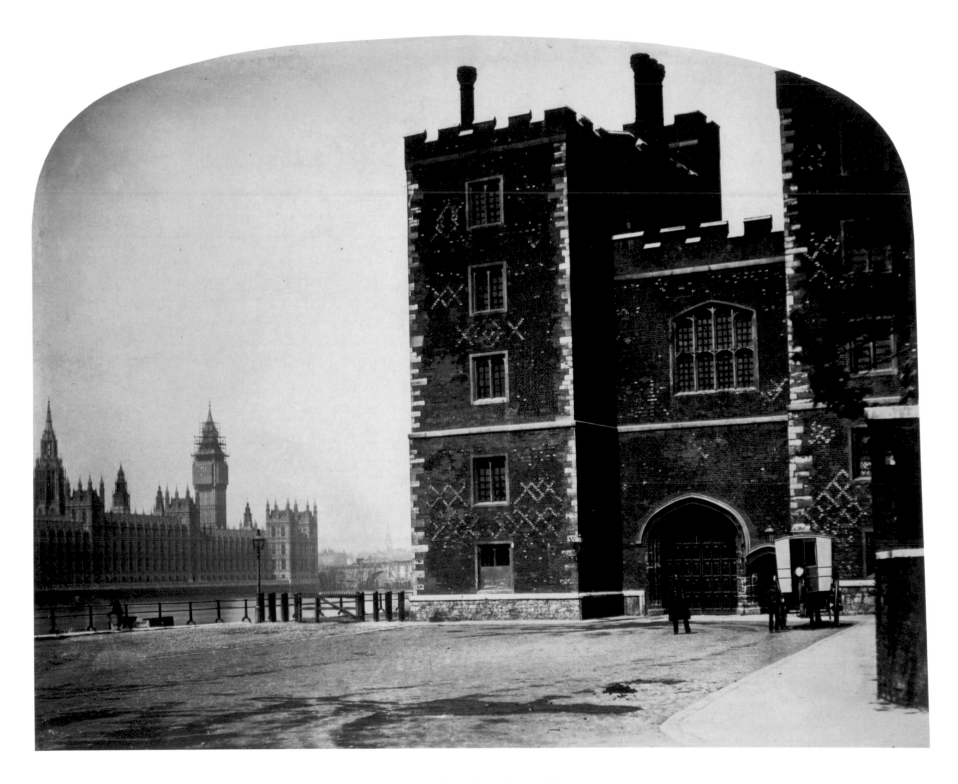

58. Lambeth Palace, [ca. 1858]

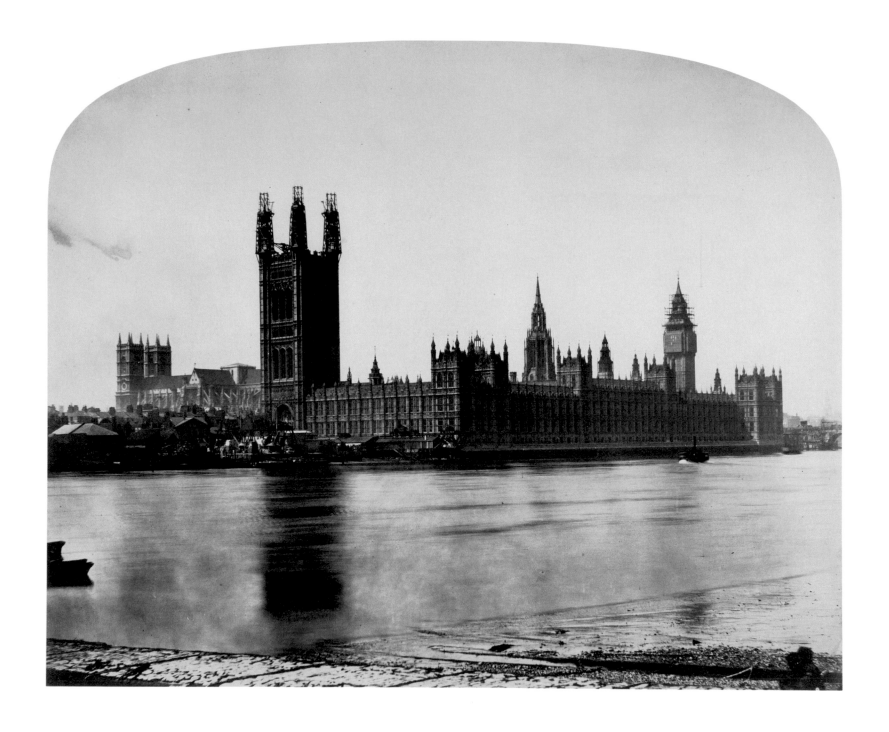

59. Houses of Parliament, [ca. 1858]

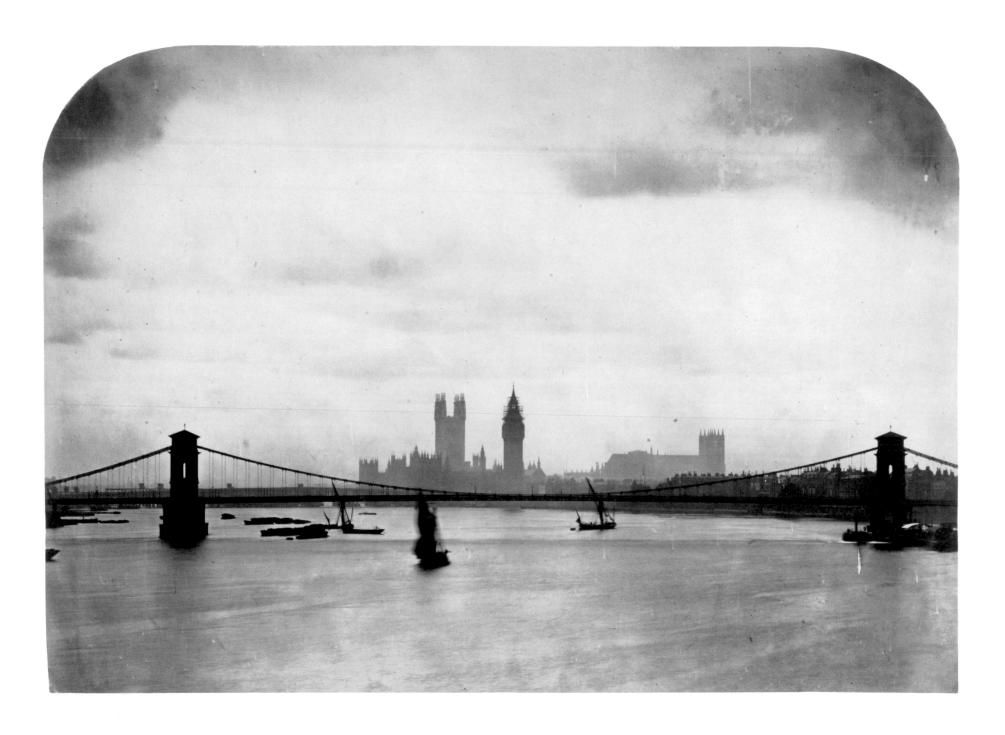

60. Westminster from Waterloo Bridge, [ca. 1858]

ORIENTALIST STUDIES, 1858

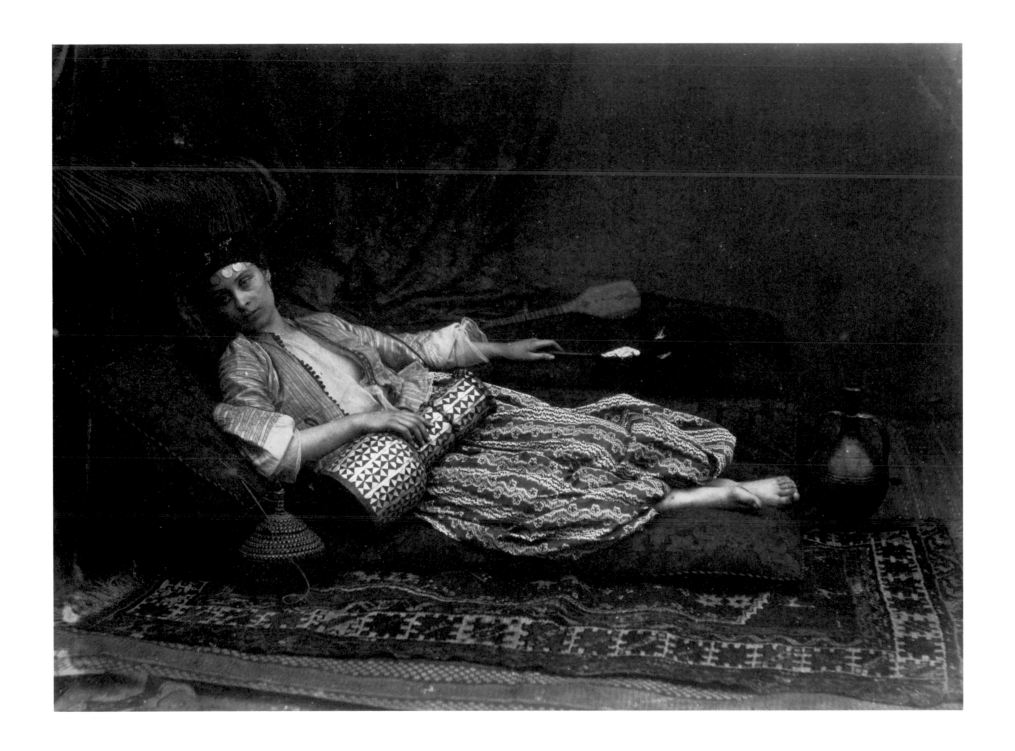

61. Reclining Odalisque, 1858

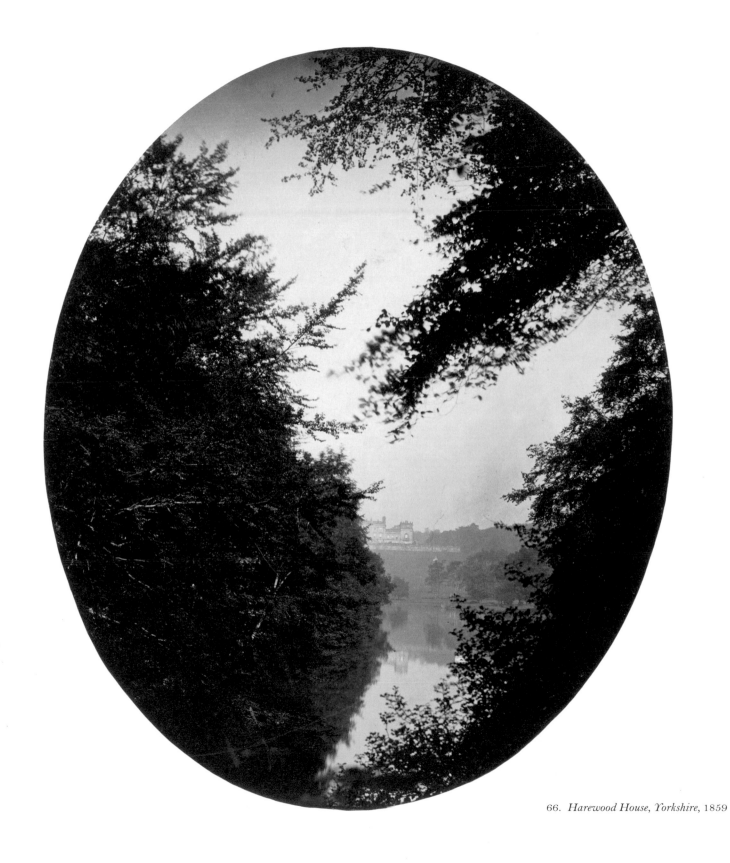

66. *Harewood House, Yorkshire*, 1859

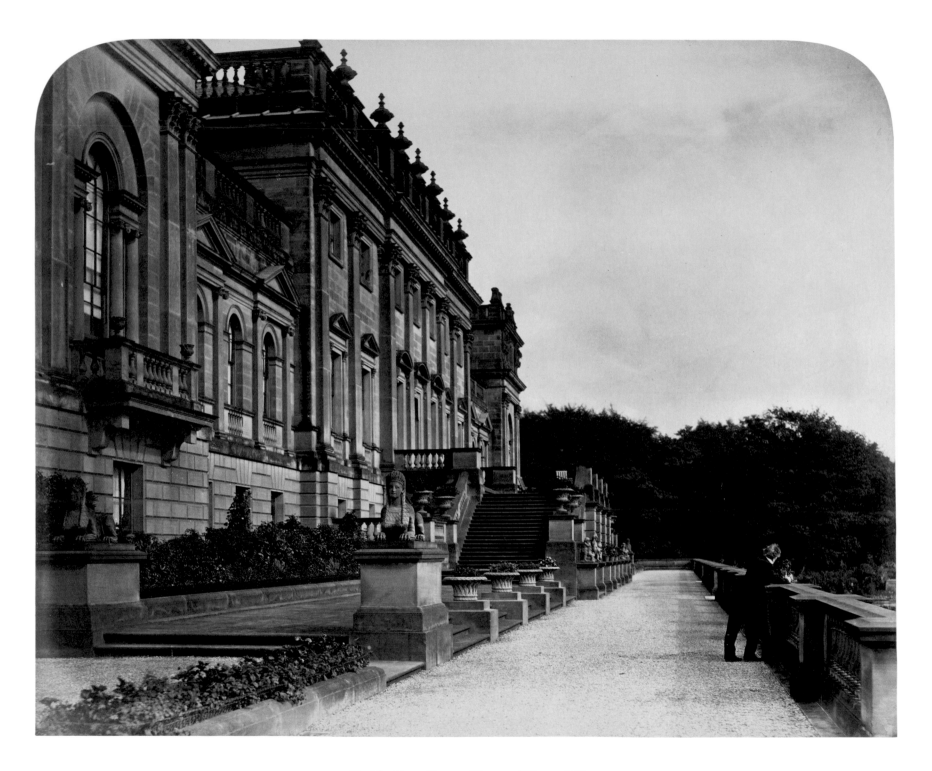

67. The Upper Terrace, Harewood House, 1859

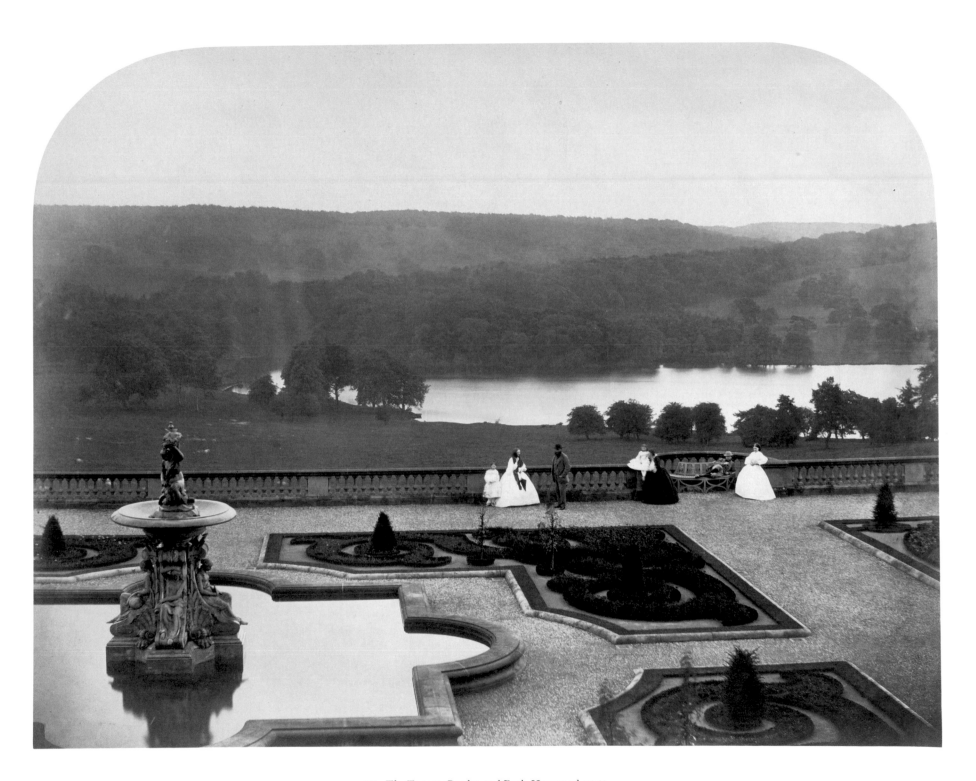

68. *The Terrace, Garden and Park, Harewood,* 1859

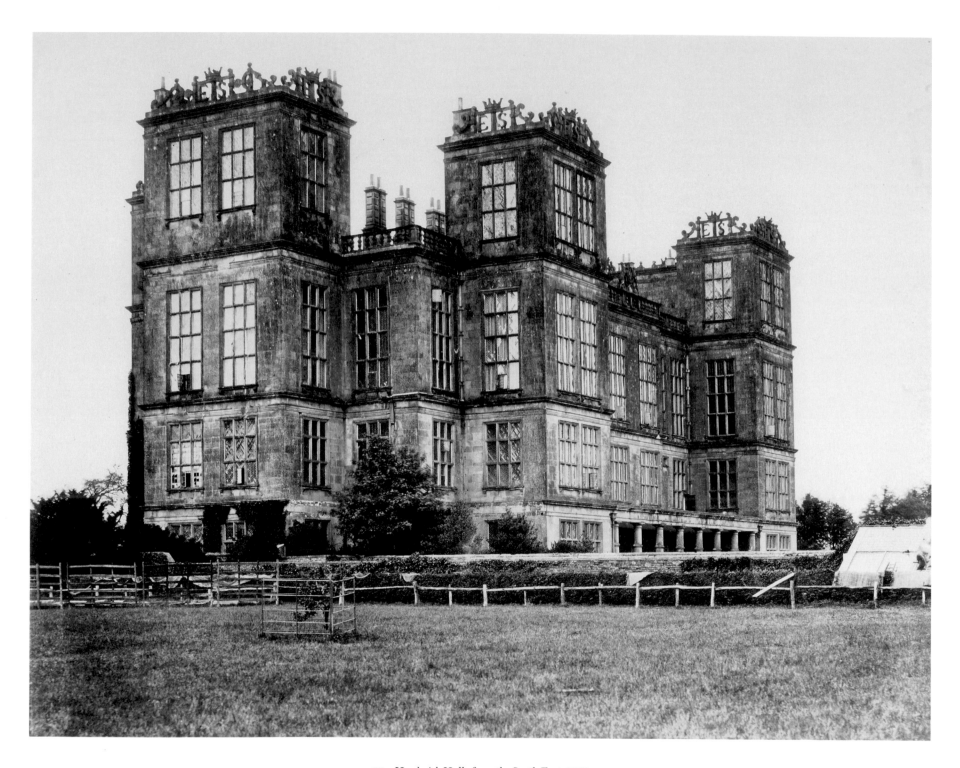

69. *Hardwick Hall, from the South East,* 1858

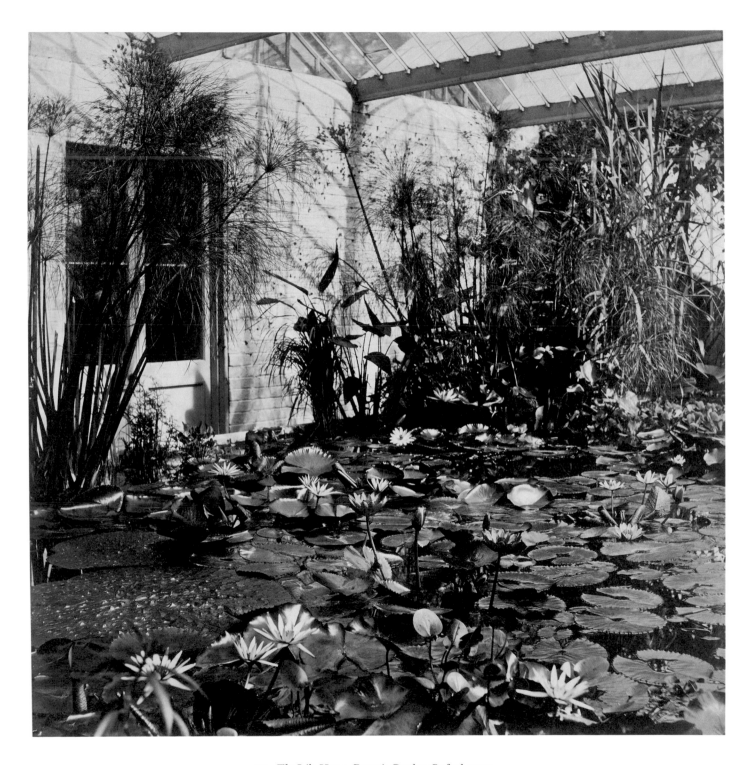

70. *The Lily House, Botanic Garden, Oxford,* 1859

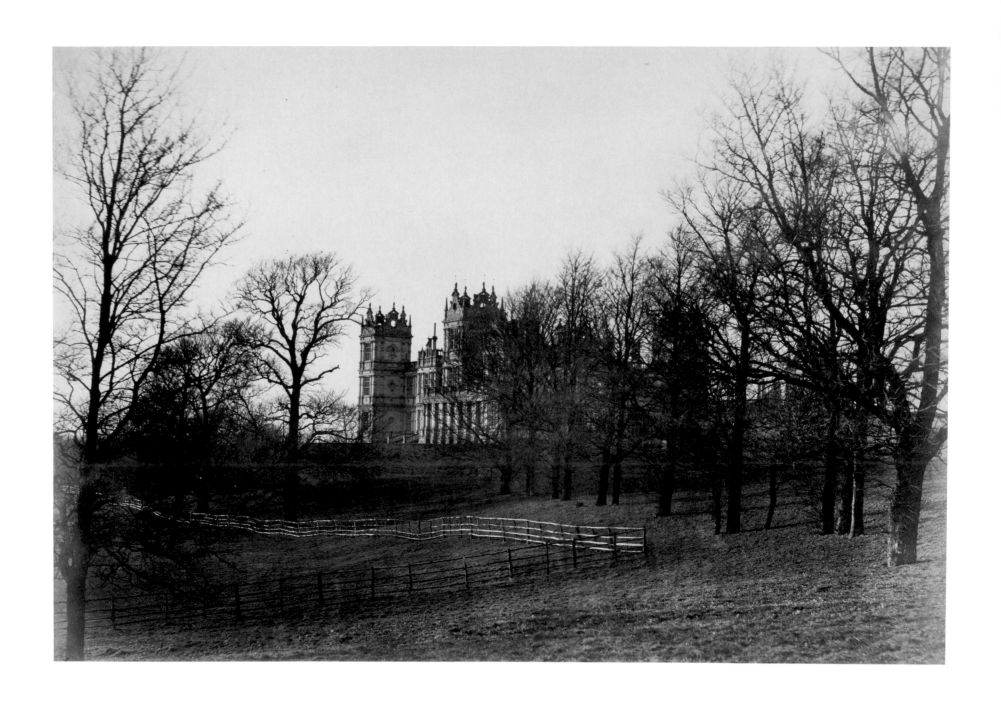

71. Wollaton Hall, [ca. 1859]

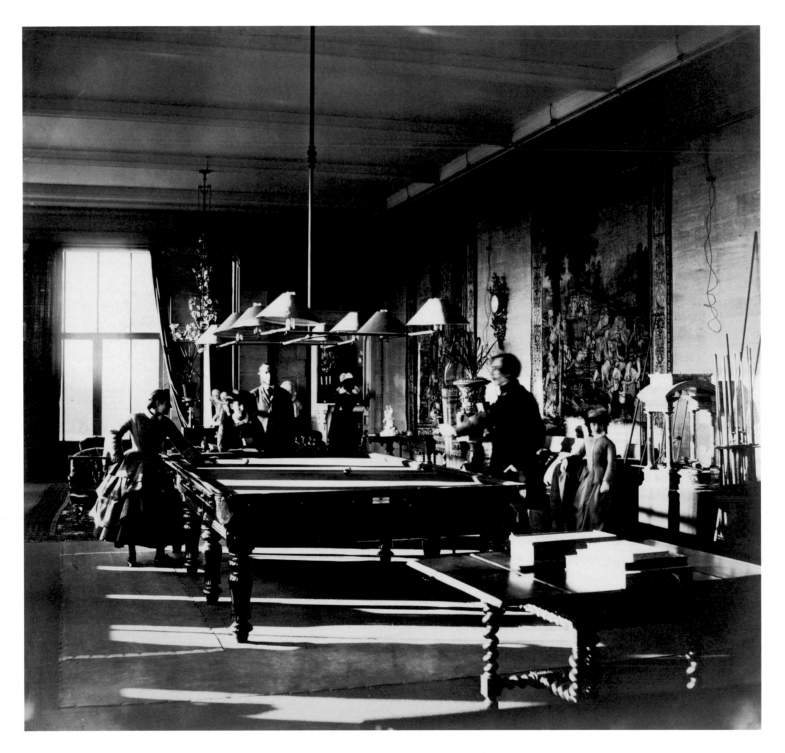

72. The Billiard Room, Mentmore, [ca. 1858]

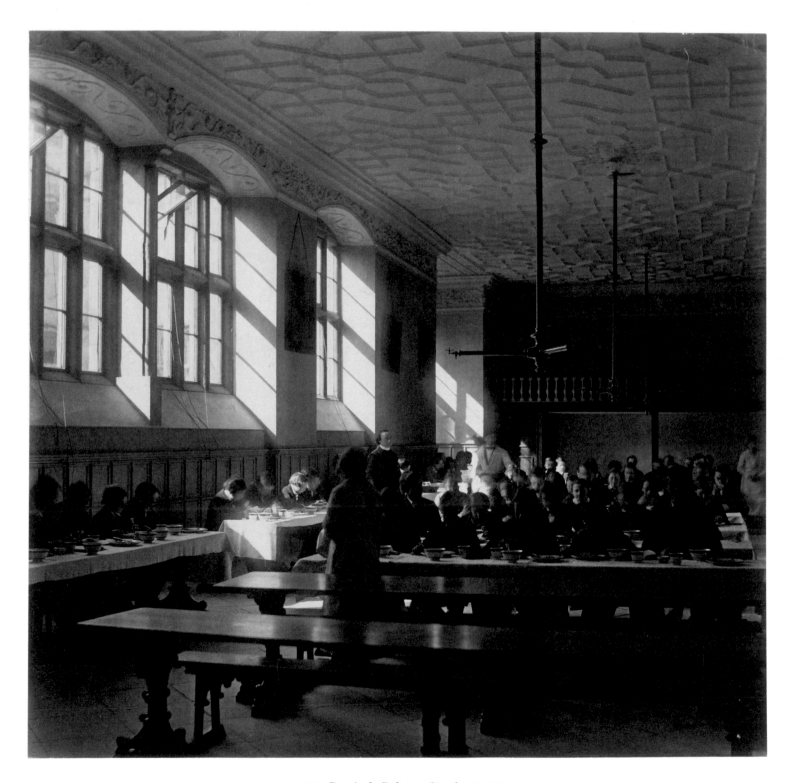

73. *Boys in the Refectory, Stonyhurst,* 1859

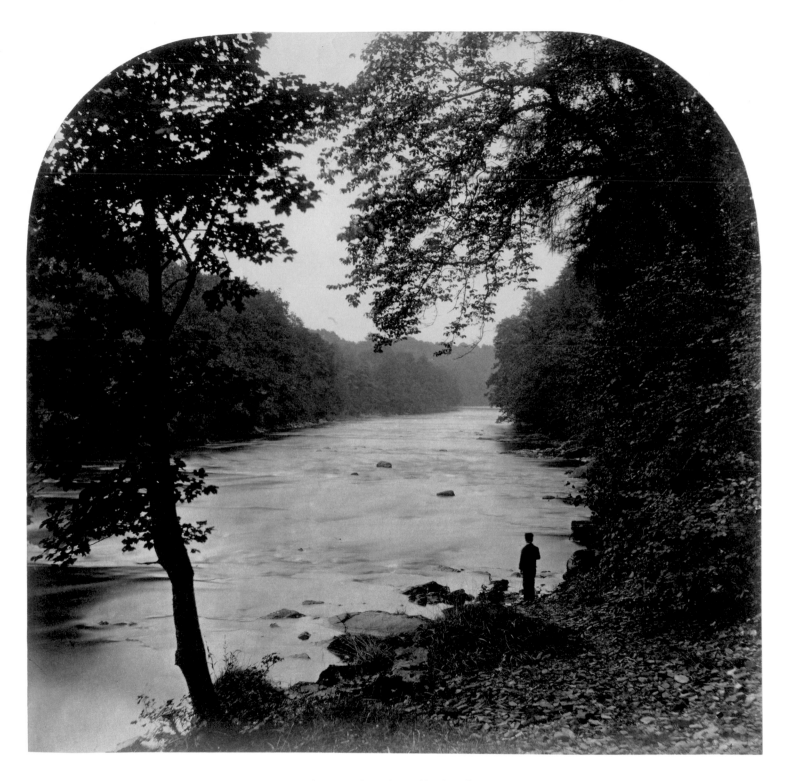

74. *Paradise, View down the Hodder, Stonyhurst,* 1859

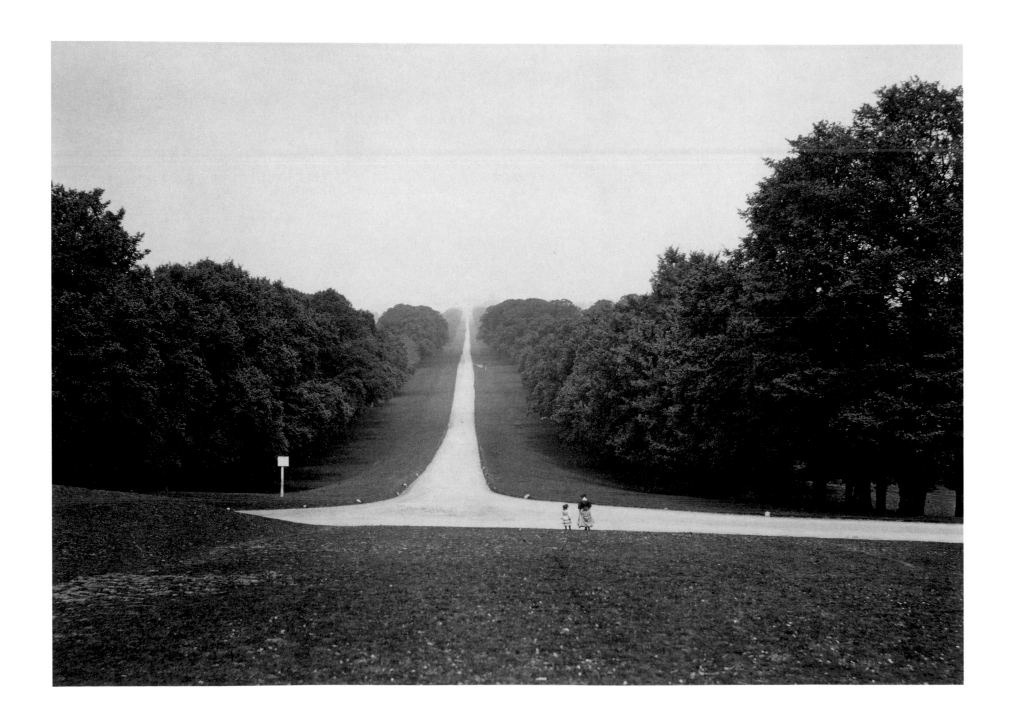

82. *The Long Walk*, 1860

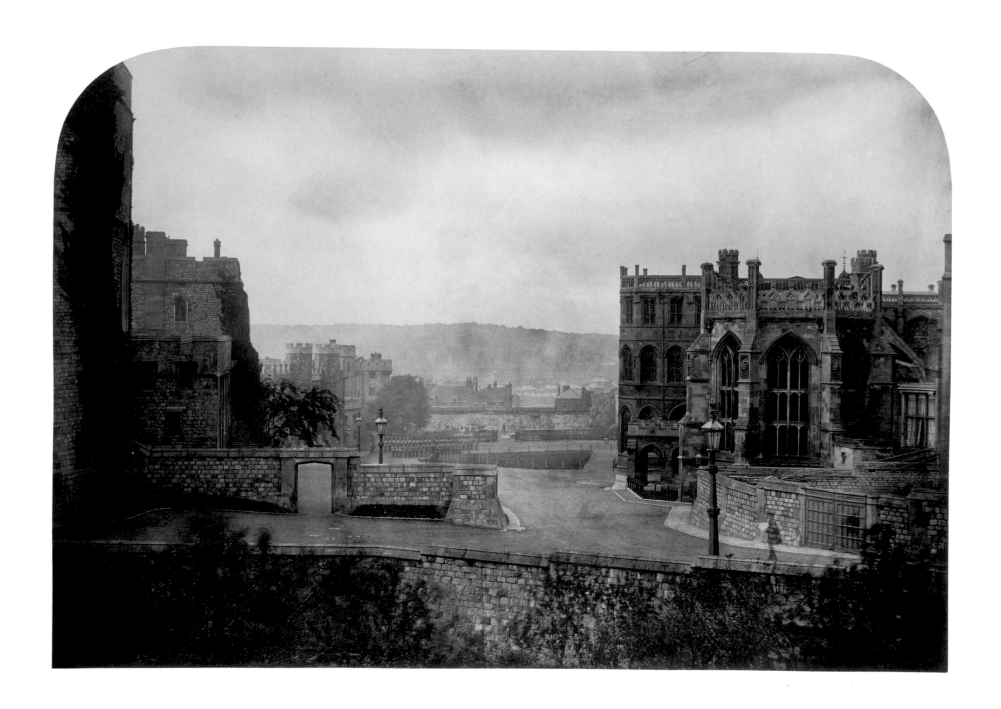

83. *View from the Foot of the Round Tower,* 1860

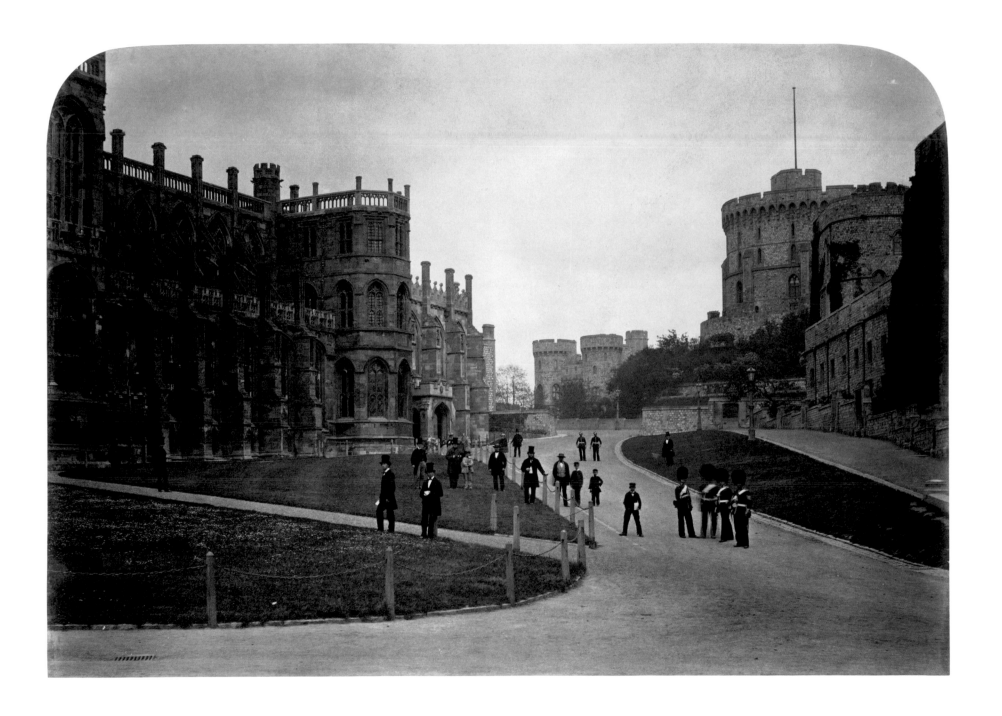

84. Saint George's Chapel and the Round Tower, Windsor Castle, 1860

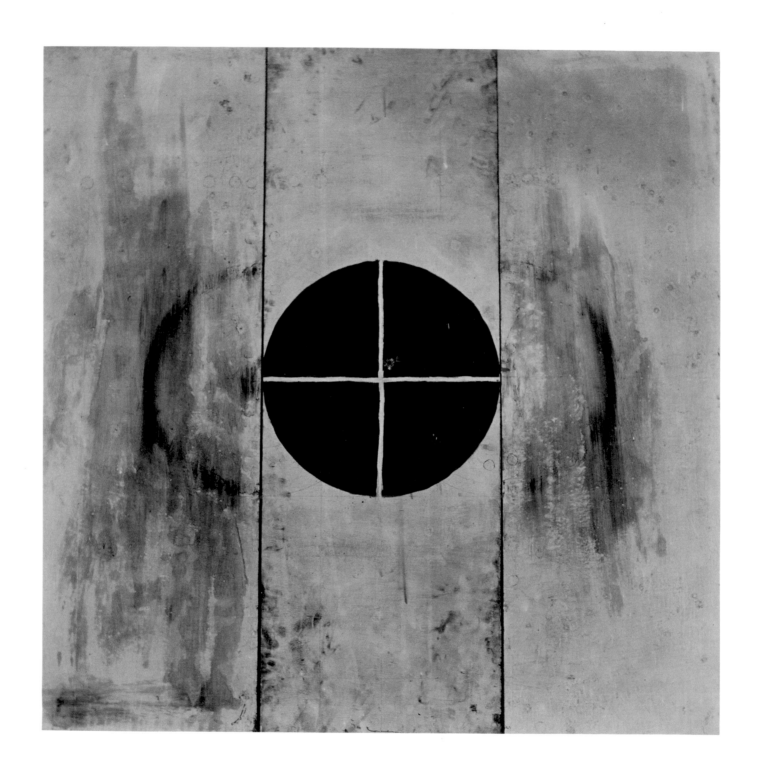

85. *The Queen's Target*, 1860

STILL LIFES, 1860

Christmas; as a result more photographs were added, a second edition of the catalogue prepared, and the closing date extended until the end of January 1853.[11] The effect of the almost eight hundred examples of British and French photography of great scope and diversity by then on display must have been overwhelming.[12] The exhibition proved a critical success, although the generally favorable reviews included one observation that some of the prints "should not have passed beyond the portfolio of the artist."[13] The exhibition also served as the setting for the founding of the Photographic Society on January 20, 1853, when Fenton was elected to the position of honorary secretary, which he had been filling informally from the outset (see "The Exertions of Mr. Fenton" by Pam Roberts in this volume).[14] At its first regular meeting the following week, Fenton set out to the membership his ambitions for the society. His vision that photography (and the society) would be well served by the "collection and the diffusion of information," with exhibitions forming "an important part of the Society's means of action," is closely aligned with his own personal ambitions.[15] By early 1853 his name was firmly linked to photography, perhaps more so than that of any other member of the Photographic Society, leading one commentator to note wryly, "Mr. Fenton is a most enthusiastic cultivator of his art."[16]

The popularity of the exhibition also prompted the Society of Arts to create a strategy for promoting photography nationally through a series of touring exhibitions. One of the powerful ideas to arise from the success of the Great Exhibition was that of "strength through unity." In a speech delivered in 1852, Prince Albert called for the continued and harmonious interchange of knowledge to bring about human advancement, and this principle was widely adopted as a rallying call by nations, industries, workmen's organizations, and educators. With mutual cooperation now high on the national agenda, the Society of Arts played its part by inviting 230 literary, philosophical, scientific, and mechanics' societies to affiliate themselves with the parent society in London and thus gain access to visiting lecturers, reduced prices on books and supplies, and other benefits. By February 1853 this important initiative had induced well over one hundred institutions to join the network.[17] The great majority of these were based in small market towns with populations of between four and five thousand souls, and many enjoyed the patronage and membership of the local aristocracy. Capitalizing on the success of its 1852 exhibition, the Society of Arts created a much reduced travel-

ing version of the show and offered it in March 1853 to these new affiliated institutions, or "institutions in union." Eighteen accepted, and a tour schedule was arranged, beginning in September, that spanned the nation from Ventnor in the Isle of Wight to Aberdeen in the north of Scotland.[18] It was an ambitious plan and not without logistical problems; nevertheless it brought eighty-three prints by twenty-four practitioners to an audience largely innocent of the appeal of photography. In addition to photographs of the displays and objects shown at the Great Exhibition, taken by Hugh Owen and Claude-Marie Ferrier, there were pictures by Cundall, Delamotte, Le Gray, Paul Pretsch, Ross & Thomson (James Ross and John Thomson), William Henry Fox Talbot, and Fenton, who contributed ten images from his series of English and Russian studies made during 1852.

Despite frequent damage done to glass and frames by a railway system better adapted to moving coal than photographs, the society decided to send works traveling the following year as well, this time creating two sets of prints for parallel exhibitions and increasing the number of photographs to 121 and 129, respectively. Fenton more than doubled the number of prints he submitted, to twenty-four in each set. With his photographs constituting about 20 percent of the total number of works on display, he had far greater prominence than any other contributor.[19] These three touring exhibitions not only legitimized photography's artistic potential in the eyes of the nation but also placed Fenton's work before the widest possible audience and were a key factor in establishing his early reputation.

Another strand of Fenton's career in photography dates from late 1852, when the prominent London publisher David Bogue issued the first two parts of *The Photographic Album*, each part illustrated with four photographic prints. Six of the total were by Fenton and two by Delamotte. The principal subject matter was Cheltenham, a Georgian spa town in the Cotswolds whose fortunes had been revived by the arrival of the Great Western Railway, providing connections to London. Bogue, Delamotte, and Fenton very likely thought that Cheltenham's quiet fashionability would be sufficient to ensure good sales of the publication. Sadly, their hopes were dashed by the appearance of Maxime Du Camp's *Egypt, Nubia, Palestine and Syria*, which had just become available in London through the efforts of the entrepreneurial publisher and picture dealer Ernest Gambart. It was inevitable that this work, one of the most important photographic publications of the mid-nineteenth century, would by its sheer size, grandeur, and ambition completely eclipse the album of the two newcomers.[20] Nevertheless, *The Photographic Album* demonstrates the scale of Fenton's ambitions for his photographs, albeit within the circumscribed market traditionally reserved for artists and engravers.

Early in 1853, Fenton's colleagues Cundall and Delamotte established the Photographic Institution in New Bond Street, London, one of the first businesses dedicated exclusively to promoting the medium. It soon became a lively center of photographic practice in which Cundall took charge of publications and Delamotte offered a whole range of photographic services, including calotype portraiture and architectural studies commissioned by members of the nobility, gentry, and clergy.[21] An essential feature of their activities, and one that drew widespread critical attention, was mounting regular exhibitions of photographs by "the best English and Continental Artists," drawn together by Delamotte.[22] Their imperative, unlike that underlying earlier exhibitions, was to bring photography into the commercial print market by appealing to collectors and connoisseurs.[23] When their first show opened on April 28, 1853, there were 250 framed photographs and three portfolios on display at prices ranging from three shillings to two guineas per print.[24] Fenton was well represented, with forty-eight works offered for sale at prices ranging from three shillings each (the British studies) to twelve shillings (the *Monastery at Kiev*). All the other Russian studies were priced at seven shillings and sixpence each. We have little idea why one print was priced at three shillings and another at four times that amount. Fenton's prices were modest in comparison with those of other photographers represented, perhaps indicating the value he placed on his own work at the time and where he saw himself within the wider field of photographic enterprise.[25]

These, briefly, are the context and history of Fenton's first years with photography. As it turned out, his timing was perfect; had he arrived on the photographic scene five years earlier or later, his influence would have been negligible. For this new field, the years 1852–53 proved critical to the way the medium advanced both artistically and technically. In 1851, photography had been poised for change; it needed only the impulse of the Great Exhibition to give it momentum and individuals like Fenton and his colleagues to carry it forward.

Fenton had the advantage of coming from a family in which self-improvement and private enterprise were highly valued. It also helped that he and his audience belonged to the same social stratum: a loosely defined body of individuals set apart by their education and financial independence.[26] By and large they were not members of the aristocracy or even the gentry but rather of a new class, that of professional gentlemen. Forward-thinking, they were comfortable with modernity and the benefits of scientific advances, especially when yoked to capitalism. Paradoxically, the same individuals revered and took comfort in traditional values and ways, viewing the past through a romantic haze of Neo-Gothic design, historical painting, and literature. They possessed both leisure time and the means to occupy it. They visited exhibitions and read the reviews. They burrowed deep into the British countryside, drawn to picturesque spots rich with literary and historical associations, and journeyed abroad following an itinerary that still carried resonances of the Grand Tour. These were the individuals who established the Photographic Society in 1853, made up its membership, and became the audience for Fenton's photographs—as he knew full well.

Knowing your public is one thing, reaching them another matter entirely. For a conventional artist or a member of the new generation of artist-photographers such as Fenton, the issue remained the same: how does an audience get to know, understand, and appreciate one's work in the most effective way? Then as now, self-promotion through the media provided the answer, and in the 1850s, newspapers and periodicals were the media that reigned supreme. In addition to daily newspapers, a staple in many households, the mid-Victorian period witnessed a most extraordinary growth in weekly, monthly, and quarterly periodicals serving the diverse tastes and inclinations of the articulate classes.[27] Many were aimed at special-interest groups ranging from antiquarians and architects to Zionists and zoologists. Photographers were increasingly well served; by 1860 there were four competing publications, although their circulation figures probably remained low, and their reviews and opinions barely touched the wider public.[28] It was the newspapers and periodicals with high circulation figures and widespread distribution throughout Britain, particularly the *Athenaeum*, *Art-Journal*, *Literary Gazette*, and *Illustrated London News*, that wielded great influence through their comprehensive coverage of literature, music, fine arts, and photography. Detailed and scholarly (but unattributed) reviews were frequently written by leading authorities who endeavored to make difficult and complex subjects more understandable. Within the exhibition system these periodicals played an important role well beyond the announcement of forthcoming events. Their critics passed judgment, praised individual merit or dismissed it, offered opinions and influenced public taste; they had the power to shape or destroy a reputation. The *Illustrated London News* frequently published wood engraving illustrations of works of art under review—a novel approach that undoubtedly contributed to the popular success of the newspaper, which boasted a weekly circulation of 123,000.[29]

Between February 1852, the date of his earliest known photographs, and January 1854, when the Photographic Society held its first annual exhibition, Fenton achieved a significant number of objectives that advanced his photographic career. The first was his involvement in the founding and management of the Photographic Society. This brought opportunities for new friendships and alliances, some of which, like those with Cundall and Delamotte, became relationships of mutual advantage. The Photographic Society was widely regarded as the parent society for photography, and as its honorary secretary Fenton occupied a pivotal position in the profession throughout Britain. Undoubtedly he was in correspondence with fellow photographers, knew when new photographic societies were being formed, and was involved with the leading photographic issues of the day. His close association with the Society of Arts gave him opportunities to exhibit his work both in London and throughout Britain, and of these he took full advantage, while the contributions of fellow photographers were relatively few in number. Determined not to remain an enthusiastic amateur, Fenton from the outset had commercial ambitions for his work. In the space of two years he seemingly did everything possible to position himself favorably. At the opening of the first annual exhibition of the Photographic Society in January 1854 he showed no fewer than seventy-three prints. The exhibition was widely reviewed in both the photographic and the national press, and, more importantly for his future status, Fenton, along with Sir Charles Eastlake, was chosen by his colleagues to conduct a tour of the exhibition for Queen Victoria, Prince Albert, and the royal party. This was a defining moment, elevating him to a position that distinguished him from other photographers and shaped the direction of his career (see "Mr. Fenton Explained Everything" in this volume).

For the next eight years, until his retirement in 1862, Fenton used photographic exhibitions as the principal means of promoting his work. He contributed, broadly speaking, to three very different types of exhibition: annual exhibitions of photographic societies in Britain, Belgium, and Holland; the international exhibitions held in 1855, 1857, and 1862 in Paris, Manchester, and London respectively; and his own "Exhibition of the Photographic Pictures Taken in the Crimea," which was seen in eight venues during 1855 and 1856.[30] While these exhibitions served very different audiences, both geographically and culturally, all acted to showcase Fenton's latest work and—implicitly with the photographic societies, explicitly with the Crimean photographs—to promote the sale of prints.[31] Fenton made greatest use of the annual exhibitions of photographic societies, whose numbers were rapidly increasing; some thirty-five were established during the 1850s.[32] An annual exhibition was central to their activities, and in most cases they followed the example of the Photographic Society in London, adopting a system of open submission so that photographers were encouraged to submit work outside their immediate region. The general principle of interchange was here being applied in an artistic context.

Since the exhibition season usually fell in the winter, it provided an opportunity for photographers to show work taken in the previous spring and summer months, when the light was at its most expressive. For Fenton this cycle of photographing and exhibiting dictated the pattern of his working year: the photographs made during his tour of Yorkshire in the summer of 1854 he exhibited in January 1855, those taken of Scotland in 1856 were shown in 1857, and those taken in North Wales during the summer or fall of 1857 were exhibited in January 1858.[33] With mid-nineteenth-century London the cultural and economic focal point around which the rest of Britain revolved, he understandably chose the annual exhibitions of the Photographic Society to foreground his latest work, but his photographs were also exhibited in Birmingham, Nottingham, Macclesfield, and Manchester in central England; Norwich in the east; and Edinburgh, Glasgow, and Dundee in Scotland. While it was generally Fenton who submitted his own works, occasionally local printsellers used the annual exhibitions as showcases in which to promote their latest stock. For example, Colin Sinclair, a stationer who sold photographs from his premises at 69 George Street, Edinburgh, submitted a number of prints to exhibitions in Edinburgh and Glasgow in 1858 and 1859 respectively, among them Fenton's celebrated genre study *Pasha and Bayadère*, which was thus exhibited in Edinburgh before being shown in London (pl. 62).[34] As long as the work was new to the market it mattered little to Fenton who entered it, whether he himself, a printseller, or a local collector anxious to demonstrate his good taste. Although all this exhibiting proved an effective and cheap form of publicity, it established a cycle of work that must have been extraordinarily demanding and by its very nature almost impossible to sustain. Fashion, public whim, and changing circumstance would see to that.

One reason Fenton's name became so well known throughout Britain and Europe was that critical responses to his work appeared across the whole spectrum of the press, from daily and weekly newspapers to specialized photographic periodicals. It was not unusual for an exhibition to be more widely reviewed than we would expect even in today's media-oriented world. For example, when *Pasha and Bayadère* was shown at the 1858 annual exhibition of the Photographic Society of Scotland, it attracted reviews from nine local newspapers; the fullest coverage was in the Scottish *Daily Express*, which published three separate notices.[35] A survey of the exhibition reviews proves invaluable for understanding the critical influences that helped shape and direct Fenton's work year by year. Some samplings follow.

They have all the appearance of being mildewed, or seen through a mist, or as if half obliterated by a sponge.

—Review of *The Photographic Album*, in *Athenaeum*, November 1852[36]

It is quite evident that when the pictures were taken, the photographic artist consulted his convenience, and aimed only at making the best of the bad subjects which the neighbourhood of Cheltenham afforded.

—Review of *The Photographic Album*, in *Art-Journal*, December 1852[37]

The productions, which are numerous, by Mr. R. Fenton . . . are of a most interesting character . . . he will excuse us from suggesting that he would do well in future to avoid subjects involving very high lights,—*particularly many points of light,—and* very deep shadows.

—Review of the photographic exhibition at the Society of Arts, *Art-Journal*, February 1853[38]

The editor of the *Art-Journal*, Samuel Carter Hall, had worked with Fenton on the management committee of the North London School of Drawing and Modelling in 1850 and was also a fellow of the Society of Arts.[39] Indeed, they may even have been friends, but any familiarity made not the slightest difference and, true to form, Hall expressed his opinion bluntly and directly.[40] Rather than being oppressed by this criticism, Fenton learned from it and took care never again to issue technically inferior or poorly composed photographs.

Further examples:

In these little pictures the gradation of tone is as perfect as in any sun pictures which we have seen, and the gradual falling off of the outlines of the objects as they are respectively more and more distant from the eye, yet still retaining their distinctness, is beautifully artistic and at the same time natural. The productions of Mr. Fenton are more varied than those of any other exhibitor.

—Review of the First Annual Exhibition of the Photographic Society, *Art-Journal*, February 1854[41]

The specimen we have engraved ("Valley of the Wharfe") illustrates the chief features of the exhibition. . . . There is a soft and mellow tone about this picture of Mr. Fenton's, and a richness of atmospheric colour, which has never been surpassed, if equalled, by the previous attempts of any photographer [fig. 65].

—Review of the Second Annual Exhibition of the Photographic Society, *Illustrated London News*, February 1855[42]

Mr. Fenton is one of the most brilliant examples of the close union of the artist and the practical photographer.

—Review of the Exposition Universelle, Paris, *Bulletin de la Société Française de Photographie*, December 1855[43]

These three slightly later reviews display a radically changed response to Fenton's work. He was now hailed for ideally combining artistic sensitivity with the technical competence necessary to produce photographs that are "perfect," "soft and mellow," and in tune with the public sensibility. Clearly his new ally was the *Illustrated London News*, in which a half-page wood engraving of *Valley of the Wharfe* was published alongside a lengthy review. Both tone and content suggest that Fenton had been "taken up" by the newspaper.

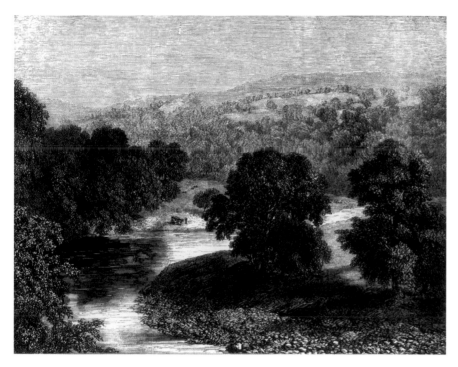

Fig. 65. *Valley of the Wharfe*, after a photograph by Roger Fenton. Wood engraving, 17.3 x 23.1 cm (6 ¹³⁄₁₆ x 9 ¹⁄₁₆ in.). From *Illustrated London News*, February 17, 1855, p. 165

It was reported in the review that he was on his way to the Crimea, and the unnamed authors noted how much they were looking forward to seeing "the results of his labours in the East"; on his return these photographs became a prominent feature of the paper's reportage of the war.[44]

The French review was prompted by Fenton's submission to the 1855 Paris Exposition Universelle, where he won a first class medal (silver) for the excellence of his photographs, and probably also reflects France's appreciation of Fenton's recent photographic activities in the Crimea.[45]

It would be needless to eulogize the extraordinary breadth and detail of these "children of light," and it would be impertinent to praise the art with which momentary expressions, a smile or a glance, are fixed, to be now perpetuated in a work that may be read and obtain an almost European circulation. . . . Men will fall before the battle scythe of war, but not before this infallible sketcher has caught their lineaments and given them an anonymous immortality. . . . As photographists grow stronger in nerve and cooler of head, we

shall have not merely the bivouac and the foraging party, but the battle itself painted; and while the fate of nations is in the balance we shall hear of the chemist measuring out his acids and rubbing his glasses to a polish.

—"Photographs from the Crimea," *Athenaeum*, September 1855[46]

We were much surprised to find a collection embracing subjects to which the artist could not have had access without influential introductions—but so it was—the artist was, we believe, recommended by H.R.H. Prince Albert to the notice of officers in high command.

—"Photographs from Sebastopol," *Art-Journal*, October 1855[47]

Here we see reviewers struggling to find an appropriate definition of Fenton's role in the Crimea. The references to him as an "artist" and to the "battle itself painted" locate him in the company of war artists such as William Simpson, whose "Authentic Sketches" of the Crimea were also showing in London.[48] What distinguished Fenton from Simpson was the reality of his photographs; his "children of light," with their clear and unequivocal gaze, offered a new kind of witness to the conduct of war. It is not only the scope of photography that is being redefined here, but also Fenton's role as a photographer; he is transposed from the tranquillity of the British landscape to the dangers of working under "fire from the Russian batteries."[49] He has become the heroic photographer with something to communicate. The prescient reviewer for the *Athenaeum* understood the significance of Fenton's role in the Crimea and accurately predicted the way photography would evolve several decades later into a powerful and influential tool of reportage. At a number of levels, Fenton's photographic expedition to the Crimea was of central importance for his career, perpetually linking his name to the event in the popular imagination during the Victorian period and, subsequently, identifying him as the first war photographer (pls. 14–21).

If Fenton hoped that sales of the Crimean photographs would create a regular income, his expectations were never realized. A joint publishing venture with Thomas Agnew of Manchester proved a commercial failure, and the negatives and remaining stock of prints were sold off in December 1856. As one venture was fading, Fenton launched himself upon another—perhaps reflexively, in the manner of his mercantile ancestors. During the spring of

1856 he became involved with the photographer Paul Pretsch and the Patent Photo-Galvanographic Company he had established in North London.[50] The photogalvanographic process was in essence a photomechanical halftone printing process capable of reproducing photographs in printer's ink. The ability to print photomechanically had been a central ambition for photography from its very conception and appealed to the Victorians for its combination of visual accuracy with mechanical utility. The process clearly interested Fenton, who likely saw it as the next logical step for photography, and by late 1856 he had been named a partner and photographer for the company.[51] He must have been delighted when the first part of a portfolio called *Photographic Art Treasures*, with four studies by him, appeared on what was hailed as "a memorable day in the history of Graphic Art" (fig. 66).[52] Sadly, though, the project was encumbered from the outset, and by May 1857 the company was reported to have suffered losses of about 4,000 pounds, with the profit from sales amounting to only 120 pounds.[53] If Fenton had a personal stake in the company, losses of this scale must have come as a hard blow; in 1857, 4,000 pounds was a considerable sum.

At about the same time the Patent Photo-Galvanographic Company was being established, Fenton became involved in another photographic business venture, one that raises questions about his ethics as an artist and photographer. In May 1856 the Photographic Association was announced as a provisionally registered company seeking to raise ten thousand pounds of capital through the sale of shares at ten pounds each.[54] Its prospectus reveals that although the company shared many aims and objectives with the Photographic Society, it was nevertheless a commercial enterprise that expected to return a 10 percent dividend to shareholders, all of whom would become members of the Photographic Association.[55] This was a new type of photographic society, adequately capitalized and with shareholders as members, and in these respects the antithesis of the Photographic Society. With ten thousand pounds capital the association could pay the bill for premises, darkrooms, a studio, a laboratory, a library, and full-time staff to run the business—the management of which was destined to lie in the capable hands of Delamotte, Fenton, Thomas Minchin Goodeve, Thomas Frederick Hardwich, William Lake Price, Lewis Pocock, and Charles Blacker Vignoles. With the exception of Pocock, who belonged to the Art Union of London, all were members of the Photographic Society.

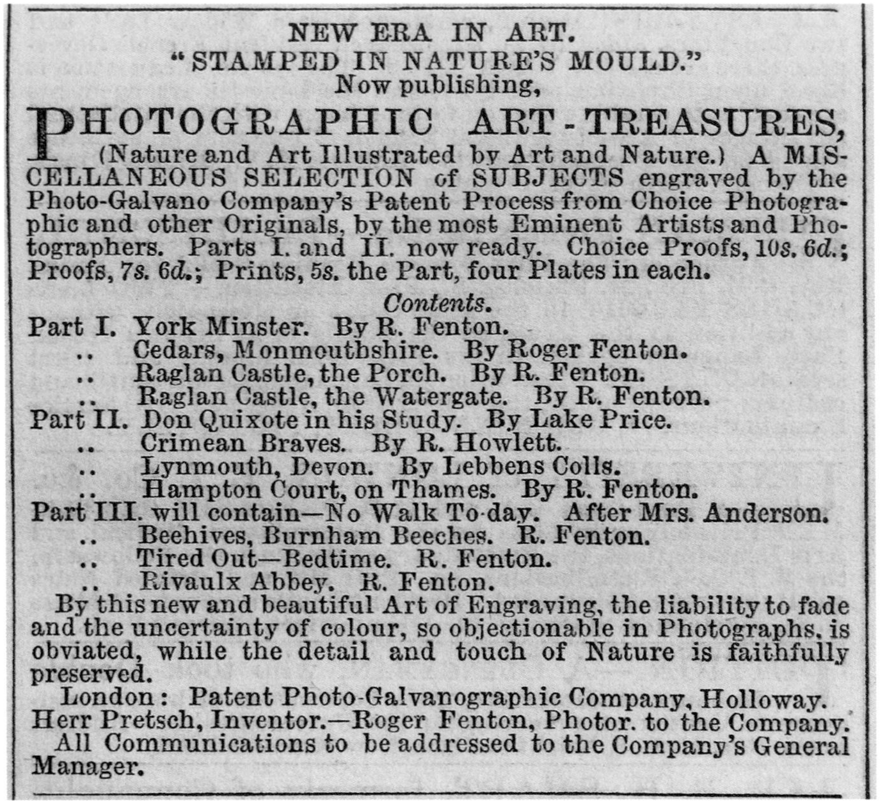

Fig. 66. "Photographic Art Treasures," advertisement. From *Athenaeum*, February 14, 1857, p. 198

Little wonder the Photographic Society felt threatened. It had neither the funds nor the facilities to compete with such an attractive scheme. To members it was unthinkable that Fenton, who had worked so hard to foster the society, should now pose such a direct threat to its future welfare. Perhaps Fenton believed that the two schemes could peacefully coexist; but whatever his motives, he and his colleagues were soon brought to account at a meeting of the Photographic Society on May 1, 1856.[56] Not surprisingly, the tone of the meeting was hostile, with calls for those involved with the Photographic Association to resign from the prestigious Council of the Photographic Society. Everything rested upon a regulation stating that a photographer "trading in photography" would not be eligible for the Council.[57] It was the view of those assembled that under the terms of their association Fenton and his colleagues would be "trading" and must therefore retire. Embedded in this position was an issue far more serious and far-reaching than the immediate problem posed by the Photographic Association.

From the beginning the notion had been generally accepted that trained artists such as Delamotte, Fenton, and Lake Price practiced on a higher level than those "trading in photography." Although they sold their works, their manner of operation and the social class to which they appealed categorized them as above trade. Increasingly, though, these distinctions were being called into question, as a growing number of photographers, especially portrait photographers, began to join the ranks of the Photographic Society. It seemed unreasonable that photographers of this type be excluded from the Council because of their "trade," when others who also sold their work were admitted on the basis of the implicit understanding that they belonged to a higher stratum of society.[58] But despite the logic of fairness, the Council ruling enshrined a fundamental aversion of many members of the Photographic Society to the very notion of trade. To them trade represented everything they were not. They were gentlemen, professional gentlemen at that, involved in photography as a vocation. It mattered little whether they actually sold photographs; their income came from elsewhere. They had the leisure time, education, and social background to set them fundamentally apart from those in trade. In mid-Victorian society, the social hierarchy was clearly defined and rigidly observed. With the benefit of hindsight, however, we can see that the decade of the 1850s introduced a period of social change that would allow far greater mobility between the classes than ever before. In part this was due to the growing importance of a whole new category of professionals, such as engineers, surveyors, and physicians, whose place in society began to be properly acknowledged. Many photographers too—especially those with fashionable portrait studios or successful topographic publishing enterprises—resented being classified as mere tradesmen and wanted more than anything to be regarded as professionals.

The double standard that allowed Fenton and others to sell photographs openly while remaining eligible for the Council was an issue that had to be resolved if the equilibrium of the Photographic Society was to be restored. But rather than amend the rules to give more open access, justice was seen to be done by having Fenton and four of his colleagues resign their positions on the Council.[59] As it happened, the Photographic Association apparently did not progress beyond provisional registration, since it was never heard of again; and the status of "tradesmen" photographers within the Photographic Society was never properly resolved, leaving the way open for further tension in the future.

The immediate impact on Fenton of this brief episode was minimal. Although his good name and reputation may have been bruised, he emerged relatively unscathed and was reelected to the Council the following year.[60] Nevertheless, he must have been aware that the status quo within the Photographic Society had been challenged by photography's capacity to evolve and adapt to the pressures of an increasingly commercial world. No longer was photography the province of the upper classes; by the mid-1850s it had become a retail commodity and was on the way to being a major economic and cultural force. If there was a lesson to be learned from this incident, it was that Fenton too had to evolve and adapt to changing circumstances in order to survive artistically and professionally, and in just this sense 1856 proved to be a pivotal moment in his photographic career.

On one level Fenton continued much as before, photographing and exhibiting with his usual enthusiasm and regularity. In September 1856, as if to put London and the affair of the Photographic Association as far behind him as possible, he traveled to the very north of Scotland, to Deeside and the estates of the royal family at Balmoral (pls. 28–30). The following year it was North Wales (1857). Thereafter his trips gradually became more circumscribed; they were visits to cathedrals, stately homes (1857–58), and places perhaps familiar to him in Derbyshire, Lancashire, Yorkshire, and the Lake District (1859–60). Although Fenton's output each year was not large, he made certain that the photographs he produced were widely distributed throughout the network of available exhibitions. His most prolific season of all was in 1859, when his work was seen in eight cities and towns across Britain, from London to the far north of Scotland, and a further eleven prints were included in the annual exhibition of the Société Française de Photographie in Paris.[61] This significant range of shows gave Fenton a wider geographic exposure than any other photographer at the time; it was an achievement that he never repeated.

By any measure Fenton's photographs from this period are among his finest, and not surprisingly they elicited flattering reviews, strewn with such phrases as "Mr. Fenton's pictures may be identified anywhere,"[62] and "no one can touch Fenton in landscape: he seems to be to photography what Turner was to painting—our greatest landscape photographer."[63] It was generally acknowledged that with each new season's work "Mr. Roger Fenton keeps ahead of his contemporaries."[64] What distinguished Fenton from most other photographers was not just skillful composition and superlative technique but an appreciation of light and the ability to capture its most expressive moments on collodion. Although light is of course essential to photography, very few photographers of this era appreciated its value beyond the taken-for-granted role it played in making an exposure. Many of the new generation of photographers had not trained as artists but rather had come to photography through other avenues; moreover, the commercial pressures under which they often worked meant they were unlikely to sit around waiting for the weather to clear. Fenton was either extraordinarily fortunate with the weather or extremely patient, or most likely a combination of both. Repeatedly it is the pattern of light within the overall composition that holds our attention, and critics frequently remarked upon his appreciation of light. One response in 1858, to a study of Tintern Abbey, typifies them all and reveals why Fenton's work was held in such high regard: "The play of light through the beautiful windows of the abbey ruin shows that the artist has watched, with all an artist's care, the ever-changing effects produced by the movement of the shadows, and seized upon that moment when the blending of light and shade developed that peculiar beauty which 'subdues, yet elevates, the gazer's soul.'"[65] That Fenton's photographs might be spiritually uplifting may surprise us today, but to a Victorian audience, weighed down with religious anxiety and burdened by social ills, the desire to seek consolation and reassurance in a photograph was quite normal. These viewers observed divine truth everywhere, in the smallest feather or the sublime grandeur of a thundercloud. Perhaps the real key to Fenton's appeal is the comfort his photographs provided, fulfilling a very real need in a troubled and apprehensive society.

Sadly, no statistics have survived to tell us what kind of client patronized photographic exhibitions or bought photographs. The social background and class of viewers can only be guessed at and cautiously extrapolated from print prices. We know from exhibition catalogues, for example, that in 1859 Fenton charged from seven shillings and sixpence to ten shillings and sixpence for his prints, making his work relatively expensive. His audience was most likely drawn from the Upper Ten Thousand, who, with the aristocracy,

were the only ones with sufficient disposable income to afford such prices. We can be reasonably certain that Fenton never directly advertised in newspapers or periodicals to sell his photographs, since that would have irrevocably classified him as a tradesman; instead he placed his work with publishers and printsellers who acted as intermediaries on his behalf. As a result there is virtually no trace of his commercial activity other than the records of exhibitions to which printsellers submitted Fenton's work as a means of promoting their business.[66]

The first indication that Fenton's attitude had changed (or adapted to circumstance) came in 1858 with an advertisement in the national press by Thomas Gladwell, a London printseller, offering the photographer's "Series of 100 exquisite Views of Dove-Dale, the Cheddar Cliffs, Haddon Hall, Hardwick Hall, Chatsworth and surrounding scenery; Lichfield, Gloucester, Wells, and Salisbury Cathedrals, Malvern Priory; Tintern, Tewkesbury, and Glastonbury Abbeys" as well as prints from Fenton's series "Public Buildings and Parks of London" (fig. 67).[67] The tone and style of the advertisement reveal that Gladwell belonged not to the well-established coterie of London fine-art dealers and printsellers but rather to a different group entirely, of importers, publishers, wholesalers, and retailers of British and foreign photographic views.[68] A keenly motivated businessman, he was one of the new photographic entrepreneurs and manufacturers who moved into the photographic market just as soon as its wider commercial potential was recognized. Though we cannot be certain, it seems likely that Gladwell was Fenton's sole London agent and acted as a wholesaler of his prints, supplying the burgeoning photographic print trade elsewhere in Britain.[69] The rising tide of tourists that had begun to spread out across Britain, traveling by rail and coach to the remotest corners, very likely created a demand for Fenton's views at every spot he had photographed. His name was so widely known and well regarded that all he needed was to place his work with an agent who would take care of orders and distribution, and that is the service Gladwell offered, promising to send "a single Specimen, or any number of Photographs, securely packed and forwarded to any part of Great Britain" for one shilling.[70] Here we see the process of commercialization at work, the very thing that had caused so much hostility at the Photographic Society just two years earlier. If Fenton's engagement with Gladwell was meant to keep him at arm's length from the more commercial aspects of

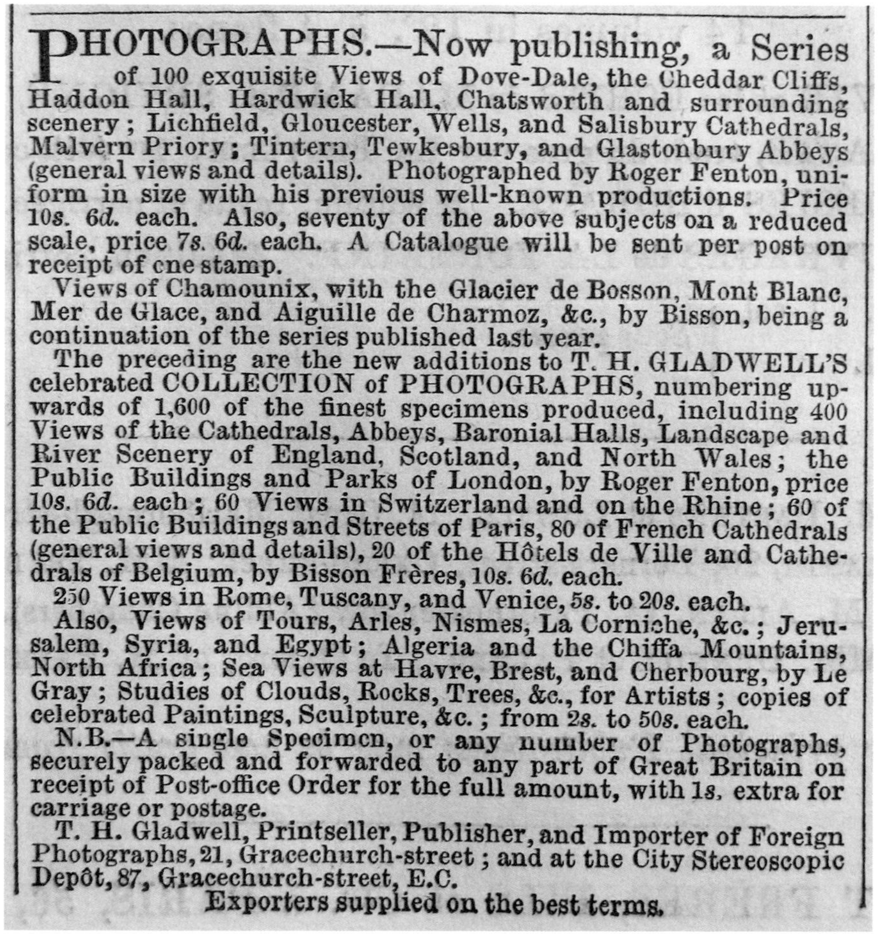

Fig. 67. "Photographs," T. H. Gladwell advertisement. From *Athenaeum*, November 27, 1858, p. 694

trade, it was probably successful, but undoubtedly he was sailing very close to the margins of acceptability.

The key issue that had surfaced in the acrimonious debate over the Photographic Association—whether the Photographic Society existed to serve the interests of amateur photographers or should transform itself to accommodate the needs of professional photographers—had never been properly resolved. By 1858 there were two quite distinct factions within the society. On one side were the old-school amateur photographers happy to explore with their cameras the visual syntax of the countryside; on the other lay the professional portrait photographers, whose technically superb results

were, however, little more than merchandise. Ideologically, aesthetically, and perhaps even socially the two were poles apart, and in truth, their interests could never be reconciled. The annual exhibitions of the society became a battleground in which both sides competed for dominance, but as there was no limit to the number of photographs a member could submit, the portrait photographers were able to overwhelm the exhibitions with their prints. The exhibition of 1858 was dominated, one reviewer commented, by "*profes-sional* [rather] than *amateur* photographers,"[71] and it was asked whether the Photographic Society had remained true to its original purpose of "cultivat-ing and promoting 'the Art and Science of Photography.'"[72]

In 1859, with the matter still unresolved, the annual exhibition prompted this critical response:

We have heard the exhibition of the Royal Academy quoted as an excuse for the exhibition of the Photographic Society. There is no parallel between them. The efforts of mind displayed in the production of a picture have nothing in common with the mechanical process of obtaining a photograph. . . . The trading character is, too, most offensively obtruded in the catalogue. . . . Our remarks are dictated by the most friendly feeling; we admire photography, and we desire to see the Photographic Society taking and maintaining its proper place amidst the societies established for the advancement of Science and Art in this country. It has allowed itself to be overridden by the commercial ele-ment; and unless, ere yet it be too late, the council resolves to return to and maintain a far more independent position, the fate of the Society is sealed.[73]

Throughout this uncomfortable period of transition, Fenton continued to photograph and exhibit as if nothing had changed. His rather ambiguous status, hovering between artist, amateur, and professional photographer, was never called into question, and each new season's work won critical tributes. But it must have been abundantly clear even to him that the golden days of the Photographic Society were now drawing to a close as photography entered its next, more commercial phase of development. When photo-graphic exhibitions became little more than shop windows for commercial photography, there were no longer any meaningful contexts in which Fenton could operate. Everything that he had achieved during the decade of the 1850s was done against the wider background of the Photographic Society and the ideals that inspired it. Once it became clear that the society had lost its sense of purpose and succumbed to the workings of capitalism, Fenton's decision to abandon photography seemed inevitable. When he submitted a group of prints to the 1862 International Exhibition held in London, the decision, one senses, had already been made. In fourteen prints he encapsulated almost his complete repertoire, choosing examples of his work at the British Museum, views of architecture, landscapes, still lifes, and Orientalist studies. The jury conferred on him its highest award, a Prize Medal, commending the "great excellence in fruit and flower pieces, and good general photography."[74] Three months later Fenton announced his complete retirement and sold his entire stock of negatives, cameras, and equipment in order to "deprive himself of all that might be a temptation . . . to revert to past occupations."[75] After a decade of unparalleled success, the end was swift, absolute, and irrevocable.

"The Exertions of Mr. Fenton": Roger Fenton and the Founding of the Photographic Society

PAM ROBERTS

Throughout his career, Roger Fenton was a man who got things done. He was indisputably the driving force that brought the Photographic Society into existence in January 1853 and set its principles and agendas.[1]

There is no extant proof that Fenton showed any interest in photography until about the time of the Great Exhibition of the Works of Industry of All Nations held at the Crystal Palace in Hyde Park, London, from May to October 1851.[2] The next year Fenton threw all his undoubted energy, artistry, enthusiasm, diplomacy, and organizational and communicative skills not only into learning the complex processes of photography but also into setting up a formal learned "society that shall be as advantageous for the art as is the Geographical Society to the advancement of knowledge in its department."[3] The objective of the new Photographic Society was "the promotion of the Art and Science of Photography, by the interchange of thought and experience among Photographers."[4]

Fenton's involvement with the Photographic Society extended from 1852 to 1862, almost as long as his involvement with photography itself. In addition to being its principal founder, he was honorary secretary (that is, unpaid chief administrator) for three years, vice president for three years, and organizer of the annual exhibitions. He served more or less continually on the society's Council and on a variety of committees and judging panels, both within the society and as its external representative. During those same years he was building a dazzling career in photography, working for the British Museum, traveling and exhibiting widely, intermittently practicing law, and raising a family.

From 1843 to 1847, Fenton had lived principally in Paris, where he studied painting. Once back in London he moved into an area that was something of an artistic coterie. With a group of other artists, Fenton founded (1850) and served on the management committee of the very successful North London School of Drawing and Modelling, an organization set up with Prince Albert as patron. Its purpose was to improve industrial design by offering evening classes to workingmen in such subjects as drawing, modeling, carving, and cabinetmaking. From this participation Fenton derived not only organizational experience but doubtless also an appreciation of the exceptional advantages that flowed from Prince Albert's energetic patronage.

When Fenton underwent his sudden conversion to photography, inspired by the photographs he saw at the Great Exhibition, it was largely the French material—works by Hippolyte Bayard, Louis-Désiré Blanquart-Evrard, Comte Frédéric Flacheron, Gustave Le Gray, Henri Le Secq, and Frédéric Martens—that caught his eye and galvanized him into action. In January 1851 these same photographers had been instrumental in establishing the Société Héliographique, the world's first photographic society, and in October 1851, Fenton went to Paris to visit it.

Britain did have an informal organization, the Photographic Club (also known as the Calotype Club). Its existence was first reported in the pages of the *Athenaeum* in December 1847, "a dozen gentlemen amateurs associated together for the purpose of pursuing their experiments in this *art-science*,"[5] although the club may have been meeting unreported prior to this date. It was roughly modeled on the more formal Graphic Society in London, whose members, mostly painters, engravers, and architects,[6] had since 1839

211

occasionally viewed photographs at their monthly meetings, and which sponsored an exhibition of calotypes in 1847.[7]

Known members of the Photographic Club included Richard Ansdell, James Archer, Joseph Cundall, Peter Wickens Fry (a lawyer like Fenton), John Rogers Herbert, Robert Hunt, Edward Kater, James Payne Knight, Sir William Newton (the latter two also members of the Graphic Society), Hugh Owen, and Sir Thomas Maryon Wilson.[8] They exchanged correspondence, experiments, advice, and prints, and those who were in town met a couple of times a month at one another's homes. Present at some of the early 1850s meetings, although not mentioned in press reports, was the sculptor and inventor of the wet collodion process, Frederick Scott Archer, who demonstrated his process to a club meeting in 1850.[9] Archer "first explained the process to his friends on the 21st of September 1850, at which time he was as well acquainted with its valuable properties as he was at the time he published it in March 1851, in 'The Chemist.'"[10] The "friends" were most likely members of the Photographic Club. Archer is known to have attended at least one meeting of the club in 1851 at Fry's home, where he exhibited a collodion image on glass, whitened by mercury bichloride and mounted over black velvet, showing the entrance to Beddington Park.[11]

While the new process seemed to open exciting possibilities for photographic expansion, and members of the Photographic Club were eager to transform their organization into a formal society along the lines of the Société Héliographique, the situation in Britain was far less favorable than that in France. William Henry Fox Talbot, the inventor of the paper negative (or calotype), had placed patent restrictions on the use of his method. He had subsequently relaxed the restrictions to charge no fees for genuine amateur or scientific use, but if a photographer sold his work he was subject to all the restrictions. Now Talbot intended to expand his patent specifications to include Archer's collodion process. These measures had a seriously inhibiting effect on the growth of photography in general and on the establishment of a more formalized photographic society (which might have some commercial activity, at least indirectly) in particular.[12] Fenton later described the situation: "It was now obvious that at this time the existence of the patent was the great obstacle, not only to the formation of the society, but to the improvement of the art itself. Few were willing to expend much time and labour upon an art, upon the study of which they were told they had no right to enter without permission."[13] (While Talbot had registered his patents in France as well as in Britain, French photographers largely ignored the patent restrictions, with impunity.)

Discussions with Talbot aimed at persuading him to relax his patent rights for members of a hoped-for photographic society had been going on for some time. Just a few weeks before the opening of the Great Exhibition in May 1851, Robert Hunt, photography critic of the *Art-Journal*, wrote to Talbot about "the Photographic Club matter." Hunt—the keeper of the Museum of Practical Geology in London, a keen photographic experimenter, and, with Fry, the founder of the Photographic Club—had since 1841 been in frequent amicable correspondence with Talbot about matters photographic, and the two men seemed to respect and trust each other. Hunt wrote, on March 23, 1851: "I have submitted your letter to some of the more influential movers in the Photographic Club matter—I have not yet their reply—On Thursday there is to be a meeting if you have any proposition to make I shall be glad to be in possession of it on Thursday morning."[14] The letter from Talbot to which Hunt alludes has not survived. It may have been one element in the ongoing discussions over a relaxation of Talbot's patent rights on the calotype, so that members of an expanded Photographic Club would not need to pay a fee. Or it may, possibly, have been a response to an unsigned and undated draft proposal that seems to have been written soon after the news of the establishment of the Société Héliographique in Paris in January 1851. Drafted by a member of the Photographic Club, possibly Fry, the paper proposes the establishment of a Photographic Society in London similar to the French society.[15]

Equally frustratingly, no surviving letters between Talbot and Hunt fill the gap between May and November 1851. But in a draft of a letter Talbot wrote to Hunt on November 6 and 7, 1851 (but did not send), Talbot refers to recent correspondence (no longer extant) and expresses a fair degree of annoyance with members of the Photographic Club: "With reference to your observation yesterday respecting a Photographic Club, I would mention that so long as gentlemen few in number were practising this fascinating art for their amusement I had no wish to interfere—I only regretted that so few of them either sent any courteous acknowledgement to myself or adhered to their promise of dealing with my Licensees Messeurs Henneman & Company for their photographic materials."[16]

Into these entrenched discussions and seeming stalemate at the end of 1851 entered Roger Fenton, thirty-two years old, artistic, independently wealthy, well connected, with time at his disposal, and an enthusiastic convert to photography, having had lessons in Paris from Monsieur Puech and Vicomte Vigier. Even better, he was possessed of a young legal brain that might help him find a solution to the patent problem. Impressed by the way the French had organized the Société Héliographique, he published an article about it in early 1852 and determined to attempt something similar in London.[17] The Société Héliographique was comfortably housed at the home of its founder, Colonel Benito de Montfort, in the classy center of Paris at 15, rue de l'Arcade, a short stroll north of the Champs-Élysées and the Madeleine. The premises held rooms for conducting meetings, lectures, experiments, and discussions; an office in which the distinguished weekly publication of its proceedings, *La Lumière*, was produced; even a roof garden! The initial forty members of the *société*, under the presidency of Baron Jean-Baptiste-Louis Gros, were a starry mix of artists, scientists, writers, photographers, optical instrument makers, and aristocrats. The likes of Eugène Delacroix, the physicist Edmond Becquerel, the writer and critic Francis Wey, and the engraver Augustin-François Lemaître rubbed shoulders with the photographers Bayard, Eugène Durieu, Le Secq, Édouard Baldus, and Le Gray. Fenton must have been deeply impressed.

A month after his article on the Société Héliographique, Fenton published his "Proposal for the Formation of a Photographical Society," which included an invitation for interested parties to contact him directly. He proposed a society "of those eminent in the study of natural philosophy, of opticians, chemists, artists, and practical photographers, professional and amateur. . . . Such meetings should be periodically held, for the purpose of hearing and discussing written or verbal communications on the subject of photography, receiving and verifying claims as to priority of invention, and for the exhibition and comparison of pictures produced by different applications of photographic principles."[18] Another, undated version of the proposal, with two sentences crossed out in ink, shows that Fenton contemplated, but decided against, including the following passage: "The heaviest expense attendant upon the plan would be the leasing or construction of convenient premises, and this expense might be lessened by the letting off the lower part as a shop for the sale of photographic chemicals, and the upper part to some person who would form a commercial establishment for the printing of positives" (fig. 68).[19]

On March 5, 1852, probably after reading Fenton's published proposal and a subsequent interchange with Talbot—who was unlikely to have been happy with Fenton's emphasis on "professional" photographers or the phrase "receiving and verifying claims as to priority of invention"—Hunt wrote to Fry, "Mr. Fox Talbot knows nothing whatever of Mr. Fenton or his society schemes and I don't fancy Sir David Brewster [the Scottish physicist, a close friend of Talbot's] knows anything of it. I have not the slightest knowledge of Mr. Fenton but I somewhat doubt from the conversation I had with him if such a society as he proposes would have, and maintain, the required respectability."[20] However, Talbot had agreed, Hunt also wrote, that "if a Photographic Society is formed upon a very respectable basis, he will give a licence to every member of the Society to practise the Art"—with five conditions, most of which related to the process not being used for commercial gain.[21] The "respectability" that Talbot repeatedly stressed meant the amateur practice of photography as a gentlemanly pursuit, untainted by trade and commerce.

It seems that while the Photographic Club had been, through Hunt, very slowly working toward formalizing its position with Talbot, Fenton had suddenly stirred things up with his energetic and dynamic approach. (The fact that Hunt did not know Fenton indicates that Fenton was not a long-standing member of the Photographic Club and was still an unknown quantity.) As a reading of the continuing correspondence between Talbot, Hunt, and others reveals, Fenton seems to have had the effect of binding the members' various opinions into a whole. Hunt's future letters to Talbot became much shorter and sharper on legalities, perhaps with the help of Fenton the barrister.

On March 19, 1852, Hunt wrote again to Talbot, informing him that "a great many good names have been received for the Photographic Society—as yet nothing has been done—There will be a meeting when Mr. Fenton, who is now in Lancashire, returns to London."[22] Two weeks after the letter quoted above, Hunt not only knows who Fenton is but seems to be working with him. Hunt also emphasized that prospective members of a Photographic Society were wary of joining until the question of Talbot's patent rights was finally resolved. In his reply, Talbot agreed to meet a committee of five gentlemen to discuss his patent rights. "I assure you that I have

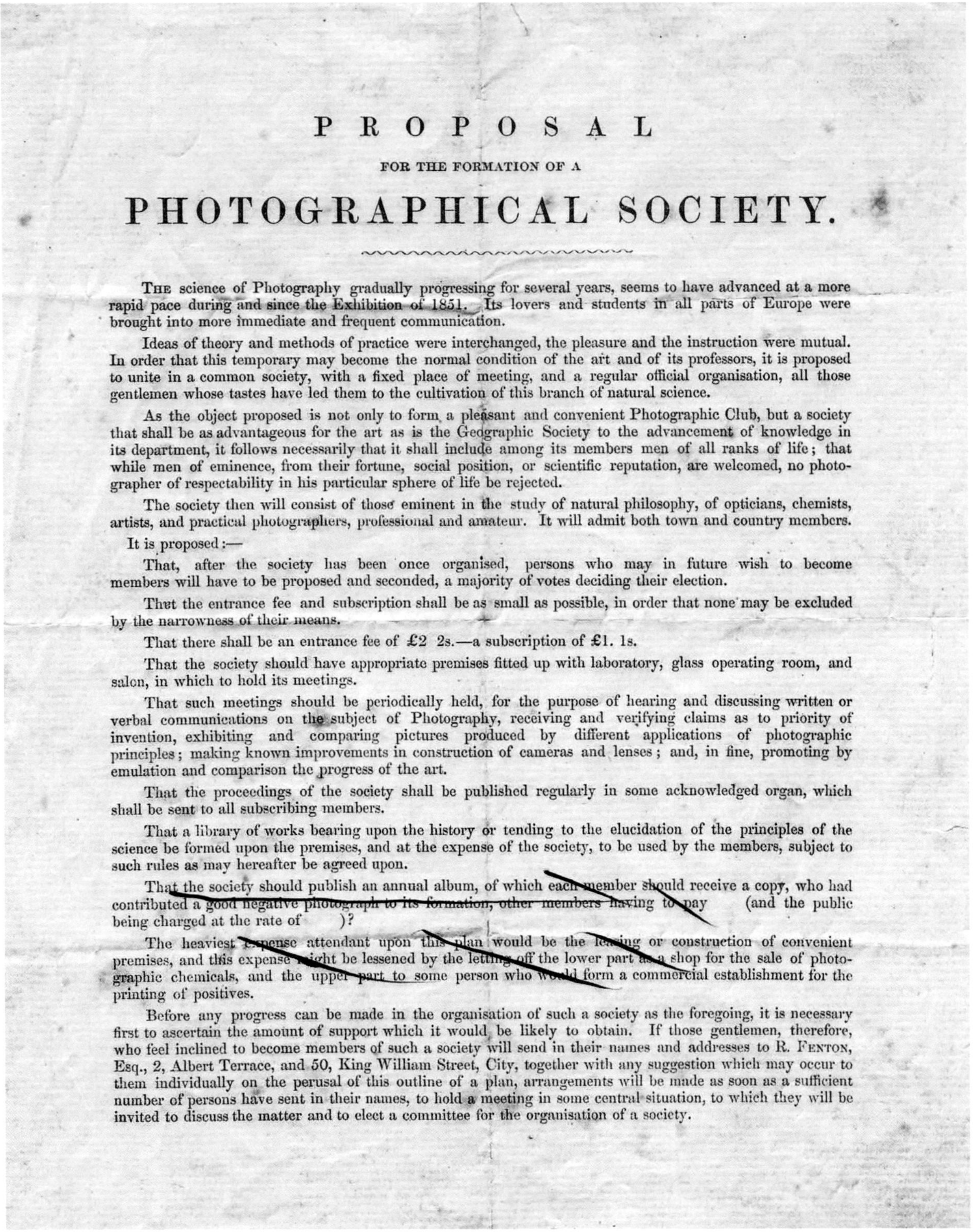

PROPOSAL

FOR THE FORMATION OF A

PHOTOGRAPHICAL SOCIETY.

THE science of Photography gradually progressing for several years, seems to have advanced at a more rapid pace during and since the Exhibition of 1851. Its lovers and students in all parts of Europe were brought into more immediate and frequent communication.

Ideas of theory and methods of practice were interchanged, the pleasure and the instruction were mutual. In order that this temporary may become the normal condition of the art and of its professors, it is proposed to unite in a common society, with a fixed place of meeting, and a regular official organisation, all those gentlemen whose tastes have led them to the cultivation of this branch of natural science.

As the object proposed is not only to form a pleasant and convenient Photographic Club, but a society that shall be as advantageous for the art as is the Geographic Society to the advancement of knowledge in its department, it follows necessarily that it shall include among its members men of all ranks of life; that while men of eminence, from their fortune, social position, or scientific reputation, are welcomed, no photographer of respectability in his particular sphere of life be rejected.

The society then will consist of those eminent in the study of natural philosophy, of opticians, chemists, artists, and practical photographers, professional and amateur. It will admit both town and country members.

It is proposed:—

That, after the society has been once organised, persons who may in future wish to become members will have to be proposed and seconded, a majority of votes deciding their election.

That the entrance fee and subscription shall be as small as possible, in order that none may be excluded by the narrowness of their means.

That there shall be an entrance fee of £2 2s.—a subscription of £1. 1s.

That the society should have appropriate premises fitted up with laboratory, glass operating room, and salon, in which to hold its meetings.

That such meetings should be periodically held, for the purpose of hearing and discussing written or verbal communications on the subject of Photography, receiving and verifying claims as to priority of invention, exhibiting and comparing pictures produced by different applications of photographic principles; making known improvements in construction of cameras and lenses; and, in fine, promoting by emulation and comparison the progress of the art.

That the proceedings of the society shall be published regularly in some acknowledged organ, which shall be sent to all subscribing members.

That a library of works bearing upon the history or tending to the elucidation of the principles of the science be formed upon the premises, and at the expense of the society, to be used by the members, subject to such rules as may hereafter be agreed upon.

That the society should publish an annual album, of which each member should receive a copy, who had contributed a good negative photograph to its formation, other members having to pay   (and the public being charged at the rate of   )?

The heaviest expense attendant upon this plan would be the leasing or construction of convenient premises, and this expense might be lessened by the letting off the lower part as a shop for the sale of photographic chemicals, and the upper part to some person who would form a commercial establishment for the printing of positives.

Before any progress can be made in the organisation of such a society as the foregoing, it is necessary first to ascertain the amount of support which it would be likely to obtain. If those gentlemen, therefore, who feel inclined to become members of such a society will send in their names and addresses to R. FENTON, Esq., 2, Albert Terrace, and 50, King William Street, City, together with any suggestion which may occur to them individually on the perusal of this outline of a plan, arrangements will be made as soon as a sufficient number of persons have sent in their names, to hold a meeting in some central situation, to which they will be invited to discuss the matter and to elect a committee for the organisation of a society.

Fig. 68. Roger Fenton, "Proposal for the Formation of a Photographical Society," 1852. Courtesy of Hans P. Kraus Jr., Inc., New York

the best wishes for the formation of a prosperous society, but it appears to me that there is not much reciprocity of feeling on the part of those who would naturally take a leading part in it" (Talbot's underlining). On the back of this letter Hunt listed six men to meet Talbot: Frederic W. Berger, Peter Le Neve Foster, Fry, Newton, himself, and Roger Fenton.[23]

Although the meeting occurred in late March or early April, negotiations about the waiving of Talbot's patent were still going badly, and on April 28, 1852, Hunt wrote to Talbot, "So very strong was the expression of feeling on the subject of the Society under the circumstances I believe we must abandon for the present any attempt to form a society—into which any considerations of your patent rights shall enter."[24] Nevertheless, Hunt had approached the Society of Arts about the use of a large room for the new Photographic Society's inaugural meeting and a small room for future fortnightly meetings, and on April 21, Professor Charles Wheatstone, the physicist and inventor, had agreed to be one of the three vice presidents of the society, should it be formed—at Talbot's particular request.[25] Talbot perhaps wanted to have a sympathetic colleague and fellow scientist on the society's Council. (Wheatstone may already have known Fenton as well, since less than two months later Fenton made pairs of images to be viewed in Wheatstone's reflecting stereoscope.[26] The next year, Wheatstone recommended Fenton for the job of photographer at the British Museum.)[27] Members of the Organizing, or Provisional, Committee for the proposed Photographic Society were Berger, Fenton, Fry, Le Neve Foster, Thomas Minchin Goodeve, Hunt, Newton, Dr. John Percy, and Wheatstone. In a meeting held at the Society of Arts on June 19, 1852, Fenton was elected honorary secretary to the Organizing Committee.

Taking the advice given him by his uncle Lord Henry Lansdowne and by Wheatstone, Talbot engaged in correspondence with Sir Charles Lock Eastlake—artist, president of the Royal Academy, and soon to be the Photographic Society's first president—and William Parsons, 3rd Earl of Rosse—astronomer, Member of Parliament, and president of the Royal Society—whom Talbot recognized "as being the acknowledged heads of the artistic and scientific world."[28] Eventually Talbot was presented with a joint letter from the two men, in which, using wording that he himself had proposed, they requested that he abandon his patent rights. Unless Talbot made some alteration in the exercise of his patent rights, wrote Eastlake and Lord Rosse, British photography might "be left behind by the Nations of the Continent." The letter ends, "We beg to make this friendly communication to you in the full confidence that you will receive it in the same spirit, the improvement of Art and Science being our common object."[29] On July 30, 1852, Talbot agreed to relinquish his patent rights, except on photographic portraits for sale to the public. (In 1854 he would abandon all patent rights.) The Eastlake/Rosse letter and Talbot's response were subsequently published in the *Times*.[30]

The way was now clear for the formation of the Photographic Society. An exhibition composed solely of photographs was organized after a letter to the Society of Arts suggesting such an undertaking from Joseph Cundall, a publisher as well as a photographer, was read and approved by the society's Council on November 17.[31] Fenton's absence for three months while he was photographing in Moscow and Kiev meant that the preparations were carried out largely by Cundall and Philip Henry Delamotte. The exhibition, "Recent Specimens of Photography," opened at the Society of Arts on December 22, 1852.

At the opening,[32] Fenton read a paper, "On the Present Position and Future Prospects of the Art of Photography." After paying tribute to Talbot as the "inventor of photography upon paper," he continued in honorary secretary vein:

To the commercial principle just now beginning to be applied to this art, may be safely left the development and the reward of practical skill. But these more abstract questions [concerning physical, optical, and chemical aspects of photography] will not be likely to receive the attention due to them, until photographers are united together in a society which shall give a systematic direction to their labours, and which shall keep a permanent record of the progressive steps from time to time, and of the authors of them. Such a society will be [the] reservoir to which will flow, and from which will be beneficially distributed, all the springs of knowledge at present wasting unproductively. Such a society is within one step of complete organization, and awaits only the general co-operation of the whole body of photographers to enter upon an active and useful existence.[33]

This first purely photographic exhibition in Britain, consisting of almost eight hundred photographs, attracted an enthusiastic audience and was

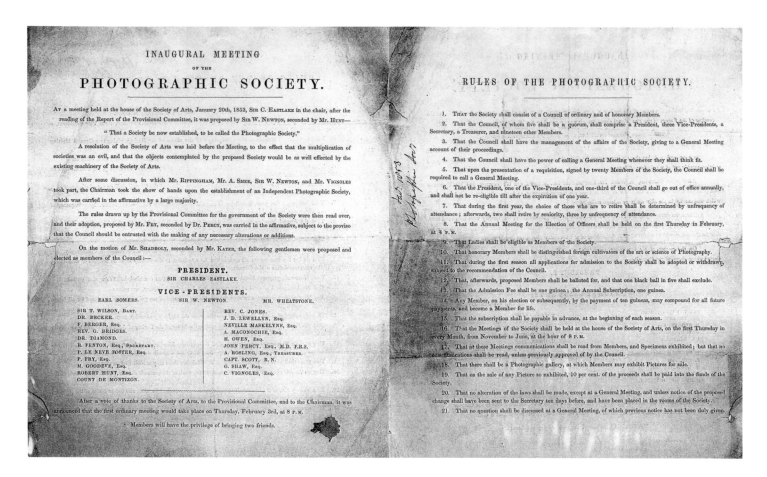

INAUGURAL MEETING
OF THE
PHOTOGRAPHIC SOCIETY.

At a meeting held at the house of the Society of Arts, January 20th, 1853, Sir C. Eastlake in the chair, after the reading of the Report of the Provisional Committee, it was proposed by Sir W. Newton, seconded by Mr. Hunt—

"That a Society be now established, to be called the Photographic Society."

A resolution of the Society of Arts was laid before the Meeting, to the effect that the multiplication of societies was an evil, and that the objects contemplated by the proposed Society would be as well effected by the existing machinery of the Society of Arts.

After some discussion, in which Mr. Rippingham, Mr. A. Smee, Sir W. Newton, and Mr. Vignoles took part, the Chairman took the show of hands upon the establishment of an Independent Photographic Society, which was carried in the affirmative by a large majority.

The rules drawn up by the Provisional Committee for the government of the Society were then read over, and their adoption, proposed by Mr. Fry, seconded by Dr. Percy, was carried in the affirmative, subject to the proviso that the Council should be entrusted with the making of any necessary alterations or additions.

On the motion of Mr. Shadbolt, seconded by Mr. Kater, the following gentlemen were proposed and elected as members of the Council:—

PRESIDENT.
SIR CHARLES EASTLAKE.

VICE-PRESIDENTS.
EARL SOMERS. SIR W. NEWTON. MR. WHEATSTONE.

SIR T. WILSON, Bart.
DR. BECKER.
F. BERGER, Esq.
REV. G. BRIDGES.
DR. DIAMOND.
R. FENTON, Esq., Secretary.
P. LE NEVE FOSTER, Esq.
P. FRY, Esq.
M. GOODEVE, Esq.
ROBERT HUNT, Esq.
COUNT DE MONTIZON.

REV. C. JONES.
J. D. LLEWELLYN, Esq.
NEVILLE MASKELYNE, Esq.
A. MACONOCHIE, Esq.
H. OWEN, Esq.
JOHN PERCY, Esq., M.D. F.R.S.
A. ROSLING, Esq., Treasurer.
CAPT. SCOTT, R.N.
G. SHAW, Esq.
C. VIGNOLES, Esq.

After a vote of thanks to the Society of Arts, to the Provisional Committee, and to the Chairman, it was announced that the first ordinary meeting would take place on Thursday, February 3rd, at 8 P.M.

* Members will have the privilege of bringing two friends.

RULES OF THE PHOTOGRAPHIC SOCIETY.

1. That the Society shall consist of a Council of ordinary and of honorary Members.
2. That the Council, of whom five shall be a quorum, shall comprise a President, three Vice-Presidents, a Secretary, a Treasurer, and nineteen other Members.
3. That the Council shall have the management of the affairs of the Society, giving to a General Meeting account of their proceedings.
4. That the Council shall have the power of calling a General Meeting whenever they shall think fit.
5. That upon the presentation of a requisition, signed by twenty Members of the Society, the Council shall be required to call a General Meeting.
6. That the President, one of the Vice-Presidents, and one-third of the Council shall go out of office annually, and shall not be re-eligible till after the expiration of one year.
7. That during the first year, the choice of those who are to retire shall be determined by unfrequency of attendance; afterwards, two shall retire by seniority, three by unfrequency of attendance.
8. That the Annual Meeting for the Election of Officers shall be held on the first Thursday in February, at 4 P.M.
9. That Ladies shall be eligible as Members of the Society.
10. That honorary Members shall be distinguished foreign cultivators of the art or science of Photography.
11. That during the first season all applications for admission to the Society shall be adopted or withdrawn, subject to the recommendation of the Council.
12. That, afterwards, proposed Members shall be balloted for, and that one black ball in five shall exclude.
13. That the Admission Fee shall be one guinea; the Annual Subscription, one guinea.
14. Any Member, on his election or subsequently, by the payment of ten guineas, may compound for all future payments, and become a Member for life.
15. That the subscription shall be payable in advance, at the beginning of each season.
16. That the Meetings of the Society shall be held at the house of the Society of Arts, on the first Thursday in every Month, from November to June, at the hour of 8 P.M.
17. That at these Meetings communications shall be read from Members, and Specimens exhibited; but that no communications shall be read, unless previously approved of by the Council.
18. That there shall be a Photographic gallery, at which Members may exhibit Pictures for sale.
19. That on the sale of any Picture so exhibited, 10 per cent. of the proceeds shall be paid into the funds of the Society.
20. That no alteration of the laws shall be made, except at a General Meeting, and unless notice of the proposed change shall have been sent to the Secretary ten days before, and have been placed in the rooms of the Society.
21. That no question shall be discussed at a General Meeting, of which previous notice has not been duly given.

Fig. 69. Council of the Photograph Society, "Inaugural Meeting of the Photographic Society & Rules of the Photographic Society." The RPS Collection at the National Museum of Photography, Film & Television, Bradford

extended until January 29, 1853. It even drew Dante Gabriel Rossetti, who visited the exhibition on its closing day.[34]

The inaugural meeting of the Photographic Society was held in the Great Room of the Society of Arts on Thursday, January 20, 1853, at 4:00 p.m. (the time of day suggests that participants were gentlemen with time to spare). Eastlake was elected president; Talbot—hardly surprisingly, after the patent discussions of the last two years—had declined the offer of the presidency. The question of independence or affiliation was raised by Le Neve Foster, member of the Council of the Society of Arts, who declared that "the multiplication of societies was an evil, and that the objects contemplated by the proposed Society would be as well effected by the existing machinery of the Society of Arts."[35] Acutely aware of the momentum that photography was rapidly gaining, and encouraged by the success of the recent exhibition, the Society of Arts was keen to have the fledgling society established under its own wing. To this end, Le Neve Foster offered "funds, rooms, officers and publications, with such other facilities as may be necessary for the full development of photographic art."[36] But the majority of those at the meeting agreed with Newton, who "thought it essential for the Artist that there should be a separate independent Photographic Society";[37] and the Photographic Society was born (fig. 69).

Members of the Council were elected. Earl Somers (brother-in-law of the not-yet-practicing photographer Julia Margaret Cameron), Sir William John Newton (1785–1869), and Charles Wheatstone (1802–1875) became the three vice presidents, and Alfred Rosling (1802–1882), later the father-in-law of Francis Frith, was chosen to be treasurer. Other Council members were Prince Albert's librarian, Dr. Ernst Becker (1826–1888); Frederic W. Berger; the Reverend George Bridges; Dr. Hugh Welch Diamond (1809–1886), who afterward replaced Fenton as honorary secretary and also served as editor and vice president; Peter Wickens Fry (d. 1860); Thomas Minchin Goodeve; Robert Hunt (1807–1887); the Reverend Calvert Jones (1802–1877); Peter Le Neve Foster (1809–1879); John Dillwyn Llewelyn (1810–1882); A. Maconochie; Nevil Story-Maskelyne (1823–1911); Count Juan Carlos de Montizon (1822–1887); Hugh Owen (1804–1881); Dr. John Percy (1817–1889); Captain Scott; George Shaw (1818–1904); Charles Blacker Vignoles (1798–1875); and Sir Thomas Maryon Wilson (1800–1869). Twenty-one rules were drawn up and with slight emendations published in the *Journal of the Photographic Society* on March 3, 1853.[38] Fenton was formally elected honorary secretary, a position he held until his resignation in February 1856.

The first ordinary meeting of the new society was held on February 3 at 8:00 p.m. There were four papers read: Newton's on photography and its relations to the arts; Percy's on the applicability of the waxed paper process to hot climates; Vignoles's on the usefulness of photography to engineers; and Fenton's "Upon the Mode in Which It Is Advisable the Society Should Conduct Its Labours." They were published in the *Journal of the Photographic Society* a month later.[39]

During its first few meetings the society rapidly established specific activities that it intended to carry out. In addition to conducting ongoing experimentation and discussion, plans were made for the publication of a journal; the holding of frequent exhibitions to show the best new work by both members and nonmembers; the display of portfolios of new work to a critical elite; the provision of darkrooms; and the establishments of a library, a photographic collection, a museum, and a separate gallery for the exhibition of members' work (with the society taking a 10 percent cut on any photographs sold, as had been suggested by Talbot). Many of these aims would be rapidly realized. Professor Arthur Henfrey became honorary editor of the *Journal*.

It was Fenton who made the society work. Influenced by the model of Victorian art institutions and learned societies, he saw it as his new society's role to champion a particular idea of professional identity and individuality, encourage the association of photography with national pride, share knowledge and expertise, and create a distinctive arena for the viewing, discussion, and selling of works. To these ends the society on May 30, 1853, secured the patronage of Queen Victoria and Prince Albert. Although the Council considered asking for permission to change the group's name to the Royal

Photographic Society, no action was taken at this early date, and it would be 1894 before the society finally assumed that title.

As Fenton, perhaps still thinking of the glamorous headquarters of the Société Héliographique, had predicted, ultimately the society's heaviest expenditures were for suitable premises. Ordinary meetings and Council meetings continued to be held at the Society of Arts, and in February 1853, Vignoles briefly provided a room at 4 Trafalgar Square for clerical work. But by May 1853, the Council was leasing a room from the Botanical Society in Bedford Street, Strand, for thirty pounds a year. After July 1854, all meetings were held in a room rented from the Horticultural Society at 21 Regent Street for thirty pounds per annum plus five pounds per annum for the attendance of a servant. In the same year applications were made to the government for space in Burlington House on Piccadilly, where the tenants over the years were to be an assortment of "metropolitan societies for the promotion of natural knowledge,"[40] including the well-established Royal Academy, the Royal Society, the Linnaean Society, the Geological Society, the Royal Astronomical Society, and the Royal Society of Chemistry. For the Photographic Society, which encompassed both art and science, this location shared with like-minded institutions would have been the perfect home, but, alas, nothing came of the attempt.[41] (It was not until November 1857 that the society would move to far more prestigious and expensive premises, at 1 New Coventry Street, above the Union Bank on the corner of Leicester Square. Here there were meeting and reading rooms, a laboratory, a glasshouse, and "other conveniences." However, after paying rent of three hundred pounds per annum and a further seven hundred pounds for fixtures and fittings, the society could not afford to stay at the address for long.)[42]

The society's first annual exhibition, organized by six Council members including Fenton and thrown open to international entries, contained 980 items and was held at the Suffolk Street Gallery of the Society of British Artists in January and February 1854. Exhibitors and members were admitted free, while the public paid one shilling entrance fee, sixpence for a catalogue; the exhibition was hugely popular, and a small profit was made. Queen Victoria and Prince Albert, accompanied by Viscountess Jocelyn,[43] Colonel Bouverie, and Lieutenant Colonel F. Seymour, were shown around the exhibition by Eastlake, Fenton, Hunt, and Wheatstone. The royal patrons bought several photographs, including six of Fenton's

Russian prints,[44] and thus began their deep commitment, especially on Prince Albert's part, to the affairs of the new society. In the years that followed, Albert scrupulously attended every annual exhibition and often purchased prints. He also took an interest in the process of photography, experimenting with it himself and partially funding (with a donation of fifty pounds) the committee set up in 1856 to investigate the permanency of photographs.

The new society earned mixed reviews. The majority were favorable; the *Morning Chronicle*, for instance, gave the Photographic Society credit for "the rapid progress and development of photography . . . during the last two years."[45] But the *Athenaeum* commented dryly, "Should a few real men of business be added to the Council the permanence of this useful Society might perhaps be considered as established."[46] And a lengthy complaint was voiced by the *Builder:* "We had hoped that the formation of the Photographic Society would have led to a more systematic investigation of the chemical agencies upon which the art is based, and to a prompt and unreserved publication of the result of such investigations. . . . The council have done nothing more than call the members together seven times within the twelvemonth to talk the matter over among themselves, without, as a body, having issued or sanctioned a single communication tending to the improvement of the art, or even having made an attempt to publish a clear and minute account of the several processes already in use."[47]

The range of opinions did not prevent the Photographic Society from concluding its first year in a very healthy position, with a membership of 370; an immense circulation figure for its *Journal*, four thousand copies per month (hinting at a huge untapped audience for photography); and a credit balance of 406 pounds 17 shillings.

The patent difficulties with Talbot continued to rumble on, however. In 1854 Talbot took out injunctions against the professional portrait photographer Martin Laroche for infringing his patents by using the collodion process in a commercial portrait business. The Council of the Photographic Society, led by the lawyers Fry (Laroche's attorney), Hunt (Talbot's former correspondent), and perhaps Fenton himself, supported Laroche. They feared that a validation of the patents' extension to the collodion process would strangle the further development of photography and discourage potential membership in their society. Talbot appealed to Story-Maskelyne,

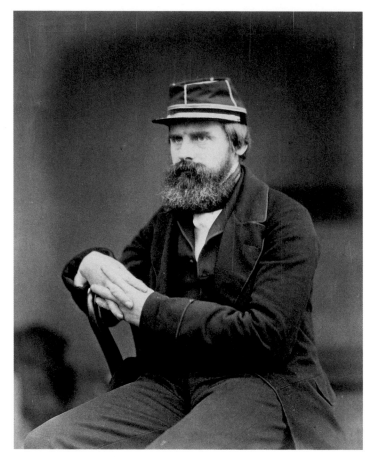

Fig. 70. Attributed to Hugh Welch Diamond or Roger Fenton, *Portrait of Roger Fenton*, 1856. Salted paper print, 19.5 x 15.2 cm ($7^{11}/_{16}$ x 6 in.). From *Rules of the Photographic Society Club Album*, 1856. The RPS Collection at the National Museum of Photography, Film & Television, Bradford

then a lecturer on mineralogy and chemistry at Oxford University and an experimental photographer, who was one of Talbot's few supporters on the Council of the Photographic Society. Talbot wrote to him bitterly, "The Photographic Society will hold a meeting on Wednesday next, I believe, to make their final arrangements for my destruction at the Trial. It is evident they will do their uttermost, (the same body that asked me to be their President!)"[48] The always delicate relationship between Talbot and the Photographic Society fractured completely when, in December 1854, with the society's help (and possibly an injection of its finances), Laroche won his case. Talbot soon withdrew his remaining patent restrictions.

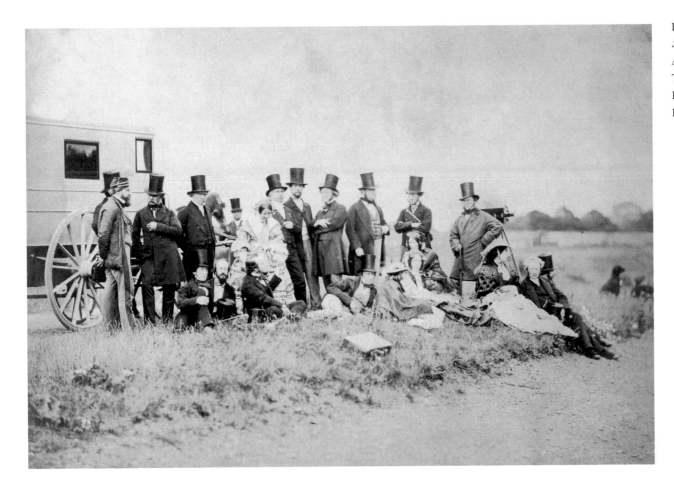

Fig. 71. Roger Fenton, *Members of the Photographic Society Club at Hampton Court, July 18, 1856.* Albumen silver print, 24.2 x 33.3 cm (9⁹⁄₁₆ x 13⅛ in.). The RPS Collection at the National Museum of Photography, Film & Television, Bradford, Gift of Fenton descendants, 1934, 2003-5000/12787

In February 1856, Fenton resigned as honorary secretary, the society having accrued enough money to pay the Reverend John Richardson Major of King's College, London (one of forty-four applicants for the job), a salary of two hundred pounds per annum for carrying out the combined duties of secretary and editor of the *Journal*. In May of that year, Fenton and several others resigned from the Council because of their association with a commercial organization, the Photographic Association.[49] He was back on the Council a few months later and became vice president of the society in December 1857.

Simultaneously the Photographic Society Club, an informal and social grouping within the Photographic Society, was established "to promote union and friendly feeling amongst the members of the Photographic Society."[50] Made up of an elite inner core of Photographic Society members and, with its social, dining, and information-exchange functions, resembling the Photographic Club of old, it had an annually elected president, treasurer, and combined secretary-caterer and was limited in membership to twenty-one.[51] Members dined together five times a year, "one of which dinners shall take place in some country locality favourable to photographic pursuits."[52] The club's best-known country outing was one to Hampton Court on July 18, 1856; a group photograph taken by Fenton on that occasion, with contemporary annotations identifying members, shows them with attendant cameras, some accompanied by their wives and the occasional dog. Fenton's wife appears seated with one of their daughters, while Fenton himself poses alongside his photographic van (fig. 71).

The year 1856 was a good one for the society, which at its annual general meeting in February 1857 declared a reserve fund of 1,060 pounds and a much increased membership. The journal circulation had gone down slightly, to three thousand a month (other photographic publications had by now

Baldus, whose landscapes figure in his railway albums principally as parts of a description of the iron way or as conspicuous landmarks that leaven the record of architectural marvels along the route. With their lyric portrayal of varied landforms, from the wildnesses of northwest Wales to the cultivated and orderly river valleys of the Midlands, Fenton's images present a range of responses to landscape that had no rivals until the emergence of the great American landscape photographers of the 1860s and 1870s such as Carleton Watkins and Timothy O'Sullivan. The landscape these men photographed was itself of a heroic nature unavailable in the more tempered countryside of the British Isles.

Underlying all Fenton's landscape work is an ideal, an effort to preserve the image of a land that was diminishing and increasingly exploited. Even in North Wales, still one of the remote fastnesses of Britain, where he photographed a slate pier (pl. 39), there was already a long history of quarrying and mining. And in the countryside in general, land that had been cultivated and productive was, with the drift to the cities, falling fallow.

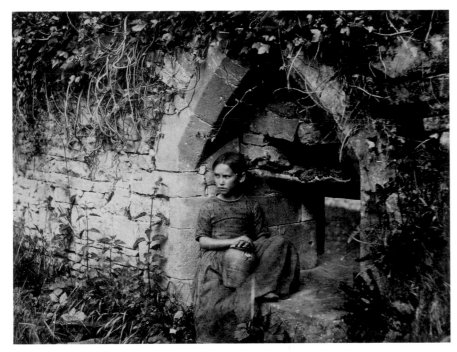

Fig. 76. Roger Fenton, *Scene in Tintern Abbey*, 1854. "Printed and Published by F. Frith, Reigate." Albumen silver print, 16.5 x 20.9 cm (6½ x 8³⁄₁₆ in.). Collection Centre Canadien d'Architecture / Canadian Centre for Architecture, Montréal, PH1980:0689

The series of images of the great monastic foundations, Tintern, Fountains, and Rievaulx, all fallen into decay after the Reformation, express the beauty of the quietist architecture of the Cistercians as well as Fenton's attachment to the English Romantic heritage (pls. 8–12). Perhaps he knew the remark John Webster gives to Antonio in *The Duchess of Malfi:* "I do love these ancient ruins. / We never tread upon them but we set / Our foot upon some reverend history."[26] But Fenton's Romanticism was not sentimental. He recognized the tangible relationship of structure to setting that the monks had understood so well in choosing the sites for their foundations.

Who are the people who appear in the pictures? Many are in mourning clothes, perhaps no uncommon sight in the years immediately after the Crimean campaign. Fenton lost three young children of his own, and some pictures have such intimacy that it seems likely the subjects are members of his immediate family. There is a quality of truth in Fenton's best photographs that is deeply moving. Few truer portraits of children exist than the touchingly lovely portrayal of a pensive child resting in an alcove of the refectory at Tintern (fig. 76),[27] while his photographs of the royal princesses, whose social position could hardly be more different, are similarly imbued with the reflective wistfulness of childhood (pls. 27, 28). Fenton seems to have recognized that the stillness required by long exposure times brought out the introspective qualities of his sitters and was something specific to portraiture in his chosen medium.

To judge from the titles of the academic paintings he produced early in his artistic career, Fenton began picture making with an approach governed by sentiment. When he turned to photography one might have expected that this member of the wealthy professional classes would take no more than a dilettantish interest in the medium. Well placed, a barrister, financially secure, he had no reason to exert himself and could easily have adopted the genteel role of an amateur. Instead the medium liberated him and gave his work the edge of discovery and rigor that has assured his place in the photographic pantheon. His search to extend the limits of photographic seeing seems to rest on curiosity about the very substance of picture making.

The fittingness of his interpretation to the materials is always apt. The early salt prints display a relish for form and massing and effectively utilize the particular qualities of the paper structure. In the later large glass plates

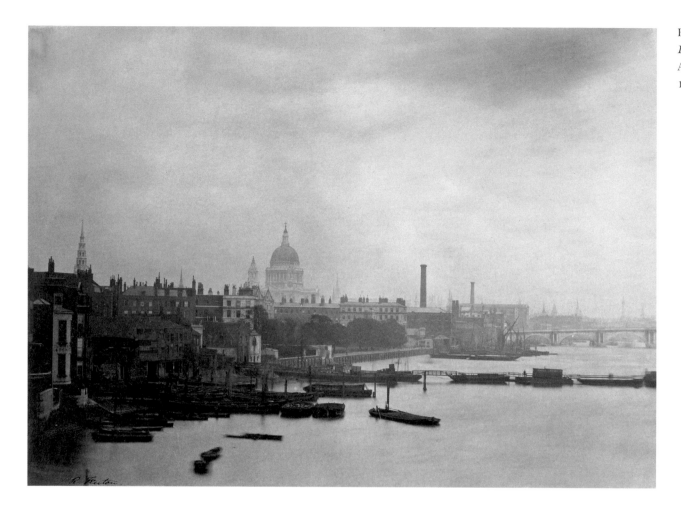

Fig. 77. Roger Fenton, *The Thames and Saint Paul's, Looking Downstream from Waterloo Bridge*, ca. 1858. Albumen silver print, 31.5 x 42.5 cm (12⁷⁄₁₆ x 16¾ in.). Tolstoy Museum, Moscow

this evolves into an overwhelming, nigh hallucinatory revelment in the rendering of detail. The obsession with detail reaches its apogee in the still lifes that represent the culmination of his career in photography, if not its zenith. One can seek a hidden iconography in these late images, but their deeper meaning remains obstinately unreachable, and instead we become fascinated by the richly rendered surfaces and the distortions in color caused by the spectral response of the photographic emulsion. The Victorian tendency to embellish is reflected in these hothouse productions, and elaboration and density of texture seem the predominant motifs. Qualities of surface fix our attention on the bloom of freshly gathered fruit and then the fragility of that bloom already brushed aside. Themes of temporality and mortality are also present in the earlier and less studiously arranged images of fish and game, which through the act of photographing suspend the inevitable decay of their subjects, capturing the ephemeral sheen of a fish's flank and the still-supple bodies of birds and rabbits.

There is in Fenton's best works a kind of charged serenity that undoubtedly has its roots in a highly complex eye educated in the interpretation of space. He had the ability to recognize a latent order, something that had remained undiscovered, and to conduct the eye of the observer in such a way that revelation occurs.

In a photograph made at Rievaulx, the reading woman sitting before the doorway leading from the monks' burial ground is in contemplative counterpoint to the dynamic of the white-dressed child venturing out into the fields beyond (pl. 10). Mortality and nascence are encapsulated in one picture. It is clear that the figures in these highly staged images were not there by chance; the spontaneity comes from the creative tension of the idea being introduced

Fig. 78. Roger Fenton, *Westminster Abbey and the Houses of Parliament, Saint Stephen's Tower, and the Victoria Tower, from Great Smith Street*, ca. 1858. Albumen silver print, 31 x 42 cm (12⁵⁄₁₆ x 16⁹⁄₁₆ in.). Tolstoy Museum, Moscow

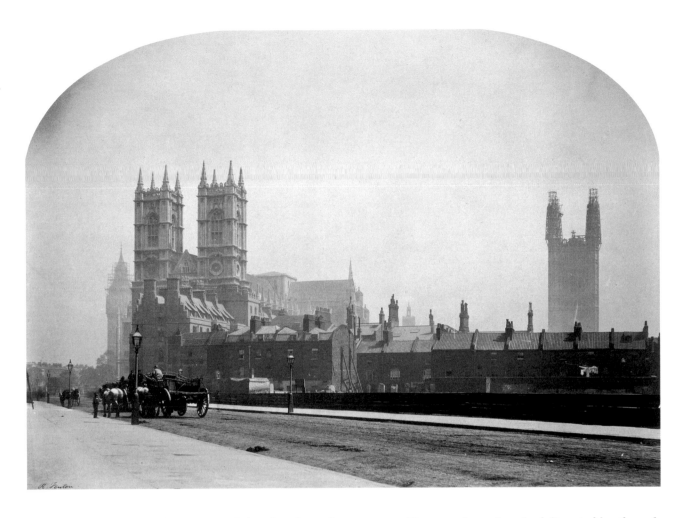

into the mind of the observer. In almost every case the inclusion of the human element in Fenton's photography is far more than a simple indication of scale. In some of the river landscapes the figures are so small as to be almost insignificant and become an experiment in the question of proportion, the balancing of attention between animate beings and the living landscape. How small can the fulcrum in a picture be? On another level they seem a reminder of the smallness of human endeavor in the continuum of time. Outbreaks of disease, child mortality, and, during these years, death and disintegration from war were never far out of mind. In this age of revolutions, the precariousness and imminent collapse of the balance of power in Europe were matters of daily conjecture. Almost as if in a deliberately constructed counterpoise are Fenton's images of perfect stability, demonstrations of order and hierarchy. The strikingly minimalist *Long Walk* at Windsor

and the view from the terrace at Harewood, so sharply delineated by the cultivated English landscape tradition and the architecture that accompanies it, are examples (pls. 82, 68). Such images stand for order and the persistence of tradition, the apparently irreducible foundations of British society, the basis of Empire.

Fenton made two pictures from Waterloo Bridge looking upstream and down, creating works of very different character. The view downstream to Saint Paul's is a dark and foreboding rendering of the "chartered Thames," with the dome of the cathedral floating unchallenged over the city (fig. 77).[28] To the left is another of Christopher Wren's masterpieces, the steeple of Saint Bride's, the tallest in London. Looking upstream, toward the Houses of Parliament, the whole temperament of the image is different (pl. 60). Fenton reduces the composition to three bands: the sky, the city, and the river. It is an elemental image in which the bridge seems literally to be bearing the great monuments of London in suspension. Photographing into the light was a technical tour de force at this stage in the evolution of the medium, and a brooding atmosphere results from this use of contre-jour. Yet it also creates luminosity, giving the picture an airy quality of suspension entirely fitting to its subject. Further, the photographer takes note of significant alterations to the skyline of London, which for hundreds of years had remained virtually unchanged. The secular New Palace of Westminster (the newly completed Houses of Parliament) rises as the symbol of imperial might to dominate the sacred abbey of Westminster, where British monarchs have been crowned in succession since 1066.

From across the river at Lambeth Fenton developed further ideas on the balance of secular and ecclesiastical power. Lambeth Palace, the principal subject of this composition (pl. 58), is the seat of the Archbishop of Canterbury, here placed in dialogue with the new Parliament on the other side of the river. In a fourth image from the series (fig. 78), Fenton achieves an effective counterplay between the immediate foreground, strongly laid out in rushing and vigorous geometry, and the beautifully described towers by Nicholas Hawksmoor at the west end of Westminster Abbey. Here this venerable ecclesiastical symbol of the monarchy dominates the shadowy mass of the new Victoria Tower to the right.

Some of Fenton's images stand out even from the overall accomplishments of his career.

The Queen's Target (pl. 85) is a picture filled with artifice. A rifle had been clamped on a tripod and aimed at the target; by pulling a lanyard Queen Victoria was assured a direct hit. Thus the whole apparatus had been elaborately rigged to yield a satisfactory, if entirely artificial, result. Ultimately this picture is a rendering of an abstract idea. Its visual audacity is the complete separation from any kind of context.

A print of the image prepared for the album presented to the queen was strategically retouched to almost completely eliminate the gestural marks left by the brush of the preparer of the target.[29] It is as though it was deemed necessary to correct a courtly oversight in which the appearance of the target had not been considered. The retouching robbed the image of most of the characteristics that probably pleased Fenton in his original conception, including its temporal aspects and attendant layers of meaning.

A very different picture, that of Ely Cathedral from the south (pl. 50), is suffused with the kind of English peacefulness epitomized by cathedral precincts, those enclaves left from the days of the great monasteries when the religious foundations were vast landholders. Here the cathedral towers rise up in the ethereal light of a summer morning. A tree described with great subtlety perfectly holds the center; the whole picture conveys serenity and a sense of peace. The rightness of fit between the subject and the materials and process at hand, the scale of the print, and the synchronicity of these different aspects of the art of picture making are what make this image succeed. It sums up at once the very quintessence of a particularly English place: the calm of the cloister, the resonance of long centuries of observance carried out with unvarying regularity. Fenton's ecclesiastical images are about more than the representation of architecture, for they constitute a native response to a subject richly enveloped in the history of the nation and in the recollection of turbulent times long ago. They form a beautifully rendered account of a deeply humanistic landscape and architecture that had been managed by the inhabitants of the land for centuries. Pictures like this of Fenton's remain unequaled in the subsequent history of the photograph.

A Chronology of the Life and Photographic Career of Roger Fenton

ROGER TAYLOR AND GORDON BALDWIN

1819

March 28 Roger Fenton born at Crimble Hall, near Bury, Lancashire, fourth child of John Fenton (1791–1863) and Elizabeth Aipedaile Fenton (1792–1829) of Crimble Hall, and grandson of Joseph Fenton (1756–1840), cotton merchant and banker. Already in the family are two brothers, John (born February 11, 1814) and Joseph (born September 7, 1817), and a sister, Elizabeth (born May 10, 1815).

November 9 Christened at Bamford Independent Chapel, near Bury, by Thomas Jackson.

The same year, Joseph Fenton establishes the Fenton, Eccles, Cunliffe & Roby bank (later J. & J. Fenton and Sons), in Rochdale.

1820

Joseph Fenton purchases Bamford Hall from last surviving Bamford descendant and occupies it henceforth.

June 15 Birth of third brother, William.

1822

February 6 Birth of second sister, Sarah.

1824

June 21 Birth of third sister, Ann.

1826

Joseph Fenton starts construction of Hooley Bridge Mill, a gaslit five-story brick building, alongside river Roch, near Heywood. Some three hundred workers' dwellings are later built nearby. Firm quickly establishes a good reputation as a fair employer.[1]

1828

March 28 Burial of eldest brother, John, at age fourteen.

1829

July 22 Death of mother, Elizabeth, at age thirty-seven.

September 24 Joseph Fenton signs agreement with Thomas Weld to purchase, for then-considerable sum of thirty-six thousand pounds, 3,250 acres of land at Aighton, Bailey, Chaigley, Dutton, and Ribchester, along with ancient manorial rights and lordships to a further 4,250 acres. Estate is contiguous with Stonyhurst College and includes village of Hurst Green, with water-powered bobbin mills.[2]

1830

Father, John, marries second wife, Hannah Owston, of Brigg, Lincolnshire; they will have ten children.

1832

December 11 John Fenton elected Whig (Liberal) Member of Parliament for new constituency of Rochdale. Except for period 1835 to 1837, remains an MP until retirement in 1841.[3] Twenty years later, Roger Fenton will consider putting himself forward as candidate for Parliament.[4]

1836

Goes to London with brother William and enters University College. Studies Latin, Greek, English, mathematics, literature, and logic for next four years.

1839

May 29 Admitted to Honourable Society of the Inner Temple at Inns of Court, London, the first essential stage to becoming a barrister.[5]

1840

Graduates from University College with Bachelor of Arts degree.

June 18 Joseph Fenton dies, leaving estate worth more than five hundred thousand pounds.[6] Each grandchild receives one thousand pounds; Roger, having passed age of majority, inherits immediately.

1841

Begins law studies at University College.

Resides at 11 Gower Place, London, giving profession in 1841 census as "Templar," a title given to law students.

University College appoints Charles Blacker Vignoles professor of civil engineering.[7]

1842

June 28 Passport number 719 issued to Mr. Roger Fenton on recommendation of Mr. Cunliffe, banker, 21 Bucklersbury, London.[8]

1843

August 29 Marries Grace Elizabeth Maynard, daughter of John Charles Maynard of Harlsey Hall, Northallerton, Yorkshire, in Harlsey Parish Church.[9]

1844

May 17 Watercolor (private collection) titled and dated "Roger Fenton, Paris, May 17, 1844."[11]

June 29 Registers as copyist at the Musée du Louvre, naming as his teacher Michel-Martin Drolling (1786–1851), history and portrait painter and professor at École des Beaux-Arts.[10]

1845

Birth of first child, daughter Josephine Frances, possibly in Paris.

1846

Birth of second daughter, Annie Grace, in Paris.[12]

1847

Probably this year, begins study in London under the history painter Charles Lucy (1814–1873), a member of the Royal Academy; the two will become friends.

December Moves to newly completed house at 2 Albert Terrace, Regent's Park, London.[13]

December 18 First mention of "Calotype Society," described as "a dozen gentlemen amateurs" meeting informally at the home of Peter Wickens Fry.[14] This group, consisting of Fry, Joseph Cundall, Hugh Owen, and others (but not Fenton), first regular gathering of photographers held in London, will later promote idea of a photographic society for the city.[15]

1848

February 25 Mentioned in diary of Ford Madox Brown (FMB): "French Revolution proclaimed . . . went at eleven at night to see Lucy, found him in great excitement about Paris, Fenton his pupil in a sad state about it. We all three have associations with Paris."[16]

June 3–December 12 FMB records further encounters with Fenton.[17]

1849

March 19 FMB: "repainted at the head of Cordelia . . .

Lucy and Fenton called in, did not like her." (Brown was painting *Cordelia at the Bedside of Lear*, now in the collection of the Tate Gallery, London.)

May Exhibits painting at Royal Academy of Arts (no. 603): *You must wake and call me early . . .*, illustrating scene from Alfred, Lord Tennyson's ballad "The May Queen."[18]

1850

March 12 Death of eldest daughter, Josephine Frances, at age five.

March 13 FMB: "went to Fenton to paint his dead child."

March 14 FMB: "to Fenton's, finished the head—and back to work."

May Exhibits painting at Royal Academy (no. 71): *The letter to Mamma: What shall we write?*[19]

May 1 North London School of Drawing and Modelling opens under patronage of Prince Albert, offering evening classes intended to teach workmen and artisans "true knowledge of form." Fenton, Lucy, Brown, George Godwin, Samuel Carter Hall, J. Scott Russell, Thomas Seddon, and Digby Wyatt serve on Management Committee.[20]

June 6 Birth of third daughter, Aimée Frances, at home on Albert Terrace; she will die in infancy.[21]

July 25–26 With Grace, visits at Crimble Hall until about September 4.[22]

November 8 Being in area "alone," dines with brother-in-law Edmund Maynard, a captain in Eighty-Eighth Regiment, at barracks in Bury.[23]

1851

February 17 Having let membership lapse while in Paris, is readmitted to Inner Temple as a student, a prerequisite to being called to bar.[24]

May Exhibits painting at Royal Academy (no. 148): *There's music in his very steps as he comes up the stairs.*[25]

May 1 Great Exhibition of the Works of Industry of All Nations at Crystal Palace, Hyde Park, opened by

Queen Victoria and Prince Albert. Photographs widely distributed throughout exhibition, including in foreign courts, but British photography, especially amateur work, poorly represented.[26]

May 9 Called to bar; business address given as 50 King William Street, City of London.[27]

October On trip to Paris, meets Gustave Le Gray and other French photographers; visits Société Héliographique.[28]

1852

February Publishes article describing importance of Société Héliographique to French photography and asking that similar association be established in London.[29]

February 18 Date of earliest known photographs by Fenton, which include studies of Regent's Park, Albert Road, and Saint Mark's Church, a self-portrait, and five other portraits of unidentified persons, perhaps including his wife and a daughter.[30]

March *Chemist* publishes Fenton's "Proposal for the Formation of a Photographical Society," encouraging interested parties to apply directly to its offices or to Fenton at Albert Terrace.[31] Other notices of intent are published elsewhere.

March–July Robert Hunt corresponds with William Henry Fox Talbot on behalf of those seeking to establish a photographic society, arguing that Talbot's patents would unfairly restrict practice of members of proposed society. With the further intervention of Sir Charles Eastlake and Lord Rosse, the matter is resolved on July 30, when Talbot agrees to relinquish most patent rights.[32]

March 19 Letter from Hunt to Talbot notes that Fenton is currently in Lancashire.[33]

April 10–13 Photographs in Gloucester and surrounding region.[34]

June 15 Photographs dead game in Zoological Gardens, Regent's Park.[35]

June 19 Meeting at Society of Arts names provisional committee to establish a photographic society.[36]

August Fifth edition of W. H. Thornthwaite's *Guide to Photography* contains new chapter by Fenton that explains and modifies waxed paper process developed by Le Gray.

August 17 Departs for Russia with Vignoles and John Cooke Bourne, artist and photographer, to make pictures of construction of a suspension bridge across Dnieper River in Kiev, commissioned by Czar Nicholas I and designed by Vignoles.[37] Will also make extensive series of photographs in Moscow, Kiev, and elsewhere, often in trying circumstances.[38]

August 25 Fenton, Vignoles, and Bourne disembark in Saint Petersburg, where "the Photographic Apparatus was not allowed to pass" through customs and was only released six days later. Fenton and Bourne go to Moscow ahead of Vignoles.[39]

September 24 Reaches Kiev with Bourne and meets up with Vignoles, who had arrived the previous week.[40]

October–December Reviews of first two parts of *The Photographic Album*, published by David Bogue, which contain a total of eight photographic prints, six by Fenton and two by Philip Henry Delamotte.[41]

November 10 Departs Kiev with Vignoles, arriving in London on November 20. Bourne remains in Kiev to continue photography.[42]

December 8 Elected member of Society of Arts, having been proposed by Peter Le Neve Foster.

December 22 "Recent Specimens of Photography," first exhibition in Britain devoted exclusively to photographs, opens at Society of Arts, Adelphi theater, London.[43] Fenton, who contributes forty-one prints, all employing the waxed paper process, reads his paper "On the Present Position and Future Prospects of the Art of Photography."[44]

1853

January 1 Illustration *Soirée of Photographers, in the Great Room of the Society of Arts* (fig. 64) appears in *Illustrated London News.*[45]

January 19 Attends meeting of Society of Arts at which Antoine Claudet delivers paper on stereoscope.[46]

January 20 Inaugural meeting of Photographic Society held in Great Room of Society of Arts. Eastlake elected president, supported by three vice presidents and Council of twenty-one members, including Fenton, who is elected honorary secretary.[47]

January 27 At first meeting of Photographic Society Council, a committee composed of Sir William Newton, Dr. John Percy, Vignoles, and Fenton is appointed to consider future relationship with Society of Arts.[48] (For Fenton's attendance at Council meetings, see final entries in relevant years.)

February 3 First ordinary meeting of Photographic Society held at Society of Arts: Fenton reads paper "Upon the Mode in Which It Is Advisable the Society Should Conduct Its Labours" and discusses experiences with waxed-paper-negative process in Russia.[49]

February 10 Council meeting: Publication Committee, composed of Hunt, Vignoles, and Fenton, appointed to establish journal for society.[50]

February 17 Council meeting: Fenton and Foster appointed to respond to Society of Arts proposal for touring exhibition of photographs by members of society.[51]

February 24 Council meeting: Fenton and Percy are asked to register as proprietors of the journal, to be held in trust for Photographic Society.[52]

March 3 First number of *Journal of the Photographic Society* printed and laid before Council for inspection.[53] It will continue to be published under a succession of names and still exists.

March 10 Council meeting: Fenton proposes to give introductory paper on "the qualities required for a good working camera" at next general meeting of society.[54]

March 17 Birth of fourth daughter, Eva Catherine, at 2 Albert Terrace. Council receives letter explaining Fenton's "unavoidable absence" from meeting.[55]

April 21 Ordinary meeting: Fenton contributes to discussion on cameras submitted for examination, including one made by Fenton's future assistant Marcus Sparling, who is on hand to explain its features.[56]

April 28 Shows forty-eight topographic and architectural views at inaugural exhibition of Photographic

Institution, 168 New Bond Street, London, a commercial enterprise established by Cundall and Delamotte to deal with all aspects of photography, especially retailing of photographic prints.[57]

May Gives German explorer Eduard Vogel photography lessons to equip him for forthcoming expedition to Central Africa.[58]

May 5 General meeting: Fenton reads Sir Charles Wheatstone's "Note on a New Portable Reflecting Stereoscope" and joins others in exhibiting stereoscopic photographs, made by him the previous year.[59]

May 12 Council meeting: Sparling elected to society.[60]

May 24 Fenton's "Scènes de forêt" (Forest Scenes) and "Vues de Russie" (Views of Russia) are shown at Ernest Lacan's house in Paris.[61]

May 30 Queen Victoria and Prince Albert "willingly give their Patronage to the Photographic Society."[62]

June 25 Sydney Smirke, architect and designer of Reading Room at British Museum, directed "to consider the construction of a temporary Photographic Chamber on the roof of the Museum."[63]

July 14 Writes to Edward Hawkins, keeper of antiquities at British Museum, giving detailed advice on type of studio, darkroom, and equipment suitable for photographing museum's objects.[64]

September 14 Touring exhibition of photographs organized by Society of Arts opens at Woburn Literary and Scientific Institution; ten of its eighty-three prints are by Fenton.[65]

October 4 Writes to Sir Henry Ellis, principal librarian, offering his services as photographer to the British Museum.[66]

October 6 Wheatstone writes to Hawkins, recommending Fenton as museum photographer. Fenton appointed to make "some experimental trials" and authorized to spend up to 180 pounds on additional apparatus.[67]

November 3 Reads paper on use of nitrate baths with collodion negative process at meeting of Photographic Society; transcript, sent to *La Lumière*, is published in translation.[68]

November 19   *Priest of the Greek Church*, made in Kiev, appears in *Illustrated London News*, the first illustration in that publication based on photograph by Fenton.[69]

December 1   Council meeting: Fenton reports on rental of rooms at Society of British Artists, Suffolk Street, for first annual exhibition of Photographic Society. Six members of Council, including Fenton, take responsibility for organizing exhibition.[70]

December 6   Writes to *La Lumière* inviting French photographers to participate in Photographic Society exhibition;[71] as a result, their work is well represented.

In 1853, attends Photographic Society Council meetings: January 27, 31; February 3, 10, 17, 24; March 10, 24, 31; April 7, 14, 21, 28; May 5, 12, 26; June 9, 16, 30; November 17; December 1, 8, 15, 22. Absent from Council meetings: March 17, May 19, July 28, August 8, October 20, 27.

1854

January 3   First annual exhibition of Photographic Society opens with visit from Queen Victoria and Prince Albert. Eastlake and Fenton, among others, selected to conduct royal party through gallery; queen later notes that Fenton "explained everything & there were many beautiful photographs done by him."[72] Of the 980 photographs Fenton has seventy-three prints, more than half made by waxed paper process.[73]

January 14   *Morning Post* reports that Queen Victoria so admired Fenton's Russian views during visit to exhibition that she purchased six of those on display.[74]

January 23   Photographs royal children in costumes from Nicolas-Marie Dalayrac's *Les deux petits Savoyards*, performed before their parents at Windsor Castle on January 16.[75]

January 25   Photographs Queen Victoria and children "just outside the Green Drawing-room windows."[76]

February 1   Photographs tutor Dr. Ernst Becker with Prince Alfred and the Prince of Wales.[77]

February 4   Responds belatedly to letter from Talbot about need for permanence in "positive copies," expressing hope that Talbot's experiments in photographic engraving will prove successful.[78]

Russian Peasants, after a photograph by Fenton, appears in *Illustrated London News*.[79]

February 10   Tableaux vivants of Four Seasons performed by royal children at Windsor to celebrate fourteenth wedding anniversary of parents.[80] Tableaux subsequently restaged for Fenton to photograph.

February 11   Photographic Room at British Museum completed and fitted out. Fenton makes test photographs, which are submitted to museum's trustees.[81]

March   Twenty-four prints included in photographic exhibition organized in support of Royal Infirmary Fund, Dundee.[82]

March 11   Photographs Baltic Fleet departing Spithead for the Baltic.[83]

March 27–28   After months of rising tension, Britain and France decide to support Turkish cause by declaring war on Russia.

April 10   For five negatives taken at Buckingham Palace, Fenton charges the royal family one guinea per negative and one shilling and sixpence for each print.[84]

April 17   Second tour of photographs organized by Society of Arts begins; two sets of work are sent around Britain simultaneously, to fifteen and eighteen venues respectively. Fenton has twenty-four prints of similar subjects in each set.[85]

May   Makes twenty-nine more negatives at Buckingham Palace, with sittings on May 1, 5, 6, 11, and 22.[86]

May 11   Photographs Queen Victoria in court dress at Buckingham Palace as well as with Prince Albert after a Drawing Room at Saint James's Palace (fig. 49).

May 22   Makes "instantaneous photographs"—i.e., those with short exposure times—of the queen, prince, and their eight children together on grounds of Buckingham Palace (fig. 10).[87]

June 12   Photographs Lady Harriet Hamilton in Mary, Queen of Scots, costume, worn to Bal Costumé held at French Embassy, May 12, 1854.[88]

June 20   On behalf of Photographic Society, writes Talbot asking whether Talbot's proposal to include

collodion negative process in renewal of his 1841 patent would alter his existing arrangement with the society. Talbot reassures Fenton that it was never his intention "to withdraw, or to alter, the gift" he granted the society in 1852.[89]

June 30   Photographs Queen Victoria, Prince Albert, and Dr. Becker.[90]

July 6   General meeting: Talbot's intention to renew patent discussed; Fenton supports Vignoles's resolution to oppose renewal because Talbot's claim, that collodion was chemically the same process as calotype, was mistaken.[91]

July 15   Fenton's engagement as photographer temporarily terminated by British Museum pending report to Trustees reviewing purposes and costs of photography.[92]

July 20   Receives sixty-six pounds two shillings for photographic work for royal family (portraits of family and prints; prints of views on Wye and at Tintern).[93]

July 27   Council meeting: Newton, Foster, Alfred Rosling, and Fenton nominated to arrange for members to submit work to Exposition Universelle, to be held in 1855 in Paris.[94]

Late summer–early fall   Photographs in Yorkshire at Rievaulx, Fountains, Bolton, Mount Grace, Ripon, and Helmsley, and along Wharfe River.[95] Fenton's brother William, who has gone into the family banking business and has later become financially involved with the rapidly expanding railway network in Britain—serving as a director of several railway companies and chairman of others—perhaps facilitates Fenton's rail travel with his photographic van and paraphernalia.

October 31   Photographs Prince Nicholas of Nassau.[96]

November   Photographs Princess Victoria Gouramma, daughter of former Rajah of Coorg.[97]

November 2   Nominated to committee arranging second annual exhibition of Photographic Society. At general meeting, voices disapproval of Maxwell Lyte's device for introducing skies or foregrounds into photographs by use of two negatives; shows recent views of Yorkshire.[98]

November 11   Trustees of British Museum approve report on photography and direct that a sum of one thousand pounds be inserted into budgets for following year, heralding Fenton's resumption of duties.[99]

In 1854, attends Photographic Society Council meetings: January 2, 12, 26; February 2, 9; March 2, 16, 30; April 6, 27; May 4, 18; June 19, 29; July 6, 12, 27; October 26; November 2, 9, 30; December 7, 14, 21, 28. Absent from Council meetings: February 23.

1855

January Eleven studies, taken on paper and collodion negatives, exhibited at Photographic Institution, New Bond Street, London.[100]

January 11 Shows forty-five prints at second annual exhibition of Photographic Society.[101]

February 2 Submits invoice to royal household for photography undertaken during August, November, and December 1854 for Queen Victoria. In August 1855 acknowledges full payment of seventeen pounds nine shillings and sixpence.[102]

February 17 *Valley of the Wharfe*, after photograph by Fenton, appears in *Illustrated London News* (fig. 65).[103]

February 20 Departs for Crimea from Blackwall Pier with Sparling and "the boy" William. Passage aboard HMS *Hecla* provided by Duke of Newcastle and railway entrepreneur Sir Morton Peto. On board are Fenton's photographic van, seven hundred glass plates, and thirty-six large chests of equipment and personal effects.[104]

April 27 From Gibraltar, writes first in a series of letters home describing his experiences.[105] Tells how, during a storm crossing the Bay of Biscay he "lay prostrate, groaning in spirit, unable to eat or drink."[106]

March 6 Constantinople: Calls on British Consul, using "letter from Prince Albert" to establish his credentials.[107]

March 8 Balaklava: Arrives in Crimea to begin "five months' hard labour . . . as a photographer at the seat of war."[108]

March 16 Balaklava: After a week of frustration, gets horses, carriage, equipment, and supplies unloaded and begins photographing. "In order to avoid the necessity of explaining to all comers what my carriage was for,

I had made Sparling paint on it 'Photographic Van.'"[109] Photographs regularly henceforth.

March 26–28 Balaklava: "The labour in itself is great, and many pictures are spoilt by the dust and heat, still more by the crowds of all ranks who flock around. I am afraid I shall not get away as soon as I expected . . . the distances are so great and the difficulty of getting people together whose portraits are wanted, that it will take me much time."[110]

April 4 En route to headquarters above Balaklava: Concerned about his wife's impending confinement, advises her to employ a nurse ahead of time, "as it will not do to look for one when she is needed."[111]

April 19 Above Sebastopol: "The ground here is covered with cannon balls, and I took care to keep well behind the hill in going down, for I could hear by the whir and thud that the balls were coming up the ravine on each side . . . there was no stop to the awful commotion . . . like an express train that had broken off the line and leapt up into the air."[112]

April 24 Above Sebastopol: "Anxious as I am to get back to the repose of my glass room at the Museum I will never leave my work half done here." In closing, bids "Good bye honey, keep your courage up, play the piano, [take] plenty of exercise, & go out occasionally in the evening. Thine RF."[113]

April 29 "I am sadly bothered with applications to make portraits, this after all is my chief hindrance. If I refuse to take them I can get no facilities for conveying my van from one locality to another."[114] "Of course you would expect me to sleep in a bed when I get back. I shall begin by sleeping at the top of Primrose Hill hiring some one to fire off squibs all night to prevent me from feeling the silence painful. By proper precaution perhaps I may be got to sleep in the house in a fortnight's time provided it is upon the landing with all the windows open."[115]

May 6 Balaklava: "I have made considerable progress during the past week with my work; have got several more of the generals & hope that another fortnight will finish what I have to do at the front & then I shall have nothing to do but sell my baggage & pack up."[116]

May 13 Radikoi: "I do not like living with the French, they are very kind, but their habits are so different . . .

there is one great drawback in their camp which is not very easily described (much better understood then told). There being no women here, they are not particular as to how they exhibit themselves & there has been a story going about the camp that I had given up taking views in disgust because I could never get a picture without there being in it some object not fit to show to a British Public."[117]

May 15 Exposition Universelle opens in Paris with a selection of photographs sent by Photographic Society; landscape studies by Fenton are awarded a silver medal.[118]

May 26 At headquarters: "I have sold 2 of my horses & am winding up. I have taken the portraits of 3 of our generals this morning and hope to get Lord B's & General Airey's on Monday when I shall consider that I have done."[119]

June 8 "I have nothing to do but sell my things & look out for a vessel. I am hindered by Sparling who has been drinking a good deal lately, and has in consequence a bad attack of dysentery . . . I am constantly thinking of you and wishing that I were with you. Please God! It won't be long now."[120]

June 18 Watching Russians repulse attack of British and French on Malakhov and Redan fortifications at Sebastopol: "In our confidence of success we had chosen this day, it is said, that on the anniversary of Waterloo a victory common to both nations might efface from the minds of one the recollection of their former defeat, but we reckoned too proudly, and now the 18th of June will be a glorious day to the Russians."[121]

June 22 Departing from Balaklava: "We had nearly got outside the harbour when I began to vomit. . . . By nine o'clock I was bad with the cholera, and there was no doctor on board. . . . I got them to make me some rice water and mixed lime juice with it. . . . At half past ten cramp began in my legs and I had to be held upright and rubbed. . . . William and Sparling took it in turn to watch me, and I must say they both took great care of me."[122]

June 27 or 28 Sails from Constantinople on Royal Mail steamer *Orinoco*, under lease to admiralty.

July 2 Birth of fifth daughter, Rose Maynard, at 2 Albert Terrace.

July 11   *Orinoco* arrives at Portsmouth.

August 8   Queen Victoria, at Osborne House, notes that after dinner she looked at "some interesting photos, taken by Mr. Fenton, in the Crimea, portraits & views, extremely well done."[123]

Mid-August   Photographs the Princess Royal and Princess Alice on grounds of Osborne House (pl. 27).[124]

September   "Exhibition of the Photographic Pictures Taken in the Crimea" opens at Gallery of Water Colour Society, Pall Mall, the first of three London venues. For next eight months, versions of exhibition appear in other cities and towns, notably Birmingham, Exeter, Gloucester, Leeds, Liverpool, Manchester, and Yeovil.[125]

September 7   In Paris Fenton and William Agnew Jr. summoned to palace of Saint-Cloud to show Napoléon III entire collection of Crimean photographs. Emperor spends more than an hour and a half examining and discussing the works, and gives Fenton a medal and a portrait of himself.[126]

September 12   Two studies by Fenton on show at photographic exhibition organized for Glasgow meeting of British Association for the Advancement of Science.[127]

September 22   *Photographic Pictures of the Seat of War in the Crimea*, a three-part portfolio, advertised by Thomas Agnew for sale at sixty-three pounds. Panoramas and portraits of distinguished generals available as individual prints.[128]

October 6–December 29   *Illustrated London News* publishes seven illustrations after Fenton's Crimean photographs: *General Bosquet*; *General Simpson, Commander of Her Majesty's Forces in the Crimea*; *Omer Pacha* [sic]; *General Sir William John Codrington, the New Commander-in-Chief in the Crimea* and *Spahi and Zouave*; *Mr. Fenton's Photographic Van*; and *Croats*.[129]

December   "Exhibition of the Photographic Pictures Taken in the Crimea" moves to Gallery of New Society of Painters in Water-Colours, Pall Mall.[130]

In 1855, attended Council meetings: January, 3, 4, 11, 18, 31; September 27; November 29; December 6, 13, 27. Absent from Council meetings: January 24; February 7 to July 6; October 25; November 11.

1856

January   Contributions to third annual exhibition of Photographic Society, London, include various subjects from British Museum work; portraits, among them "a Zouave"; and a study of children.[131]

January 3   Ordinary and special general meeting: Bourne describes his design for a "patent portable camera, with separate dark-chamber"; Fenton reads his "Narrative of a Photographic Trip to the Seat of War in the Crimea."[132]

January 21   Lectures on Crimean experiences at Public Hall, Rochdale, Lancashire.[133]

February 7   Resigns as honorary secretary of Photographic Society following Council's decision to combine post with that of editor of the journal. Reverend John Richardson Major is named to new position.[134]

February 27   Paul & Dominic Colnaghi & Co. chosen to act as agents for sale of Fenton's British Museum photographs.[135]

April   "Exhibition of the Photographic Pictures Taken in the Crimea" moves to new premises at The Gallery, Saint James's Street; 360 subjects presented in third and final edition of catalogue. Also shown are James Robertson's photographs of fall of Sebastopol.[136]

April 23   Presides over meeting of Society of Arts at which Paul Pretsch delivers a paper, "On Photo-Galvanography, or, Engraving by Light and Electricity."[137]

May 1   Council meeting: disagreement arises over involvement of some Council members in promoting the Photographic Association, which has commercial ambitions directly opposed to the principles of the Photographic Society. After heated debate, Fenton, Delamotte, Vignoles, William Lake Price, and Thomas Frederick Hardwich resign from Council.[138]

June 5   British Museum publishes *Photographic Facsimiles of the Remains of the Epistles of Clement of Rome* in edition of fifty, with twenty-two original unmounted salt prints by Fenton and introduction by Sir Frederic Madden, keeper of manuscripts.[139]

July 18   Photographic Society Club, an informal social and dining organization, holds annual outing to Hampton Court; group portrait of members includes Fenton (fig. 71).

August 14   At Exposition Universelle de Photographie, Brussels, Fenton exhibits topographic and landscape studies with clouds, for which he is awarded a medal.[140]

September   Forty Crimean pictures by Fenton included in Manchester Photographic Society's annual exhibition.[141]

Travels to Scotland, photographing sites and landscapes en route to Yorkshire, Holy Isle (Lindisfarne), Jedburgh, Melrose, Braemar, Dunkeld, Edinburgh, and Roslin, and along the Feugh, Clunie, and Dee rivers.[142]

At Balmoral Castle takes portraits and views commissioned by Queen Victoria; charges five guineas for each of the eight negatives, prints extra.[143]

October   Sparling publishes treatise, *Theory and Practice of the Photographic Art: Including Its Chemistry and Optics with Minute Instruction in the Practical Manipulation of the Various Processes, Drawn from the Author's Daily Practice*, which describes author as "Assistant to Mr. Fenton, in taking the Crimean Photographs."[144]

October 31   First part of *Photographic Art Treasures; or Nature and Art Illustrated by Art and Nature*, comprising four photographs by Fenton, published by Patent Photo-Galvanographic Company, of which he is a partner and the company photographer.[145]

November 6   General meeting: Fenton exhibits views of Yorkshire, and Le Gray, pictures of clouds and the sea.[146]

November 17   Participates in exhibition of Norwich Photographic Society.[147]

December 1   Shows twenty-seven prints, including Scottish and Yorkshire subjects, at second annual exhibition of Société Française de Photographie, Paris.[148]

December 15   Following commercial failure of Crimean photographs, remaining stocks of prints, and negatives, are sold at general auction by Southgate and Barrett, Fleet Street, London.[149]

December 17   Exhibits with other members of Photographic Society at evening reception, King's College, London. More than two thousand pictures are on display, Fenton's described as "grand north-country scenes."[150]

December 20 Contributes thirty-eight views to first exhibition of Photographic Society of Scotland, Edinburgh.[151]

In 1856, attended Council meetings: January 3, 24, 31; February 4, 7, 14, 28; March 6; April 4, 17, 25; May 1, 8. Absent from Council meeting: March 26.

1857

January Shows fifty-four prints at fourth annual exhibition of Photographic Society, including landscape and architectural studies made in Scotland the previous September and examples of photo-galvanographic printing.[152]

February 5 Annual general meeting: Fenton reelected to Council.

April 21 Facing legal action, Fenton writes Talbot on behalf of Patent Photo-Galvanographic Company in attempt to settle dispute arising from firm's acknowledged infringement of Talbot's patent for photomechanical printing.[153]

May 5 Manchester Art Treasures Exhibition opens. Its photographic gallery of works selected by Delamotte includes eight studies of landscape and architecture by Fenton.[154]

May 1 Patent Photo-Galvanographic Company reported to be facing losses of about four thousand pounds.[155]

May 7 Photographic Society establishes subscription fund to provide annuity to widow and children of Frederick Scott Archer; Fenton named as one of the organizers.[156]

June Exhibits prints at Colnaghi's, including views of Bolton Abbey and London parks as well as photo-galvanographs.[157]

July 25 Photographs cricket match between Royal Artillery and Hunsdonbury Club at Hunsdonbury.

August 10 Exhibits unnamed studies at Exposition Universelle de Photographie, Brussels, for which he is awarded a medal.[158]

August and/or September Photographs at Ely, Peterborough, and Lincoln.[159]

Fall Photographs in North Wales, particularly in and around Bettws-y-Coed.[160]

December 3 General meeting: Fenton formally takes office of vice president of the society, following Newton's obligatory retirement.[161]

December 12 Contributes views of Scotland to second annual exhibition of Photographic Society of Scotland, Edinburgh.[162]

December 30 Joins committee on fine-art copyright established by Society of Arts and writes editor of Photographic Society's *Journal* seeking opinion of "brother photographers" about what degree of protection to require in change in law being proposed.[163]

In 1857, attended Council meetings: February 5, 19; March 5, 9; April 16; May 7; June 4; July 16; November 5, 19; December 3, 17, 22. Absent from Council meetings: March 19, 26; April 4; May 21; June 11, 18; July 2; September 4; October 1.

1858

January 7 Shows twenty-five studies at first exhibition of Architectural Photographic Association, held at the Suffolk Street Galleries, Pall Mall, London.[164]

January 15 Contributes forty-one prints to fifth annual exhibition of Photographic Society, which opens initially at South Kensington Museum before transferring to New Coventry Street, where it will reopen on May 15.[165]

April 6 Chairs meeting of Photographic Society at which Oscar Rejlander gives his paper on photographic composition and the *Two Ways of Life*.[166]

April 27 Annual Art Union of London drawing for prizes held at Haymarket theater, London. Three hundred volumes, each containing twelve photographs, are among prizes, with Fenton contributing five prints to each volume.[167]

May 12 Council of Photographic Society of Ireland recommends presenting members with "one of Mr. Fenton's views of Welsh scenery."[168]

Summer Makes series of Orientalist studies in his London studio.[169]

July 1 Lovell Reeve publishes first issue of *Stereoscopic Magazine*, a monthly periodical containing three stereoscopic views in each issue.[170]

Summer–early fall Photographs in two expeditions: one to Salisbury, Glastonbury, Wells, and Cheddar, the other to Lichfield, Hardwick, Haddon, and Chatsworth.[171]

November 27 Thomas Gladwell, London printseller and retailer of photographic views, advertises latest series by Fenton.[172]

December 18 Shows thirteen prints at third annual exhibition of Photographic Society of Scotland, Edinburgh. Among these are four Orientalist studies: "Turk and Arab," "Pasha and Dancing Girl," "The Water Carrier," and "Reverie."[173]

In 1858, attended Council meetings: January 5, 19, 26; February 16; March 2, 9, 16: April 6, 20; May 4, 11, 18; June 1, 8, 15, 22; July 7; August 3; October 8, 19; November 2, 16; December 7, 16. Absent from Council meetings: February 2; July 20; August 5.

1859

January 6 Prince Albert visits sixth annual exhibition of Photographic Society, at which Fenton shows forty-two of his latest works.[174] These include architectural studies of stately homes and cathedrals at Hardwick, Chatsworth, Haddon, Lichfield, Salisbury, Wells, and Glastonbury, as well as seven Orientalist studies.[175]

January 7 Contributes landscapes to first exhibition of Nottingham Photographic Society.[176]

January 8 Acquires large plot of land at Potter's Bar, then a rural hamlet north of London; adds two lots on January 10 and other parcels at later dates. A few years later this will become the site for his new house.[177]

January 13 Birth of only son, Anthony Maynard, at 2 Albert Terrace.

January 17 Contributes a series of views of Welsh scenery to first annual exhibition of Macclesfield Photographic Society.[178]

January 28–February 1 Reviews of Orientalist studies published. *Photographic Journal* praises "admirable illustrations of Eastern scenes of actual life," *Art-Journal* does not "regard them as a success," and *Photographic News* criticizes use of string to hold up model's hands.[179]

March   Murray & Heath advertises "Smartt's Photographic Tent," as used by Roger Fenton.[180]

April   Shows fifty-one prints at exhibition of Glasgow Photographic Society, Buchanan Street, Glasgow.[181]

April 15   Shows eleven prints at third exhibition of Société Française de Photographie, Palais des Champs-Élysées, Paris.[182]

April 26   Annual Art-Union of London prize drawing held at Adelphi theater, London. Seven hundred volumes, each containing twelve photographs, are among prizes, with Fenton contributing eight prints to each volume.[183]

May   Makes first contributions to *Stereoscopic Magazine*: views of Ely Cathedral and the Pont-y-Pant bridge in North Wales.[184]

June–July   At Stonyhurst College, most likely at behest of Father William Kay, professor of chemistry. Photographs college gardens and buildings, including newly built Sodality Chapel; also photographs along Hodder and Ribble rivers and in Hurst Green, subjects related to Fenton estate purchased from Thomas Weld in 1829.[185]

July   After protracted and acrimonious negotiations, Fenton's employment at British Museum is terminated following Trustees' decision to transfer his negatives to South Kensington Museum.[186]

September   Exhibits seven photographs, including "Pacha and Dancing Girl," at meeting of British Association for the Advancement of Science, Union Street, Aberdeen.[187]

November 1   Council meeting: Fenton discusses results of his experiments with lenses conducted over the summer.[188]

December 17   Contributes to fourth annual exhibition of Photographic Society of Scotland, George Street, Edinburgh. Works include "The reed deep on the Ribble, and Pendlehill" and "Paradise View on the Hodder" along with studies of Stonyhurst College.[189]

December 23   Photographs at Stonyhurst College in wintry conditions.[190]

In 1859, attended Council meetings: January 4, 18; February 1, 15; March 1, 15; April 5; May 3; July 11; November 1, 8; December 16. Absent from Council meetings: May 17; November 15; December 6.

1860

January   *The Conway in the Stereoscope*, illustrated by Roger Fenton Esq. M.A., is published by Lovell Reeve, London; contains twenty albumen stereo prints taken in valleys of the Conway and tributaries, North Wales.[191]

January 13   Contributes thirty-seven prints to seventh annual exhibition of Photographic Society at Gallery of the Society of Painters in Water-Colours, 5A Pall Mall East, London.[192]

February   Has become a member of Hythe School of Musketry, where he is placed in the First Section of volunteers, participating in a fashionable pastime given status through the patronage of Queen Victoria. Takes a series of seventeen studies including *Volunteer Class* and an extended sequence showing rifle exercises.[193]

April 20   Death of Marcus Sparling.[194]

April 24   Death of only son, Anthony Maynard, age fifteen months.

May   Becomes captain in London University Corps, where he is known as the "Crimean celebrity, Volunteer and Photographer"; continued visits to Hythe School of Musketry prompt publication of five studies of rifle volunteers.[195]

May 15   Benjamin Brecknell Turner, Henry White, and Fenton each send fifty prints to Photographic Society for distribution to members contributing to Archer Memorial Fund.[196]

Summer   Photographs in the Lake District and at Furness Abbey.[197]

Executes series of fruit and flower still lifes, probably in late July and early August.[198]

July 7   Takes thirteen studies at National Rifle Match, Wimbledon Common, attended by Queen Victoria, who fires first shot—a prearranged bull's-eye at four hundred yards.[199]

July 17   Gives detailed evidence to House of Commons Select Committee on South Kensington Museum concerning his activities as photographer at British Museum and effect of government decision to sell photographs cheaply through Department of Science and Art.[200]

September 17   Royal family pays invoice for twenty-four pounds eight shillings for prints from Hythe, Wimbledon, Windsor Park, and two copies of "studies from life."[201]

December 4   Having served the statutory period in office, retires as senior vice president of Photographic Society and is replaced by Professor Thomas Bell, whose position he assumes on Council.[202]

In 1860, attended Council meetings: January 3, 17, 24, 31; March 20; April 3; June 5; October 8. Absent from Council meetings: February 7, 21; March 6; May 1; November 6; December 4.

1861

January 12   Contributes thirty-nine prints to eighth annual exhibition of Photographic Society, London, including landscapes from Lake District, views at Harewood House, and Fruit and Flower series.[203]

April 7   Gives occupation as "barrister" to census enumerator. The census return reveals that in addition to Fenton's wife and children, a governess, cook, and housemaid live in the house—a modest household for the period.[204]

August 7   Attends Council meeting as regular participant for the last time.

September 5   Contributes to photographic exhibition organized in conjunction with annual meeting of British Association for the Advancement of Science.[205]

December   Lancashire cotton trade severely depressed following outbreak of America's Civil War and subsequent blockade of its southern ports, cutting off supply of cotton; layoffs of British mill workers increase. These factors and a family dispute cause closing of Hooley Bridge Mill.[206]

December 14 Photography loses an advocate when Prince Albert dies unexpectedly following a brief illness.

In 1861, attended Council meetings: May 3, 7; June 4; July 8; August 7. Absent from Council meetings: February 1, 5; March 5; April 2; May 22, 25.

1862

May 1 Shows fourteen prints at International Exhibition, London, drawn largely from earlier landscape, topographic, and still-life studies. This will be his last exhibition.[207]

May 15 Review of *Ruined Abbeys and Castles of Great Britain* by William and Mary Howitt, illustrated with photographic plates by Francis Bedford, Fenton, William Russell Sedgfield, George Washington Wilson, and others.[208]

July 11 Awarded a Prize Medal for "great excellence in fruit and flower pieces, and good general photography" at International Exhibition.[209]

October 15 Retirement from photography announced with editorial in *Photographic Journal* and preliminary notice of sale of entire apparatus and stock of almost one thousand large-format negatives.[210]

November 11 Sale of equipment and negatives, Stevens Rooms, King Street, London, is well attended and realizes good prices, especially for lenses.[211] Negatives, reportedly in bad condition with "blistered and cracked varnish," do less well.[212]

In late 1862, still resident at Albert Terrace but probably begins construction of house at Potter's Bar, named Mount Grace, that will be principal residence for remainder of his life.[213]

1863

Returns to law practice as barrister, with chambers at 4 Harcourt Buildings, Temple, London. Named as counsel for the Northern Circuit, which allows him to act as barrister in the Assize courts of Manchester, Salford, and York.[214]

February 3 Judges photographs at ninth annual exhibition of Photographic Society and awards four medals, including one to Bedford for landscape studies.[215]

July 25 Death of father, John Fenton, at age seventy-three.[216]

1865

Gives up chambers in the Temple.

March John Eastham of Manchester issues a series of portraits of Fenton and sends them to *British Journal of Photography* for review (fig. 10).[217]

1866

December 11 At meeting of Photographic Society, receives medal as "the founder of the Society." His appearance is "the signal for an outburst of loud and continued cheering."[218]

1869

May 4 Six Russian views, lent by architect Wyatt Papworth, shown at Architectural Exhibition, Conduit Street, London.[219]

August 9 Dies at his home, Mount Grace. Causes listed as "nervous exhaustion, weakness of heart, and congestion of lungs"; occupation cited as "gentleman."[220]

In will leaves house and household effects to his wife, the balance of assets put in trust for benefit of wife and children.

August 20 *British Journal of Photography* prints detailed obituary, while *Photographic News* is brief and to the point, acknowledging Fenton as "a man of considerable culture and taste."[221]

1870

June 13 Fenton's collection of paintings, watercolors, and framed engravings sold at Christie's.[222]

August 21 Fenton's books and portfolios of prints and engravings sold at Sotheby's.[223]

1871

October 5 Fenton's house and land at Potter's Bar sold.[224]

1872

April 2 Grace Fenton offers British Museum a "number of photographic negatives" of "vases, old ornaments, stuffed animals, prints &c." Offer declined a month later.[225]

1878

November Family bank, trading as J. & J. Fenton and Sons, Rochdale, goes into liquidation, with liabilities variously estimated in excess of £550,000.[226]

1886

July 14 Death of Grace Elizabeth Fenton.

1969

Fenton's grave and that of his wife destroyed when church of Saint John, High Street, Potter's Bar, is demolished. Their joint tombstone was headed with the words "God is Love."[227]

p. 1247; "Photographic Publications," *Art-Journal*, December 1, 1852, p. 374.

57. On Bourne's daguerreotypes and calotypes, see Vignoles 1982, pp. 118, 122, 128–31, 139, 142.

58. Fenton told the members of the Photographic Society that in October 1852 the temperature in Kiev had been "considerably below the freezing-point." See Percy, March 3, 1853, p. 11.

59. Hannavy 1993, p. 238, suggests that before he left England Fenton familiarized himself with the reflecting stereoscope invented by Charles Wheatstone and the stereo camera because Vignoles specifically wished to have stereo views made of his bridge.

60. See Taylor, *Photographs Exhibited in Britain*, 2002, pp. 18, 38.

61. The Society of Arts quickly realized that photography would be an immensely valuable addition to its activities and in early 1853 tried, unsuccessfully, to keep the Photographic Society from establishing itself as a separate entity. See "Photographic Society," *JSA*, January 28, 1853, p. 114.

62. Seiberling 1986, p. 127. Cundall and Delamotte sold individual prints from the exhibition for prices varying from a few shillings (Fenton and others) to more than two pounds (Martens), as well as portfolios of collected works. Most of Fenton's views from Russia were seven shillings and sixpence.

63. Philip Henry Delamotte, advertisement in *Catalogue of Photographic Pictures Exhibited at the Photographic Institution* 1853, n.p.

64. See "A Most Enthusiastic Cultivator of His Art" by Roger Taylor in this volume for a different interpretation of Fenton's prices.

65. It is possible that Fenton began working for the British Museum as early as the summer of 1852; on July 3, 1852, Wheatstone wrote to Edward Hawkins, Keeper of Antiquities, recommending Fenton "to take some photographs of the antiquities in the British Museum." See Date and Hamber 1990, p. 316. However, no further references to Fenton appear in museum records until the summer of 1853, and no surviving photographs by Fenton of British Museum objects can be conclusively dated to 1852 or 1853; thus it is likely that he was not hired by the museum until the fall of 1853.

66. Fenton to Hawkins, October 4, 1853, British Museum, Original Letters and Papers (archival source).

67. Fenton to Hawkins, July 14, 1853, British Museum, Original Letters and Papers (archival source).

68. Delamotte to Hawkins, July 25, 1853, British Museum, Original Letters and Papers (archival source).

69. Wheatstone to Hawkins, October 6, 1853, British Museum, Original Letters and Papers (archival source); British Museum, Trustee Committee Minutes (archival source), pp. 8614–15, October 8, 1853. On November 12, 1853, the trustees authorized an additional seventy-seven pounds five shillings for photographic equipment. See British Museum, Trustee Committee Minutes (archival source), p. 8619, November 12, 1853. Fenton referred to himself as "Photographer to the Museum" in 1859 (see Date and Hamber 1990, p. 322).

70. Fenton to Hawkins, July 14, 1853, and Fenton to Anthony Panizzi, July 30, 1857, British Museum, Original Letters and Papers (archival source). Sometimes Fenton's methods were risky. When he photographed the *Epistles of Clement of Rome* in 1856, Fenton, unable to make the photographs inside the studio, fastened the book's leaves to a board on an outdoor wall. The Keeper in the Department of Manuscripts, Frederic Madden, complained that the "open air . . . was rather a ruder trial than I had anticipated for the MS for the effect of the air and the sun were very powerful on it." Date 1989, p. 11.

71. British Museum, Trustee Committee Minutes (archival source), p. 8959, May 13, 1854.

72. Ibid., p. 8733, August 12, 1854; Hamber 1996, p. 381.

73. British Museum, Trustee Committee Minutes (archival source), p. 8746, October 14, 1854.

74. Ibid., p. 8751, November 11, 1854.

75. "January 21st, 1854," *JPS*, January 21, 1854, p. 153. Because Prince Albert was the patron of the North London School of Drawing and Modelling, scholars have suggested that Fenton met him as early as 1850 (see Lloyd 1988, p. 3), but this January 1854 meeting was clearly their first meaningful encounter.

76. "Photographic Society," *Athenaeum*, January 7, 1854, p. 23.

77. "January 21st, 1854," *JPS*, January 21, 1854, p. 153; *Morning Post*, quoted in "Exposition de la Société Photographique de Londres," *La Lumière*, January 14, 1854, p. 5.

78. Victoria, Queen of England, Journal (archival source), January 3, 1854.

79. See Dimond and Taylor 1987. In 1852 Prince Albert began to collect photographs of all of Raphael's works. See Robertson 1978, p. 186; Dimond in Dimond and Taylor 1987, pp. 44–49.

80. From "The Charge of the Heavy Brigade at Balaclava." At the end of his life, no doubt disturbed by the jingoistic tone of his earlier "Charge of the Light Brigade" (1854), Tennyson wrote this much more somber and ambivalent description of the infamous battle.

81. "Her Majesty 'Leading' the Fleet to Sea," *ILN*, March 18, 1854, p. 242.

82. Dimond and Taylor 1987, p. 81, no. xii.

83. "Arsenal of Portsmouth," *ILN*, March 18, 1854, p. 242.

84. Sir John Hall's diary from the Crimean War, quoted in Barnsley 1963, p. 6. My thanks to Roger Taylor for bringing this to my attention.

85. Russell 1995, p. 53.

86. Victoria, Queen of England, Journal (archival source), February 22, 1855, quoted by Taylor in Dimond and Taylor 1987, p. 39.

87. Barnsley 1963, p. 7.

88. Taylor in Dimond and Taylor 1987, p. 39.

89. See "To the Editor," *JPS*, March 21, 1854, p. 177. According to an unnamed author in the *Moniteur universel* (cited in "La Photographie et la guerre," *La Lumière*, April 15, 1854, p. 54), Lord Raglan had proposed to have a photographer with him in the Crimea, and the idea had originated with Prince Albert.

90. See "April 21st, 1854," *JPS*, April 21, 1854, p. 189.

91. Ibid.; "Photography Applied to the Purposes of War," *Art-Journal*, May 1, 1854, p. 153. A photographer, Richard Nicklin, was assigned to Captain (later Major) John Hackett of the Seventy-seventh Regiment and sailed to the Crimea in late May 1854. He and his two assistants died in the sinking of the *Rip Van Winkle* in November 1854, and no work from this endeavor appears to have survived. Gernsheim 1954, p. 12, notes that Major Hackett applied for replacement photographers and "Ensigns Brandon and Dawson" were sent in the spring of 1855, after being trained by John Mayall.

92. See *ILN*, July 15, 1854, p. 45.

93. Wilson 2003, p. 186.

94. See Knightley 1975, p. 15; Lloyd 1988, p. 14.

95. See Lalumia 1984, pp. 117, 121. Hannavy 1974, p. 11, writes that "Government officials" approached Agnew asking him to hire a photographer whose pictures "had to conform to strict official requirements." For further discussion of this issue, see Keller 2001, p. 123.

96. Keller 2001, pp. 123–26.

97. Fenton, "Narrative of a Photographic Trip," *JPS*, January 21, 1856, p. 286.

98. Ibid.

99. On the editing of this correspondence by the Gernsheims, see note 23.

100. Quoted in Gernsheim 1954, pp. 44, 45.

101. Ibid., pp. 51, 57.

102. Ibid., pp. 47, 89.

103. Ibid., p. 61.

104. Ibid., p. 58.

105. In his address to the Photographic Society on his return to England, Fenton acknowledged the omission of views of the aftermath of battle "so ably depicted by Robertson" after his departure. See Fenton, "Narrative of a Photographic Trip," *JPS*, January 21, 1856, p. 290.

106. Gernsheim 1954, p. 46.

107. These included the photograph of General Sir George de Lacy Evans, who, at nearly seventy, had been wounded in the Battle of Alma and had returned to England before Fenton arrived in the Crimea. Keller 2001, p. 138.

108. On how the officers themselves viewed the Crimean battles as spectacles, see ibid., pp. 4–8.

109. Gernsheim 1954, p. 75.

110. Wilson 2003, pp. 175–95.

111. "Report of the Council," *JPS*, February 21, 1855, p. 117; Gernsheim 1954, pp. 57, 90, 75. Fenton wrote of his diligent efforts to get the "people together whose portraits are wanted," a comment that suggests he had a list, perhaps supplied by Agnew. Gernsheim 1954, p. 57.

112. Fenton, *Photographs of the Seat of War in the Crimea*, portfolio of photographs issued 1855–1856, title page.

113. See, for example, Gernsheim 1954, p. 58.

114. Ibid., pp. 74–75. Because Napoleon was often depicted with his arm raised and hand pointed, there is no way of knowing what portrait Fenton had in mind.

115. Ibid., p. 57.

116. Ibid., p. 71.

117. Ibid., pp. 59, 68–69.

118. See, for example, "Photographs from the Crimea," *Athenaeum*, September 29, 1855, p. 1118; or *Morning Chronicle*, September 20, 1855, and *Guardian*, October 3, 1855, quoted in Keller 2001, p. 133.

119. As noted in Keller 2001, pp. 131–34, Fenton actually took two photographs of the shallow ravine from the same camera position. In the first the cannonballs lie mostly scattered by the side of the road; in the second the cannonballs have been placed more prominently on the road itself.

120. Gernsheim 1954, pp. 97, 99, 105.

121. Victoria, Queen of England, Journal (archival source), August 8, 1855.

122. "Photographs of the Seat of War," *ILN*, September 15, 1855, p. 326.

123. "Photographs from Sebastopol," *Art-Journal*, October 1, 1855, p. 285; "Photographs from the Crimea," *Athenaeum*, September 29, 1855, p. 1117.

124. "Topics of the Week," *Literary Gazette, and Journal of Science and Art*, September 22, 1855, p. 605.

125. *Scenery,—Views of the Camps, &c.*, consisted of ten parts, each containing five subjects; *Incidents of Camp Life,— Groups of Figures, &c.* had ten parts, each containing six subjects; and *Historical Portraits* had five parts, each of six subjects. A single part cost two pounds two shillings. See advertisement in *Exhibition of the Photographic Pictures Taken in the Crimea by Roger Fenton, Esq.* 1855, opening pages (unpaginated).

126. See advertisement in *Exhibition of the Photographic Pictures Taken in the Crimea by Roger Fenton, Esq.* 1855, p. 15; Gernsheim 1954, p. 27. Fenton's Crimean photographs were distributed in France by Jacques-Antoine Moulin, a French photographer, in London by Colnaghi, and in New York by "Williams," information that is printed on their mounts.

127. Elizabeth Eastlake, April 1857, p. 443.

128. "C'est la photographie paysagiste poussée à son dernier degré de perfection." Molard, October 1856, p. 283.

129. "Exhibition," *JPS*, May 21, 1858, p. 208.

130. "Photographic Society. Annual General Meeting. Feb. 7th, 1856," *JPS*, February 21, 1856, pp. 299–304.

131. *JPS*, no. 42 (May 21, 1856), pp. 37–38; "Photographic Society. Ordinary Meeting. May 1, 1856," *JPS*, May 21, 1856, p. 38.

132. Public Records Office, Kew, B.T. 41, box 560/3062, quoted in Seiberling 1986, p. 76; "Photographic Association," *JPS*, May 21, 1856, n.p.; "Manchester Photographic Society," *Photographic Notes*, May 25, 1856, p. 51.

133. See *JPS*, no. 42 (May 21, 1856), p. 37.

134. "Photographic Society. Anniversary Meeting. Thursday, February 2nd, 1854," *JPS*, February 21, 1854, p. 166.

135. "Photography and the Photographic Society," *Builder*, February 11, 1854, p. 73.

136. "To the Editor," *JPS*, September 21, 1858, p. 31; "Forthcoming Exhibition," *JPS*, September 21, 1858, p. 31.

137. Earlier that spring Prince Albert had donated fifty pounds to the Photographic Society to encourage research into this question. See "Photographic Society. Annual General Meeting. Feb. 7th, 1856," *JPS*, February 21, 1856, p. 300.

138. See Fenton to William Henry Fox Talbot, February 4, 1854, Lacock Abbey Collection LA54-007 (archival source); Talbot Correspondence Project (website), doc. 06912.

139. "Photogalvanography," *Photographic Notes*, May 25, 1856, pp. 60–62.

140. *Photographic Art Treasures* 1856, pt. 1, title page.

141. "Photo-Galvanography, or Nature Engravings," advertisement in the *Athenaeum*, May 16, 1857, p. 614.

142. John Henry Bolton to William Henry Fox Talbot, May 1, 1857, Lacock Abbey Collection LA57-015 (archival source); Talbot Correspondence Project (website), doc. 07399.

143. See Talbot to Bolton, April 24, 1857, Lacock Abbey Collection LA57-013 (archival source); Talbot Correspondence Project (website), doc. 07396. See also Bolton to Talbot, May 1, 1857, Lacock Abbey Collection LA57-015 (archival source); Talbot Correspondence Project (website), doc. 07399.

144. Bolton to Talbot, August 13, 1857, Lacock Abbey Collection LA57-022 (archival source); Talbot Correspondence Project (website), doc. 07437.

145. See "Exhibition of Art Treasures at Manchester," *Liverpool and Manchester Photographic Journal*, July 15, 1857, p. 145.

146. Dimond in Dimond and Taylor 1987, p. 43.

147. See Taylor in Dimond and Taylor 1987, pp. 15–17. Rejlander's *The Two Ways of Life* was an allegorical depiction of the choice faced by two young men between a life of virtue and one of vice. To make it, Rejlander photographed more than twenty models at different times.

148. See Dimond in Dimond and Taylor 1987, pp. 51–55.

149. British Museum, Trustee Committee Minutes (archival source), pp. 9018–19, June 7, 1856.

150. See William Jacobson et al. to Henry Ellis, February 9, 1856, and Ellis to Reverend Selwyn, February 11, 1856, British Museum, Original Letters and Papers (archival source).

151. Fenton to Panizzi, July 30, 1857, British Museum, Original Letters and Papers (archival source).

152. Ibid.

153. See British Museum, Trustee Committee Minutes (archival source), p. 9447, July 24, 1858, and p. 9484, November 13, 1858. It has been suggested that in the summer of 1858 Fenton set up a kiosk in the museum's front hall. Hannavy 1976, p. 42. Although his photographs could be purchased at the museum, there is no evidence that he had a sales booth.

154. British Museum, Minutes of the Sub Committee (archival source), pp. 1114–16, July 7, 1859.

155. Fenton to Panizzi, July 7, 1859, British Museum, Original Letters and Papers (archival source).

156. Darrah 1977, pp. 3, 4.

157. "Stereoscopic Magazine," *Literary Gazette, and Journal of Belles Lettres, Science, and Art*, April 24, 1858, p. 408. See also Stark 1981, p. 11.

158. "Stereoscopic Magazine," *Literary Gazette, and Journal of Belles Lettres, Science, and Art*, April 24, 1858, p. 408.

159. Rejlander, April 21, 1858, p. 196.

160. Ibid.

161. "London Photographic Society," *Photographic News*, January 11, 1861, pp. 18–19.

162. Quoted in Date 1989, p. 12.

163. Parliament, House of Commons, *Report from the Select Committee*, 1860, p. 89.

164. Ibid.

165. Darrah 1981, pp. 5–6.

166. Hervé, May 21, 1858, p. 223.

167. After numerous objections were raised to this proposal, the Organizing Committee established a separate hall for photography. See, for example, *Photographic Journal*, no. 109 (May 15, 1861), pp. 171–74; "Photographic Society of London . . . June 4, 1861," *Photographic Journal*, June 15, 1861, pp. 196–98; "Photographic Society," *Art-Journal*, July 1, 1861, p. 223.

168. Nadar 1899, pp. 194–96.

169. "Photographic Exhibition," *Photographic News*, January 27, 1860, p. 242.

170. "Exhibition of the Photographic Society," *Photographic News*, January 28, 1859, p. 242.

171. "Photographic Exhibition," *Photographic News*, February 3, 1860, p. 254.

172. "Exhibition of the Photographic Society of Scotland," *Photographic Journal*, January 16, 1860, p. 132; "Photographic Exhibition," *Photographic News*, January 18, 1861, p. 25.

173. "Photographic Exhibition," *Athenaeum*, January 21, 1860, p. 98; "Exhibition of the Photographic Society," *Art-Journal*, February 1, 1861, p. 48.

174. *Photographic Journal*, no. 93 (January 16, 1860), p. 115; "London Photographic Society's Exhibition," *BJP*, February 15, 1861, pp. 67–68; "Exhibition of the Photographic Society," *Art-Journal*, March 1, 1860, p. 72.

175. "Exhibition of the Photographic Society," *Art-Journal*, March 1, 1860, p. 71.

176. *Photographic Notes*, no. 98 (May 1, 1860), p. 116.

177. Parliament, House of Commons, *Report from the Select Committee*, 1860, p. 91.

178. "London Photographic Society," *Photographic News*, January 11, 1861, pp. 18–19.

179. "Photographic Society. Ordinary Meeting. May 7, 1857," *JPS*, May 21, 1857, p. 271.

180. "Archer Fund," *Photographic Journal*, May 15, 1860, p. 243.

181. "Failure as Viewed in Heywood," *Heywood Advertiser*, ca. 1878.

182. "Retirement of Mr. Fenton," *Photographic Journal*, October 15, 1862, p. 158.

183. "Mr. Fenton's Photographic Effects," *Photographic News*, December 5, 1862, p. 588.

184. *Law List* 1863, p. 45. Fenton was a barrister for the Assize (or traveling) Courts of Manchester, Salford, and York; he continued to reside at Mount Grace in Potter's Bar. It is noted in "Late Mr. Roger Fenton," *BJP*, August 20, 1869, p. 401, that at the end of his life Fenton had a "connection with the Stock Exchange."

185. "Late Mr. Roger Fenton," *BJP*, August 20, 1869, p. 400.

"On Nature's Invitation Do I Come": Roger Fenton's Landscapes

MALCOLM DANIEL

In addition to the many people whose invaluable assistance is acknowledged at the beginning of this catalogue, I wish to signal my particular gratitude to Roger Taylor. He has shared his deep knowledge of Victorian history and culture, clarified details of early photographic technique, opened his library and files, passed on specific research relevant to my topic, and—most memorably and pleasurably—led me on walks to the Strid, through the ruins of Rievaulx, and along the banks of the Ribble and Hodder. I know of no scholar more generous than he.

The exhibition and catalogue have been a very happy collaboration, and I am indebted to my co-curators, Sarah Greenough and Gordon Baldwin. They have taught me much through their discussion of Fenton's pictures, research and writing for the catalogue, and careful reading and critique of this essay.

As always, I am deeply grateful also to my partner, Darryl Morrison, who bravely sat in the passenger's seat as we explored North Wales and who patiently and lovingly endured my weekend work and evening anxiety during the writing of this essay.

The title of the essay is taken from "The Recluse" by William Wordsworth, whose Romantic reverence for nature seems to me embedded in Fenton's landscapes and whose verses are therefore frequently invoked here.

1. Howitt 1840, p. 10.

2. Ibid., p. 6.

3. Although its origins go back to antiquity, the notion of the sublime in literary and aesthetic theory was most forcefully articulated and debated in eighteenth-century Britain, notably in Edmund Burke's 1756 essay *A Philosophical Enquiry into the Origin of our Ideas of the Sublime and the Beautiful*. Vast scale, power, darkness, or ruggedness—to the point of inducing a sense of terror—characterized the sublime, and stood in contrast to the smoothness, delicacy, and lightness associated with its antipode, beauty. The idea of the picturesque—literally, the combination of qualities thought to make a scene worthy of artistic depiction—was developed in response to Burke and constituted a sort of middle ground between the sublime and the beautiful. As the idea was elaborated by its chief proponent, William Gilpin, in the 1760s through the 1780s, landscape painting (or landscape itself) was enlivened by irregular contours, decaying ruins, local color, and low vantage points that immerse the viewer in a scene. By the mid-nineteenth century the theories of the sublime and the picturesque were little debated, but they had been largely internalized into the aesthetics of landscape artists.

4. Noon 2003.

5. "Exhibition," *JPS*, May 21, 1858, p. 208.

6. For examples of such views, see Hannavy 1993, figs. 7, 8.

7. See "A New Starting Point" by Sarah Greenough in this volume, p. 14, for the photographs from this campaign.

8. For Fenton's use of paper negatives during the first year of his career, see Hannavy 1993, pp. 233–43. Regarding the many variations on the paper negative process, see also Taylor and Ware 2003, pp. 308–19.

9. The inscription in Jeuffrain's album specifies that Fenton used "papier ciré sec (Le Gray)" for these landscape views, although the album's portraits and self-portrait by Fenton, also made in February 1852, were made using collodion-on-glass negatives.

10. See Taylor, *Photographs Exhibited in Britain*, 2002, pp. 304–9. The fact that some of the Burnham Beeches pictures are identified as being from waxed paper negatives suggests a date of 1852 or 1853, as Fenton appears to have switched to collodion on glass shortly after his return from Russia in the fall of 1852. Richard Pare has suggested in a verbal communication that a series of Burnham Beeches pictures found in the "gray albums" may be Fenton's, but those albums included work by other photographers, and there is no way to determine the author of these particular images (see note 30 below).

11. Hannavy 1993, pp. 238–39, figs. 5–7. In his journals, the engineer Charles Blacker Vignoles was quite specific in noting that Fenton was to make stereoscopic views of the bridge he was constructing over the Dnieper.

12. *Scenery of the Wharf* 1855, p. 3.

13. Fenton, "On the Present Position and Future Prospects of the Art of Photography," in *Catalogue of an Exhibition of Recent Specimens of Photography* 1852, p. 5.

14. Denis Diderot, *Diderot on Art*, ed. and trans. John Goodman, vol. 2, *The Salon of 1767* (New Haven and London: Yale University Press, 1995), p. 198.

15. Howitt 1854, vol. 1, p. 241.

16. Banks 1866, p. 26.

17. Ibid., p. 28.

18. *Black's Picturesque Guide to Yorkshire* 1862, pp. 50–51.

19. "Fine-Art Gossip," *Athenaeum*, June 27, 1857, p. 826.

20. *Photographic Notes*, no. 15 (November 15, 1856), p. 235, discussing Fenton's photographs.

21. "Photographic Exhibition," *JPS*, February 21, 1857, p. 215. The phrase cited by the reviewer is a misquotation of Wordsworth's "Upon Westminster Bridge." *The Reach of the Dee* is at the NMPFT (RPS Collection 2003–5000/3012).

22. *JPS*, no. 15 (March 21, 1854), p. 178.

23. Phipson, October 21, 1856, p. 147. Neither the review nor the exhibition catalogue is specific as to the identity of the landscapes displayed; the catalogue reads simply, "Vues de Hampton-court; Cléopatre; ruines."

24. *Notices of the First Exhibition of the Norwich Photographic Society* 1857, p. 5. The exhibition opened November 17, 1856. The image of Hampton Court referred to in this review cannot now be identified. No known photograph of this subject by Fenton shows natural skies.

25. Taylor, *Photographs Exhibited in Britain*, 2002, p. 328. The exhibition opened December 20, 1856. *Photographic Notes*, in a wider review of Fenton's work, commented that "two Views entitled Evening (288 and 296) . . . are among the most conspicuous where all are artistic in a high degree." "First Exhibition of the Photographic Society of Scotland," January 1, 1857, p. 26.

26. *Photographic Notes*, no. 15 (November 15, 1856), p. 235.

27. For a full discussion and numerous reproductions of Le Gray's seascapes, see Aubenas et al. 2002. *The Great Wave* is illustrated on p. 125.

28. For the reception of Le Gray's seascapes in England, see Jacobson 2001, in which the *Times* advertisement by Murray & Heath is cited.

29. These cloud studies have traditionally been dated 1859, based on the fact that Fenton first exhibited a related work, *September Clouds* (fig. 24), at the Photographic Society in 1860 and on the assumption that he showed it at the earliest opportunity after making it. However,

Fenton frequently exhibited photographs several years after making them, or exhibited previously shown photographs with variant titles, and this might well have been the case here, since *Clouds after Rain* and *Evening* had not yet been shown outside of Scotland. Fenton's association with Thomas Gladwell, beginning in late 1858, also brought many of his older images back into play (see "A Most Enthusiastic Cultivator of His Art" by Roger Taylor in this volume). Furthermore, although we do not know if Fenton was photographing in September 1859, he was definitely off in Scotland making photographs with natural skies in September 1856. Finally, it should be noted that *September Clouds* and the related works have more in common, stylistically, with other works from Fenton's 1856 campaign such as *Loch Nagar from Craig Gowan* (fig. 22) than with the views around Stonyhurst that he made in the summer and winter of 1859.

30. Commonly referred to as the "gray albums" for the color of their pages, these three portfolios contained many rare or unique works by Fenton. They were dismantled and sold piecemeal in the late 1970s and early 1980s by Christie's, London. Since the consignor insisted on anonymity, and since the volumes were not documented before being dismembered, it is now impossible to trace their provenance or to reconstruct their full contents or sequencing. Nonetheless, it is clear that they represented a personal compendium of Fenton's work, most often in unretouched proof prints. The portfolios contained photographs from 1852 to 1859 (weighted toward the later years) and included a large number of Orientalist pictures; numerous works by other photographers were also pasted to the pages.

31. William Wordsworth, "Lines Written a Few Miles above Tintern Abbey, on Revisiting the Banks of the Wye during a Tour, July 13, 1798."

32. The two untitled prints in the Metropolitan Museum collection (pls. 22, 23) have been assumed to be coincident with *September Clouds* because of their similarity of composition, although the latter is smaller in format and known only in two albumen silver prints, one at the NMPFT (RPS Collection), the other in a private collection, New York. The difference in print size and medium is no argument against this having been made at the same time as the Metropolitan Museum prints, for Fenton used negatives of both sizes on his Scottish trip and printed some images as salted paper prints and others as albumen silver prints.

33. "Photographic Exhibition," *Photographic News,* January 27, 1860, p. 242.

34. Constable to John Fisher, October 23, 1821, Constable 1968, p. 77.

35. For a discussion of this topic, see Gage 2000, pp. 125–34; Lyles 2000, pp. 135–50.

36. Davidson 1860, p. vi.

37. See "Mr. Fenton Explained Everything" by Roger Taylor in this volume, pp. 79–80.

38. Of Fenton's pictures, it was said that "foggy and misty though they be, [they] are a higher tribute to their author's consummate skill than any success, even the most perfect, could afford." *Liverpool and Manchester Photographic Journal,* no. 4 (February 15, 1857), p. 35. Bedford's scenes were discussed on the same page. On Bedford, see Spencer 1987, pp. 237–45.

39. *Liverpool and Manchester Photographic Journal,* no. 4 (February 15, 1857), p. 35.

40. "Photographic Exhibition of the Manchester Photographic Society," *Photographic Notes,* October 15, 1856, pp. 204–5.

41. The Reverend J. B. Reade, quoted in the *Liverpool and Manchester Photographic Journal,* no. 4 (February 15, 1857), p. 37.

42. Roscoe 1853, p. 121.

43. Hansard 1834, p. 202.

44. Lord 1998, pp. 23–25.

45. Ibid., pp. 34–38.

46. *Catalogue of the Collection . . . Formed by Roger Fenton,* June 13, 1870, lots 86, 82, 81. "J. P. Jackson" listed in the auction catalogue may be a typographical error for S. P. Jackson (Samuel Phillips Jackson), listed as the artist of lot 90, for example.

47. See, for example, the list of works exhibited by David Cox in Bunt 1946, pp. 87–117.

48. Davidson 1860, p. 31.

49. Roscoe 1853, p. 216.

50. *Stereoscopic Magazine: A Gallery of Landscape Scenery, Architecture, Antiquities, and Natural History, Accompanied with Descriptive Articles by Writers of Eminence,* published by Lovell Reeve beginning in July 1858. Fenton contributed views of North Wales, Ely and Peterborough cathedrals, gallery interiors and objects in the British Museum, and scenes at and around Stonyhurst.

51. Davidson (1824–1885) was a Devon-born historian, a graduate of Trinity College, Cambridge, and a lawyer called to the bar in 1850. How he knew Fenton or became aware of Fenton's Welsh stereos is unknown. "James Bridge Davidson," *Devon Notes and Queries,* 1903, p. 129.

52. Davidson 1860, p. 1.

53. Roscoe 1853, p. 207.

54. Ibid., p. 208.

55. Davidson 1860, p. v.

56. Lord 1998, p. 59.

57. "Pont-y-Pant," *Stereoscopic Magazine,* May 1859, p. 164. See also Davidson 1860, p. 77.

58. Davidson 1860, p. 133. The bridge depicted in Fenton's photograph is said to date to the fifteenth century. The stone piers of Pont-y-Pant still stand, little changed, but the wooden roadway and rails have been replaced by a concrete bed and metal fence.

59. Ibid., pp. 131–32.

60. Roscoe 1853, p. 208.

61. At the Glasgow Photographic Society exhibition of 1859, Fenton exhibited four views: "Bed of the Lledr, near Pont-y-Pont"; "Rock in the Lledr, near Pont-y-Pont"; "Pont-y-Pont, Wales, from Above"; and "Pont-y-Pont, Wales, from Below." Taylor, *Photographs Exhibited in Britain,* 2002, p. 337.

62. This, at least, is the explicit reason provided by Davidson 1860, p. 132.

63. Ibid.

64. See Thackray 1996, pp. 65–74.

65. William Wordsworth, "Lines Written a Few Miles above Tintern Abbey, on Revisiting the Banks of the Wye during a Tour, July 13, 1798."

66. "What is here seen is a mere residuum of that irresistible flood which is sometimes hurled down this contracted gorge, powerful enough, it is presumed, to carry with it blocks of felstone of considerable size." Davidson 1860, pp. 168–69. This spot is the modern-day Ffos Noddum.

67. Davidson (ibid., p. 169) writes that "the ordinary loneliness of the scene is effectually dispelled in summer by a troop of artists, who take up various positions on the rocks, and enliven their labours with occasional chants, and other vocal efforts more or less amusing."

68. "Photographic Society," *Athenaeum,* no. 1582 (February 20, 1858), p. 246.

69. Davidson 1860, p. 168.

70. "Photographic Society," *Literary Gazette, and Journal of Belles Lettres, Science, and Art,* February 20, 1858, p. 186.

71. Ann Radcliffe's phrase from the best-selling novel *The Mysteries of Udolpho* (1794) was applied to this spot in *Black's Picturesque Guide to North Wales* 1857, p. 96.

72. Roscoe 1853, p. 118.

73. Among the photographs of Wales that Fenton may have known before setting out on his own excursion would have been Alfred Rosling's *Near the Pass of Nant Frangen, North Wales,* taken in July 1856 and published in the *Photographic Album for the Year 1857.*

74. The third view of the Nant Ffrancon pass is in the collection of the NMPFT (RPS Collection 2003-5000/3220). All three versions are illustrated in Lloyd 1988, pls. 71–73.

75. Roscoe 1853, p. 119.

76. Ibid., p. 120.

77. The Conway was navigable to Trefriw by vessels of up to sixty tons. *Black's Picturesque Guide to North Wales* 1857, p. 147.

78. Davidson 1860, p. 26. Davidson also reported (pp. 19–20) that a small steamboat carried passengers daily from Conway to Trefriw. Pleasure boats brought day-trippers from Conway to the spa at Trefriw well into the twentieth century.

79. See Taylor, *Photographs Exhibited in Britain,* 2002, p. 335–36.

William Clowes, 1899–1900), which contains a comprehensive listing of periodicals published during the nineteenth century. The entries for London alone occupy almost five hundred columns on very large pages.

28. Gernsheim 1984, pp. 131–33.

29. Circulation figures for the *Illustrated London News* are given in Altick 1957, p. 394. While in 1850 the circulation was 67,000, by 1855 it had increased to 123,000.

30. Taylor, *Photographs Exhibited in Britain*, 2002, pp. 302–43. See also *Exhibition of the Photographic Pictures Taken in the Crimea by Roger Fenton, Esq. 1855.*

31. Photographic societies used exhibitions as a means of encouraging the purchase of photographs, listing prices in the exhibition catalogues. See the rules for submission in "Photographic Society," *JPS*, December 21, 1853, p. 141.

32. Jaeger 1995, pp. 133–40. Jaeger lists thirty-five societies established between 1852 and 1861. All would have acknowledged the Photographic Society in London as the parent society to which they turned for guidance and support.

33. Taylor, *Photographs Exhibited in Britain*, 2002, pp. 302–43.

34. Sinclair submitted prints by other well-known photographers in addition to Fenton, including Édouard Baldus, Bisson Frères, Caldesi & Montecci, Le Gray, Henry Hering, and Maull & Polyblank (see individual entries in ibid.). Sinclair in later years became honorary secretary of the Edinburgh Photographic Society. I am grateful to my colleague Sara Stevenson of the Scottish National Portrait Gallery, Edinburgh, for this information.

35. Reviews for exhibitions of the Photographic Society of Scotland have been preserved as press clippings and are now kept in the National Archives of Scotland, Edinburgh, with those for 1858 in file B40438. I am grateful to Peter Stubbs for these references; see his website at http://www.edinphoto.org.uk/index.htm.

36. "Photographic Album," *Athenaeum*, November 13, 1852, p. 1247.

37. "Photographic Publications," *Art-Journal*, December 1, 1852, p. 374.

38. "Photographic Exhibition at the Society of Arts," *Art-Journal*, February 1, 1853, p. 55.

39. Full details for the Committee of the North London School of Drawing and Modelling are given in the *Almanack of the Fine Arts* 1852, p. 138.

40. Under Hall the *Art-Journal* became one of the most influential periodicals of the period and, through his forthright editorial style, did much to stimulate public appreciation of art. His autobiography contains ample indication of his position within the nineteenth-century art establishment. Hall 1883.

41. "Exhibition of the Photographic Society," *Art-Journal*, February 1, 1854, p. 49.

42. "Exhibition of Photographs," *ILN*, February 17, 1855, p. 166. This was the final review, the others having been published on January 27, 1855, p. 95, and February 10, 1855, p. 141.

43. This passage is from "English Photography," *Liverpool Photographic Journal*, December 8, 1855, p. 146, which printed a translation of a small portion of the original article in the *Bulletin de la Société Française de Photographie* (see Périer, November 1855, p. 317).

44. "Exhibition of Photographs," *ILN*, February 17, 1855, p. 166. The wood engraving was not the first reproduction of Fenton's photographs published by the *Illustrated London News*. The previous year, on February 4, 1854, a small wood engraving of his *Russian Peasants* was used to illustrate an article ("A Group of Russian Peasants," p. 88).

45. Fenton was awarded a "médaille de première classe" for photographs; see "Exposition Universelle," *Photographic Notes*, January 1 and 25, 1856, p. xix. The unprecedented entente cordiale that existed between Britain and France at this time was a direct consequence of their political alliance to go to war against Russia in the Crimea. Fenton's photographic achievements there must have been well known to the French authorities, as he was summoned to meet the emperor when he and William Agnew Jr. were visiting Paris. See entry for September 7, 1855, in the Chronology.

46. "Photographs from the Crimea," *Athenaeum*, September 29, 1855, p. 1117.

47. "Photographs from Sebastopol," *Art-Journal*, October 1, 1855, p. 285.

48. "Crimean Exhibition," *Athenaeum*, March 22, 1856, p. 363. The "Crimean Exhibition" of William Simpson (1823–1899) was held at the French Gallery, 121 Pall Mall, London, in premises adjacent to Fenton's exhibition, where it undoubtedly offered a very different view of events.

49. "Photographs from Sebastopol," *Art-Journal*, October 1, 1855, p. 285.

50. In April 1856 Fenton chaired a meeting at the Society of Arts at which Pretsch read a paper "On Photo-Galvanography, or, Engraving by Light and Electricity"; "Nineteenth Ordinary Meeting," *JSA*, April 25, 1856, pp. 385–89. See also "Photogalvanography," *Photographic Notes*, May 25, 1856, pp. 60–62.

51. "Fine Arts," *Athenaeum*, January 24, 1857, p. 120, "Photographic Art Treasures," *Athenaeum*, February 14, 1857, p. 198. For a contemporary account of the process and its history, see "Photogalvanography," *Art-Journal*, July 1, 1856, pp. 215–16. Within the history of photography, the development of photomechanical reproduction and the role of the Patent Photo-Galvanographic Company deserve wider attention.

52. *Photographic Art Treasures* 1856; *Photographic Notes*, November 15, 1856, p. 235.

53. J. H. Bolton to William Henry Fox Talbot, May 1, 1857, Lacock Abbey Collection LA57-015 (archival source); Talbot Correspondence Project (website), doc. 07399.

Bolton, Talbot's lawyer, reports that the Patent Photo-Galvanographic Company has losses amounting to four thousand pounds and is in chancery following a dispute with the manager of the company. The company was further undermined when it was recognized that Pretsch's patents conflicted with preexisting patents taken out by Talbot for his photoglyphic engraving process.

54. "Photographic Association," *JPS*, May 21, 1856, n.p.

55. The Photographic Association seems to have been established in direct response to the new opportunities offered by the Limited Liability Act, which had become law in August 1855. It allowed joint stock companies to issue shares with a nominal value of not less than ten pounds and gave new protection to shareholders. *Companion to the Almanac* 1856, p. 110.

56. "Photographic Society. Ordinary Meeting. May 1, 1856," *JPS*, May 21, 1856, p. 38. The published account of this meeting is brief. A transcription from shorthand notes taken at the meeting, which offers a fuller account, is in the NMPFT (RPS Collection); see Photographic Society, Manuscript Notes (archival source).

57. Photograph Society, Manuscript Notes (archival source), p. 9.

58. Under this ruling, even eminent photographers such as Mayall could never be admitted to the Council.

59. "Photographic Society. Ordinary Meeting. May 1, 1856," *JPS*, May 21, 1856, p. 38.

60. "Photographic Society. Annual General Meeting. February 5, 1857," *JPS*, February 21, 1857, p. 222.

61. Fenton exhibited in Aberdeen, "Notes on the Photographic Exhibition at Aberdeen," *Photographic Journal (BJP)*, October 1, 1859, pp. 243–44; Blackheath, *Photographic Journal (BJP)*, no. 93 (May 1, 1859), p. 103; Edinburgh, Photographic Society of Scotland, Records (archival source), file B40438; Glasgow, "Glasgow Photographic Society," *Photographic Journal (BJP)*, June 1, 1859, p. 139; Halifax, "Conversazione of the Halifax Literary and Philosophical Society," *Photographic News*, January 28, 1859, pp. 249–50 (in this instance work submitted by a local collector); London, "Photographic Society's Sixth Annual Exhibition," *Photographic Journal, (BJP)*, February 1, 1859, pp. 34–36; Macclesfield, "Macclesfield Photographic Society's Exhibition," *Photographic Journal (BJP)*, March 1, 1859, p. 60; Nottingham, "Nottingham Photographic Society's Exhibition," *Photographic Journal (BJP)*, February 1, 1859, p. 36; and Paris, "Foreign Science," *Photographic News*, April 21, 1859, pp. 77–79.

62. "Exhibition of Art Treasures at Manchester," *Liverpool and Manchester Photographic Journal*, July 15, 1857, p. 145.

63. "Exhibition," *JPS*, May 21, 1858, p. 208.

64. "Photographic Society's Exhibition," *Builder*, February 20, 1858, p. 133.

65. "Photographic Exhibition," *Art-Journal*, February 1, 1859, p. 46.

66. Taylor, *Photographs Exhibited in Britain*, 2002, pp. 336–38. In addition to Thomas Agnew in Manchester, Fenton seems to have been well represented by printsellers in Scotland, including Colin Sinclair, White & Barr, and John Werge; see the exhibition records for the 1859 annual exhibition of the Glasgow Photographic Society.

67. "Photographs," *Athenaeum*, November 27, 1858, p. 694.

68. Along with Fenton's photographs Gladwell advertised his "celebrated collection . . . numbering upwards of 1,600 of the finest specimens produced," including works by Bisson Frères, Le Gray, and other, anonymous foreign photographers. Ibid. The main branch of Gladwell's business was at 21 Gracechurch Street, London, the other a few doors away at 87 Gracechurch Street, where it operated under the name City Stereo-scopic Depot.

69. No other advertisements promoting Fenton's photographs in the 1850s have been located.

70. "Photographs," *Athenaeum*, November 27, 1858, p. 694.

71. "Exhibition of Photographs at the South Kensington Museum," *Liverpool and Manchester Photographic Journal*, March 1, 1858, p. 61.

72. "Photographic Exhibition," *Art-Journal*, April 1, 1858, p. 120.

73. "Photographic Exhibition," *Art-Journal*, February 1, 1859, p. 46.

74. "Photography at the International Exhibition," *Photographic Journal*, July 15, 1862, p. 80.

75. "Retirement of Mr. Fenton," *Photographic Journal*, October 15, 1862, p. 158.

"The Exertions of Mr. Fenton": Roger Fenton and the Founding of the Photographic Society

PAM ROBERTS

The title quotation is from "Retirement of Mr. Fenton," *Photographic Journal*, October 15, 1862, p. 158.

1. It was later known at different times as the Photographic Society of London, the Photographic Society of Great Britain, and finally the Royal Photographic Society (now often abbreviated RPS).

2. There have been unsupported claims that he was a member of the Photographic Club (also known as the Calotype Club) formed in 1847 by Peter Wickens Fry, Robert Hunt, and others: see Gernsheim 1969, p. 176. But these are disputed by various researchers writing subsequently: Lloyd 1988; Hannavy 1993, pp. 233–43; and the present catalogue.

3. Fenton, "Proposal for the Formation of a Photographical Society," *Chemist*, March 1852, p. 265.

4. "Introductory Address," *JPS*, March 3, 1853, p. 1.

5. "Calotype Society," *Athenaeum*, December 18, 1847, p. 1304.

6. One of the few exceptions was Charles Wheatstone, professor of experimental physics at King's College, London, and inventor of the reflecting stereoscope and later a founder and vice president of the Photographic Society.

7. Taylor 1999, pp. 59–67.

8. *Almanack of the Fine Arts* 1852, p. 155.

9. Also sometimes present was Dr. Hugh Welch Diamond; Archer had been his medical patient.

10. "Report of the Jurors," *JPS*, December 15, 1862, p. 192. Dr. Hugh Diamond was among the jurors writing this report.

11. Details of the process, location, date, and photographer are written in ink on two paper labels on the back of the glass, in two different, contemporary hands. The upper label, most likely in Archer's own hand, reads, "Entrance to Beddington Park/whitened with Bichloride of Mercury/F. S. Archer." The lower label, in an unknown hand but possibly Fry's, reads, "Exhibited at Mr. Fry's house/in 1851 to the Members of the/Photographic Club." This item, badly damaged during World War II and remounted in 1957, is in the NMPFT (RPS Collection). The 1851 date could be a reference to the 1850 meeting that is wrong by a year, but it is more likely correct. The episode suggests that there was huge interest in Archer's experiments with collodion. He became a frequent visitor at the club's meetings, although not formally a member.

12. It should be noted, however, that Talbot had offered an arrangement in which society members would be able to sell photographs from their headquarters through the secretary, with 10 percent of the profit going to form a fund for the benefit of the society.

13. "Inaugural Meeting of the Photographic Society," *JPS*, March 3, 1853, p. 3.

14. Hunt to Talbot, March 23, 1851, Lacock Abbey Collection LA51-009 (archival source); Talbot Correspondence Project (website), doc. 06399. The originally written date of 1850 was changed to 1851 in Hunt's hand.

15. NMPFT (Talbot Collection TALBT/7/5). In recent research, Marian Kamlish has suggested that Antoine Claudet, a French photographer living in England, was the author of this unsigned, undated document. While the thesis is persuasively argued, it seems unlikely: Talbot and Claudet were colleagues, even friends, and were in frequent correspondence for many years (although correspondence for the critical year of 1851 is missing), and there is no reference to this draft in their later correspondence. Moreover, Claudet was supportive of Talbot's patent rights rather than highly unsupportive, as this document is. For full details, see Kamlish 2002, pp. 296–306; Kamlish 2003, pp. 389–90; Taylor 2003, pp. 386–88.

16. Talbot to Hunt, unsent draft of a letter, November 6 and 7, 1851, NMPFT (RPS Collection 141a; archival source); Talbot Correspondence Project (website), doc. 06507.

17. Fenton, "Photography in France," February 1852, pp. 221–22. Others probably favored such a step, but Fenton seems to have galvanized the group: "Eventually Mr. Roger Fenton, aided by Mr. Vignoles, conceived the idea of a Photographic Society. The suggestion was warmly entertained by Mr. Fry, Mr. Robert Hunt and a few others." "London Photographic Society. Report," *BJP*, February 15, 1861, p. 70.

18. Fenton, "Proposal for the Formation of a Photographical Society," *Chemist*, March 1852, p. 266.

19. Fenton, "Proposal for the Formation of a Photographical Society," undated (probably January–February 1852; archival source).

20. Hunt to Fry, March 5, 1852; NMPFT (RPS Collection; archival source); quoted in full in Johnston 1946, p. 2.

21. Ibid.

22. Hunt to Talbot, March 19, 1852, Lacock Abbey Collection LA52-015 (archival source); Talbot Correspondence Project (website), doc. 06580.

23. Talbot to Hunt, March 24, 1852, NMPFT (RPS Collection T/2 1279; archival source); Talbot Correspondence Project (website), doc. 06585.

24. Hunt to Talbot, April 28, 1852, Lacock Abbey Collection LA52-023 (archival source); Talbot Correspondence Project (website), doc. 06600.

25. Wheatstone to Talbot, April 21, 1852, Lacock Abbey Collection LA52-019 (archival source); Talbot Correspondence Project (website), doc. 06596.

26. Fenton was making stereoscopic images for Wheatstone's reflecting stereoscope on June 15, 1852, and he continued to take stereoscopic images for Wheatstone later that year in Russia. For more detailed information, see Hannavy 1993, pp. 233–43. See also Joseph 1985, pp. 305–9.

27. Hannavy 1988, pp. 193–204.

28. Talbot to Eastlake, June 9 and 10, 1852, NMPFT (RPS Collection T/2 1274B; archival source); Talbot Correspondence Project (website), doc. 06639. See also Talbot to Rosse, June 10, 1852, NMPFT (RPS Collection T/2 1274E; archival source); Talbot Correspondence Project (website), doc. 06640.

29. Eastlake and Rosse to Talbot, July 1852, NMPFT (RPS Collection T/2 1273; archival source); Talbot Correspondence Project (website), doc. 06653.

30. "Photographic Patent Right," *Times* (London), August 13, 1852, p. 4.

31. Le Neve Foster (great-grandson of the Photographic Society's Peter Le Neve Foster), June 23, 1939, pp. 818–23.

32. For a more detailed description of the exhibition, see "A Most Enthusiastic Cultivator of His Art" by Roger Taylor in this catalogue.

33. Fenton, "On the Present Position and Future Prospects of the Art of Photography," in *Catalogue of an Exhibition of Recent Specimens of Photography* 1852, p. 8.

34. Dante Gabriel Rossetti to Ford Madox Brown, January 29, 1853, quoted in *Praeraphaelite Diaries and Letters*, ed. William Michael Rossetti (London: Hurst and Blackett, 1900), p. 31.

35. Photographic Society, "Inaugural Meeting of the Photographic Society & Rules of the Photographic Society," NMPFT (RPS Collection; archival source).

36. See "Inaugural Meeting of the Photographic Society," *JPS*, March 3, 1853, p. 4.

37. Ibid.

38. Ibid., pp. 4–5.

39. "Photographic Society. First Ordinary Meeting. Thursday, February 3, 1853." *JPS*, March 3, 1853, p. 5. See also Newton, March 3, 1853, pp. 6–8; Percy, March 3, 1853, pp. 9–11; Fenton, "Upon the Mode in Which It Is Advisable the Society Should Conduct Its Labours," *JPS*, March 3, 1853, pp. 8–9.

40. Quotation from an unnamed source, 1850s; website of the Geological Society, www.geolsoc.org.uk/template.cfm?name=BH520.

41. Although William Ewart Gladstone spoke in the British Parliament in 1854 in support of spending 140,000 pounds to buy the Burlington House site and relocate the various learned societies there from their former home at Somerset House (which the government wanted to use for other purposes), the move began only in 1873, after two decades of discussion.

42. Moreover, membership began to drop, and on average the rooms were visited by only a single member a week. The society vacated the premises in 1860 and resumed the frequent changes of location that have dogged it for the last 150 years.

43. The stepdaughter of Lord Palmerston (shortly to be prime minister), the viscountess was later a photographer herself.

44. "Exhibition of the Photographic Society," *Morning Chronicle*, January 4, 1854.

45. Ibid.

46. "Photographic Society," *Athenaeum*, January 7, 1854, p. 23.

47. "Photography and the Photographic Exhibition," *Builder*, January 21, 1854, p. 27.

48. Talbot to Story-Maskelyne, December 4, 1854, Lacock Abbey Collection (archival source); Talbot Correspondence Project (website), doc. 07013.

49. See "A Most Enthusiastic Cultivator of His Art" by Roger Taylor, in this volume.

50. Photographic Society Club, Rules of the Photographic Society Club Album, 1856, Rule 1, NMPFT (RPS Collection; archival source).

51. Other clubs having a crossover membership with the Photographic Society were formed around this time, including the Photographic Club (1855–57), the Photographic Exchange Club (1855–58), and, a few years later, the Amateur Photographic Association (1859–late 1860s).

52. Photographic Society Club, Rules of the Photographic Society Club Album, 1856, Rule 8, NMPFT (RPS Collection; archival source).

53. *Photographic Journal*, no. 80 (March 5, 1859), p. 203.

54. It was not until more than sixty years later, in 1926, that the society began collecting in earnest, under the honorary curatorship of John Dudley Johnston.

55. "Photography at the International Exhibition," *Photographic Journal*, July 15, 1862, p. 80.

56. "Retirement of Mr. Fenton," *Photographic Journal*, October 15, 1862, p. 158.

57. Johnston 1946, p. 30.

58. "Late Mr. Roger Fenton," *BJP*, August 20, 1869, pp. 400–401. See also "Obituary," *Photographic Journal*, September 15, 1869, p. 126, and "Obituary," *Photographic News*, August 27, 1869, p. 419.

Roger Fenton: The Artist's Eye

RICHARD PARE

1. Years of engagement with the work of Roger Fenton have brought me into contact with many like-minded colleagues. I am grateful especially to Phyllis Lambert, who entrusted me with the task of exploring the broad subject of architectural representation in photography and assembling a collection that would become one of the core holdings of the Canadian Centre for Architecture. Through this undertaking I first saw the view of Ely Cathedral from the south in the gallery of the late Harry Lunn in 1976, occasioning the first of many discussions between us on the works of Fenton. Others to whom I am indebted for insights on Fenton's photography include Robert Hershkowitz, Mark Holborn, and Hans Kraus; David Travis at the Art Institute of Chicago; and Adrienne Lundgren, Preservation Specialist, Library of Congress, who brought to my attention the prints from Fenton's own collection in the library's archives. I would especially like to acknowledge Pavel Horoshilov, Deputy Minister of Culture of the Russian Federation, who told me of the remarkable album that includes works by Fenton in the collection of the Tolstoy Museum, Moscow, and kindly arranged for photography of the two works illustrated here. I am grateful to Vitaly Remisov, Director of the Tolstoy Museum, and Anna Kolupaeva, head of its Department of Culture; to Yuri Palmin for carrying out the photography on very short notice; and to Alexander Brodsky for invaluable coordination of the work in Moscow.

2. Surprisingly few pictures were made of industrial activity in photography's early days. It was not until about 1870 that John Thomson, Thomas Annan, and James Mudd made the inner city and its inhabitants a subject of their photography.

3. Both "green and pleasant land" and "dark Satanic mills" are from William Blake's poem "Jerusalem."

4. Although according to Thomas Huxley, Chambers displayed "prodigious ignorance and thoroughly unscientific habit of mind," Chambers's work was indicative of a growing intellectual restlessness with the biblical idea of creation. Huxley's remark is quoted in Dodds 1952, p. 190.

5. William Smith, *A Delineation of the Strata of England and Wales, with Part of Scotland* (London: J. Carey, 1815). Smith's map is displayed in the rooms of the Geological Society, Burlington House, London. For a full account of his life, see Simon Winchester, *The Map That Changed the World: The Tale of William Smith and the Birth of a Science* (London and New York: Viking, 2001).

6. In a letter written while on the way out to the Crimea, Fenton mentions seeing Gibraltar for the second time. "The old Rock has got his cap on and looks very sleepy, not half so brisk as the last time I saw him; no doubt if he could speak he would say, 'And you the same, old fellow.'" Gernsheim 1954, p. 35.

7. See Hershkowitz 1980, pl. 22.

8. For a full discussion of the Crimean campaign, see Hibbert 1961.

9. See Russell 1855.

10. For a somewhat different reading of Fenton's Crimean photographs, see "A New Starting Point" by Sarah Greenough in this volume, pages 19–22.

11. Fenton's *Photographic Pictures of the Seat of War in the Crimea* was published by Thomas Agnew in three portfolios in 1855 and 1856. Panorama views were available as individual prints (see the Chronology in this volume, September 22, 1855).

12. Fenton made at least two other views of the cemetery on Cathcart's Hill; see Gernsheim 1954, pl. 48; Keller 2001, p. 157, fig. 128.

13. Plate 20 in this volume, though not presented as part of the panorama in the published portfolio, is another view from the sequence. It fits in as ninth in the series, connecting with adjacent images on both left and right. This raises questions about the selection Fenton made for the panorama and his objectives in preparing it. One possible explanation for the sequential discontinuities is that instead of working from a single vantage point and creating a 360-degree radial view of the valley (his first and last panels do not connect), Fenton made a sequence that on occasion moves laterally along the ridge. It is also worth noting that the last two images on the right of the panorama, showing the cemetery, were made later than the other photographs, at a time when the ground was more worn and more graves had been added. A set of prints from Fenton's own collection, including variants, is in the collection of the Library of Congress, Washington, D.C.

14. Gernsheim 1954, pl. 65.

15. For the photographs of Pélissier and Russell, see Hannavy 1976, pls. 21, 23.

16. This was pointed out in Keller 2001, p. 138.

17. A Soviet-era housing settlement now stands at the head of the valley where the Russian batteries were positioned.

18. For an engrossing account of the circumstances leading to the charge of the Light Brigade (immortalized by Alfred, Lord Tennyson), see Woodham Smith 1953.

19. Victoria, Queen of England, Journal (archival source), August 8, 1855, quoted in Hannavy 1976, p. 61.

20. Robert Whelan, *Robert Capa: The Definitive Collection* (London: Phaidon Press, 2001), p. 81, no. 110.

21. There are two versions of this image. In one version the cannonballs are seen as they fell (Gernsheim Collection, HRC; reproduced in Keller 2001, p. 134, fig. 100), while in the version published in this volume, shot appear to have been rearranged to produce a more dramatic rendering of the subject. It was common practice for parties to be sent out to collect the round shot so that they could be fired back again.

22. See Gernsheim 1954, p. 69.

23. "I had hoped to add to the collection of views which I had formed, photographs of the scenes since so ably depicted by Mr. Robertson, and with that view made everything ready for going into Sebastopol after the attack of the 18th of June, which we all knew to be impending, and which everybody had settled was to succeed so surely. . . . When that attempt failed, and to the list of friends already sacrificed were added new names, I felt quite unequal to farther exertion." Fenton, "Narrative of a Photographic Trip," *JPS*, January 21, 1856, p. 290.

24. Ibid.

25. It is tantalizing to speculate on the relationship between Le Gray and Fenton, two photographers whose careers run parallel in many areas. The echoes of a shared photographic vocabulary, both technical and aesthetic, are ever present.

26. John Webster, *The Duchess of Malfi*, act 5, scene 3, lines 11–13.

27. There is no known print from Fenton's hand of this image. The surviving example, which is in a small format and is in the collection of the CCA, was printed by the Frith establishment after the firm acquired Fenton's negatives in the sale of his studio contents.

28. This photograph and fig. 78 are from a group of Fenton prints in a remarkable album in the collection of the Tolstoy Museum, Moscow. The album also includes works by Bisson Frères and Baldus, and previously unrecorded major works by Fenton and Le Gray.
    The phrase "chartered Thames" is from William Blake's poem "London."

29. Dimond and Taylor 1987, p. 148, no. 115.

A Chronology of the Life and Photographic Career of Roger Fenton

ROGER TAYLOR AND GORDON BALDWIN

1. See "Failure as Viewed in Heywood," *Heywood Advertiser*, ca. 1878, n.p. This article gives a detailed historical account of the Fenton family up to the collapse of the Fenton bank in 1878 and provides many valuable insights.

2. Greenall Family of Dutton Papers (archival source), DDX 445/1/3, DDX 445/1/4. The printed particulars of the sale and the signed agreement between Fenton and Weld reveal precisely what land and buildings were acquired, including bobbin mills in Hurst Green and elsewhere.

3. Stenton 1976, p. 136.

4. Reported in "Mr. Roger Fenton's Photographs," *Rochdale Weekly Banner*, October 6, 1855.

5. Honourable Society of the Inner Temple, Admission Stamp Duty Register (archival source), 1837–42, ADM/4/12. We are grateful to Dr. Clare Rider, Archivist, Honourable Society of the Inner Temple, London, for this and other information. For a concise history of the Inns of Court and Chancery, the Inner and Outer Temples, and their place in the British legal system, see *Encyclopaedia Britannica*, 11th ed., s.v., Inns of Court.

6. Burke 1906, p. 574. Joseph Fenton's true value was rumored to be double this figure, for some estates were bought jointly in the names of his two sons and himself. His will can be downloaded at www.documents online.pro.gov.uk.

7. Boase 1965, p. 1097.

8. *Post Office London Directory, 1846* (London: W. Kelly, 1846), p. 181; Public Record Office, Kew, Register of Passports, volume beginning September 4, 1841.

9. General Register Office, London, District of Northallerton, Register of Marriages (archival source), vol. 24, p. 337. Relatively little is known of the Maynard family and the extent of their holdings in Yorkshire and elsewhere, but as with other members of the elite group known as the "Upper Ten Thousand," their lineage and family connections ensured their status in society.

10. "29 juin 1844, Roger Fanton [*sic*], [age] 25, [adresse] rue d'Alger 5, [nom du maître] Michel-Martin Drolling." Musée du Louvre, Registre des cartes d'élèves (archival source), 1840–45, p. 173, entry 2432.

11. Lloyd 1988, frontis. This work is no longer believed to be a self-portrait.

12. Family Record Centre, London, Census Returns for 1861, microfilm, RG/99/128. The entry for the Fenton

household confirms that Annie Grace was born in Paris, noting that she was nevertheless a "British subject."

13. Kamlish 2002, p. 302, n. 17.

14. "Calotype Society," *Athenaeum*, December 18, 1847, p. 1304. Two years later it was also known as "The Photographic Club"; "Photographic Club," *Art-Journal*, August 1, 1849, p. 262.

15. Although Gernsheim asserts that Fenton was a member of the Calotype Club, his name is not mentioned in the articles cited in note 14 above. See Gernsheim 1969, p. 176. See also *Almanack of the Fine Arts* 1852, p. 155, the longest account, which also fails to mention Fenton.

16. Brown 1981, entry for February 25, 1848.

17. Ibid., entries for June 3, November 29, December 2, and December 12.

18. Graves 1904–5, vol. 3, p. 98.

19. Ibid.

20. Brown 1981, p. 70, n. 2. *Almanack of the Fine Arts* 1852, p. 138, gives the best account of the school and its management committees. For a wood engraving showing the activities of the school, see fig. 7 in this volume.

21. Her name is missing from the census returns for 1861 (Family Record Centre, London, microfilm, RG/99/128) and absent from all subsequent genealogies compiled by the family.

22. Maynard, Diary (archival source), July–September 1850. We are grateful to Scott and Donise Ferrel for granting us generous access to Maynard's diaries.

23. Ibid., November 8, 1850.

24. Honourable Society of the Inner Temple, Admission Register (archival source), 1842–68, ADM/2/8.

25. "Royal Academy," *Art-Journal*, June 1, 1851, p. 153. See also Graves 1904–5, vol. 3, p. 98.

26. Auerbach 1999, p. 124; Davis 1999, p. 153. Both books offer a wide perspective on the exhibition and the processes of selection, although touching only lightly on photography.

27. Honourable Society of the Inner Temple, Call Papers (archival source), BAR/6/3. The address at King William Street is given in an advertisement for the Photographical Society; *Art-Journal Advertiser*, April 1852, n.p.

28. Fenton, "Photography in France," *Chemist*, February 1852, pp. 221–22.

29. Ibid.

30. Paul Jeuffrain album, collection of Société Française de Photographie, Paris. The page bears an inscription noting that the portraits were made by Fenton using collodion, in London in February 1852.

31. Fenton, "Proposal for the Formation of a Photographic Society," *Chemist*, March 1852, pp. 265–66.

32. Correspondence at the Birr Scientific and Heritage Foundation, Birr, Ireland, and in the Lacock Abbey

Collection and Royal Photographic Collection (archival sources); Talbot Correspondence Project (website), docs. 06580, 06585, 06598, 06599, 06600, 06602, 06621, 06622, 06623, 06624, 06625, 06632, 06638, 06639, 06640, 06641, 06643, 06644, 06647, 06648, 06649, 06653, 06666, 06668. Although Talbot's zeal in protecting his patents has become almost a legend in the history of photography, correspondence between Talbot and those seeking change reveals the situation was actually far more complex.

33. Lacock Abbey Collection LA52-015 (archival source); Talbot Correspondence Project (website), doc. 06580.

34. The dates come from the photographs, which are inscribed in the negatives.

35. Photograph dated in the negative. See sale catalogue, Christie's South Kensington, March 15, 1979, lot 254.

36. "Weekly Proceedings," *Society of Arts, Manufactures and Commerce,* June 19, 1852, n.p. The committee consisted of Frederic Berger, Fenton (honorary secretary), Peter Le Neve Foster, Fry, Thomas Minchin Goodeve, Robert Hunt, Sir William Newton, Dr. John Percy, and Charles Wheatstone.

37. Vignoles, Journal (archival source), ADD 34532, p. 193r.

38. Fenton reports that on one occasion the thermometer "was standing considerably below the freezing-point." See Percy, March 3, 1853, p. 11.

39. Vignoles, Journal (archival source), ADD 34532, pp. 197r, 200r.

40. Ibid., p. 213r.

41. "Photographic Album," *ILN,* October 30, 1852, pp. 362–63; see also "Photographic Album," *Athenaeum,* November 13, 1852, p. 1247; "Photographic Publications," *Art-Journal,* December 1852, p. 374. Cundall sent Talbot a copy of the *Album* in appreciation for his having relinquished his patent rights. Cundall to Talbot, September 2, 1852, Lacock Abbey Collection LA52-045 (archival source); Talbot Correspondence Project (website), doc. 06680. Part 3, issued in 1853, included two further studies by Fenton; advertised in Delamotte 1853.

42. Vignoles, Journal (archival source), ADD 34532, entry for November 10, 1852. Bourne subsequently showed his photographs of Russia at the annual exhibitions of the Photographic Society in 1854 and 1855. For details of the exhibitions, dates, and print titles, see Taylor, *Photographs Exhibited in Britain,* 2002, pp. 156–57.

43. Held at the Adelphi theater in London, the exhibition closed on January 29, 1853. Taylor, *Photographs Exhibited in Britain,* 2002, pp. 302–5.

44. Abstract printed in *Catalogue of an Exhibition of Recent Specimens of Photography* 1852, pp. 3–8, and *JSA,* December 24, 1852, pp. 50–53.

45. *ILN,* January 1, 1853, p. 12.

46. "The Stereoscope and Its Photographic Applications";

abstract printed in "Seventh Ordinary Meeting," *JSA,* January 21, 1853, pp. 97–100.

47. "Inaugural Meeting of the Photographic Society," *JPS,* March 3, 1853, pp. 2–5.

48. Photographic Society, Minutes of Council (archival source), pp. 2–4, January 7, 1853.

49. Fenton, "Upon the Mode in Which It Is Advisable the Society Should Conduct Its Labours," *JPS,* March 3, 1853, pp. 8–9; Percy, March 3, 1853, p. 11.

50. Photographic Society, Minutes of Council (archival source), p. 11, February 10, 1853.

51. Ibid., p. 14, February 17, 1853; "Photographic Exhibition," *JPS,* March 3, 1853, p. 12.

52. Photographic Society, Minutes of Council (archival source), p. 19, February 24, 1853.

53. Ibid., p. 21, March 3, 1853.

54. Ibid., p. 26, March 10, 1853.

55. Ibid., p. 30, March 17, 1853.

56. Halkett, April 21, 1853, pp. 36–39.

57. Taylor, *Photographs Exhibited in Britain,* 2002, pp. 303–4.

58. "Photographic Gossip," *JPS,* May 2, 1853, p. 56.

59. These included views of Russia and of the woods near London. Photographic Society, Minutes of General Meetings (archival source), pp. 13–14; "Photographic Society. Fourth Ordinary General Meeting. Thursday, May 5, 1853," *JPS,* May 21, 1853, p. 57; Wheatstone, May 21, 1853, pp. 61–62.

60. Photographic Society, Minutes of Council (archival source), p. 53, May 12, 1853.

61. "Réunion photographique," *La Lumière,* May 28, 1853, p. 87.

62. Colonel Phipps to Sir Charles Eastlake, reported at Fifth Ordinary Meeting, June 2, 1853. Photographic Society, Minutes of General Meetings (archival source).

63. British Museum, Trustee Committee Minutes (archival source), p. 8571; British Museum, Original Letters and Papers (archival source), letter, July 9, 1853. See also Date 1989, pp. 10–12; Date and Hamber 1990, p. 316. We are grateful to Anthony Hamber for his generous help with information concerning Fenton's time at the British Museum.

64. British Museum, Original Letters and Papers (archival source), July 14, 1853. In response to a letter from Hawkins, Fenton offers recommendations for the size of both studio and darkroom, as well as for the kind of fittings to be employed (including a copious supply of distilled water), before setting out the costs involved. His most novel idea for the studio was "a little movable chamber in which the camera is to be placed," provided with curtains on all sides so that "all rays of light, except those reflected from the object to be copied are prevented from falling upon the surface of the lens."

65. The tour's twenty-four venues throughout Britain included mechanics' institutes, literary societies, and schools of art, each of which hosted the exhibition for about a week. The tour closed on April 1, 1854. Taylor, *Photographs Exhibited in Britain,* pp. 304–5.

66. British Museum, Original Letters and Papers (archival source), October 4, 1853.

67. "I do not know any person better qualified to superintend the proposed photographic arrangements at the British Museum than Mr. Fenton." Ibid., October 6, 1853; British Museum, Trustee Committee Minutes (archival source), pp. 8614–15, October 8, 1853.

68. Fenton, "On the Nitrate Bath," *JPS,* November 21, 1853, pp. 133–38; Fenton, "Épreuves sur verre collodioné," *La Lumière,* November 26, 1853, pp. 191–92.

69. *ILN,* November 19, 1853, p. 425.

70. Photographic Society, Minutes of Council (archival source), p. 84, December 1, 1853; "Photographic Society," *JPS,* December 21, 1853, p. 141.

71. Fenton, "Exposition d'épreuves photographiques à Londres," *La Lumière,* December 10, 1853, p. 199.

72. Sir Charles Wheatstone and Robert Hunt were also in attendance. "Photographic Society," *ILN,* January 7, 1854, p. 6; see also "January 21st, 1854," *JPS,* January 21, 1854, p. 153; Victoria, Queen of England, Journal (archival source), January 3, 1854.

73. Taylor, *Photographs Exhibited in Britain,* 2002, pp. 305–7. Many of Fenton's prints were lent to the exhibition by R. Beard or Vignoles, not by Fenton himself.

74. Reprinted in translation in "Exposition de la Société Photographique de Londres," January 14, 1854, p. 5.

75. Victoria, Queen of England, Journal (archival source), January 16 and 23, 1854.

76. Ibid., January 25, 1854.

77. Inscribed and dated print, Photograph Collection, Royal Archives, Windsor Castle.

78. Fenton to Talbot, February 4, 1854, Lacock Abbey Collection LA54-007 (archival source); Talbot Correspondence Project (website), doc. 06912.

79. *ILN,* February 4, 1854, p. 88.

80. Victoria, Queen of England, Journal (archival source), February 10, 1854.

81. British Museum, Trustee Committee Minutes (archival source), p. 8652.

82. Taylor, *Photographs Exhibited in Britain,* 2002, p. 305.

83. The sequence of eight prints is included in *Calotypes,* vol. 2, Photograph Collection, Royal Archives, Windsor Castle. For a detailed account of the departure of the fleet to the Baltic, see "Baltic Fleet," *ILN,* March 18, 1854, pp. 242–44. This maneuver was largely tactical and designed to force the Russians into war.

"Laws of the Photographic Society of London." *Journal of the Photographic Society*, no. 39 (February 21, 1856). [Insert following vol. 2.]

"Lecture in Relation to the Theatre of War." Handbill for Roger Fenton's lecture, "The Crimea," given January 21, 1856, at the Public Hall, Rochdale, Lancashire. Copy in Local Studies, Rochdale Public Library, Lancashire.

"London Photographic Society." *Liverpool Photographic Journal*, no. 30 (June 14, 1856), p. 84. [Fenton's resignation as member of the Council of the Photographic Society.]

Manchester Photographic Society *Exhibition of Photographs, at the Mechanics' Institution.* Manchester: Cave & Sever, 1856.

"Manchester Photographic Society. General Meeting Held April 3rd, 1856." *Photographic Notes*, no. 6 (May 25, 1856), p. 51.

Molard, Humbert de. "Exposition Universelle de photographie à Bruxelles." *Bulletin de la Société Française de Photographie* 2 (October 1856), pp. 278–93.

"Mr. Fenton's Crimean Photographs." *Birmingham Journal*, February 9, 1856, p. 7.

"Nineteenth Ordinary Meeting, Wednesday, April 23, 1856." *Journal of the Society of Arts*, no. 179 (April 2, 1856), pp. 385–89.

Norwich Photographic Society. Norwich: Fletcher and Alexander, [1856.]

Phipson, T. "Universal Exhibition of Photography, Brussels." *Journal of the Photographic Society*, no. 47 (October 21, 1856), pp. 146–49. [Reprinted in translation from *Cosmos* 9 (October 3, 1856), pp. 345–50; (October 10, 1856), pp. 370–72.]

"The Photo-Galvanographic Company." *Chemist* 3 (May 1856), pp. 499–500.

"Photogalvanography." *Photographic Notes*, no. 6 (May 25, 1856), pp. 60–62.

"Photogalvanography; or, Engraving by Light and Electricity." *Art-Journal* 18 (July 1, 1856), pp. 215–16.

Photographic Art Treasures; or Nature and Art Illustrated by Art and Nature. London: Patent Photo-Galvanographic Company, 1856.

"The Photographic Association." *Journal of the Photographic Society*, no. 42 (May 21, 1856), n.p.

"Photographic Exhibition of the Manchester Photographic Society." *Photographic Notes*, no. 13 (October 15, 1856), pp. 204–6.

Photographic Notes, no. 15 (November 15, 1856), pp. 235–37. [Review of *Photographic Art Treasures*, presumably written by Thomas Sutton.]

Photographic Notes, no. 16 (December 1, 1856), p. 259. [Advertisement for *Photographic Art Treasures*.]

Photographic Society. *Exhibition of Photographs and Daguerreotypes at the Gallery of the Society of Water Colour Painters.* London, 1856.

"The Photographic Society." *Athenaeum*, no. 1472 (January 12, 1856), pp. 46–47. [Discussion of Fenton's portraits.]

"Photographic Society. Annual General Meeting. Feb. 7th, 1856." *Journal of the Photographic Society*, no. 39 (February 21, 1856), pp. 299–304. [Fenton retires as secretary.] [Also mentioned in "Photographic.—Feb. 7.—Annual Meeting," *Athenaeum*, no. 1478 (February 23, 1856), p. 236, and "London Photographic Society," *Liverpool Photographic Journal*, no. 27 (March 8, 1856), p. 42.]

"Photographic Society. Ordinary Meeting. April 3, 1856." *Journal of the Photographic Society*, no. 41 (April 21, 1856), pp. 18–19. [Fenton on fading of watercolors.]

"Photographic Society. Ordinary Meeting. December 4, 1856." *Journal of the Photographic Society*, no. 49 (December 22, 1856), pp. 173–74. [Fenton retires from the Council; Fenton on modifications of paper processes.]

"Photographic Society. Ordinary Meeting. March 6, 1856." *Journal of the Photographic Society*, no. 40 (March 21, 1856), pp. 2–6. [Fenton on British Museum negatives.] [See also "London Photographic Society," *Liverpool Photographic Journal*, no. 28 (April 12, 1856), p. 52.]

"Photographic Society. Ordinary Meeting. May 1, 1856." *Journal of the Photographic Society*, no. 42 (May 21, 1856), p. 38. [Fenton on conflict of interest among members of the Photographic Society and Photographic Association.]

"Photographic Society. Ordinary Meeting. November 6, 1856." *Journal of the Photographic Society*, no. 48 (November 21, 1856), pp. 155–57.

"Photographic Society of London. Ordinary Meeting and Special General Meeting. January 3, 1856." *Journal of the Photographic Society*, no. 38 (January 21, 1856), pp. 281–82. [Fenton on the Crimea and proposed appointment of a paid secretary.]

"Photographic Society of Scotland." *Photographic Notes*, no. 7 (June 25, 1856), pp. 76–77. [Discussion of photogalvanographic patent process of Paul Pretsch and others.]

"The Photographic Society's Exhibition." *Illustrated London News*, January 19, 1856, p. 74.

"Photographic Views of Sebastopol, Taken Immediately after the Retreat of the Russians." *Notes and Queries*, 2nd ser., no. 11 (March 15, 1856), p. 220. [Mention of Fenton's photographs of the Crimea.]

"Rapport du jury: Chargé de juger la section de photographie à l'Exposition Universelle des Arts Industriels de Bruxelles."

Bulletin de la Société Française de Photographie 2 (November 1856), pp. 344–52.

Sparling, Marcus. *Theory and Practice of the Photographic Art; Including Its Chemistry and Optics with Minute Instruction in the Practical Manipulation of the Various Processes, Drawn from the Author's Daily Practice.* London: Houlston & Stoneman, 1856.

Société Française de Photographie. *Catalogue de la deuxième exposition annuelle des oeuvres des artistes et amateurs français et étrangers.* Paris: Société Française de Photographie, 1856.

1857

"The Archer Testimonial." *Notes and Queries*, 2nd ser., no. 77 (June 20, 1857), p. 493. [Mention of Fenton as treasurer of Archer committee.]

Black's Picturesque Guide to North Wales. Edinburgh: Adam and Charles Black, 1857.

Catalogue de la quatrième exposition instituée par l'Association pour l'Encouragement et le Développement des Arts Industriels en Belgique. Brussels: Guyot, 1857.

"Documents officiels pour servir à l'histoire de la photographie: Extrait des rapports de jury mixte international de l'Exposition Universelle." *La Lumière* 7 (May 9, 1857), p. 75.

[Eastlake, Lady Elizabeth.] "Art. V. Photography." *Quarterly Review* 101 (April 1857), pp. 442–68.

"Exhibition of Art Treasures at Manchester." *Liverpool and Manchester Photographic Journal*, no. 14 (July 15, 1857), pp. 144–45.

Exhibition of the Art Treasures of the United Kingdom. Supplemental Catalogue. Drawings and Sketches of Old Masters, Engravings, Photographs. Manchester, 1857.

"Exhibition of the Photographic Society." *Photographic Notes*, no. 25 (April 15, 1857), pp. 140–42.

"Exposition de Bruxelles.—1857." *Bulletin de la Société Française de Photographie* 3 (December 1857), pp. 364–66.

"Exposition de Bruxelles. Récompenses distribuées aux photographes exposants." *Cosmos* 11 (December 18, 1857), p. 689.

"Exposition de la Société Photographique d'Écosse." *La Lumière* 7 (December 12, 1857), p. 198.

"Fine-Art Gossip." *Athenaeum*, no. 1548 (June 27, 1857), pp. 826–27. [Mention of Fenton's photographs of Bolton Abbey exhibited at Colnaghi's.]

"Fine Arts." *Athenaeum*, no. 1526 (January 24, 1857), p. 120. [Discussion of Fenton's association with the Patent Photo-Galvanographic Company and review of his work in *Photographic Art Treasures*.]

"First Exhibition of the Photographic Society of Scotland." *Photographic Notes*, no. 19 (January 1, 1857), pp. 24–26.

"First Exhibition of the Photographic Society of Scotland." *Photographic Notes*, no. 20 (February 1, 1857), pp. 45–46.

Journal of the Photographic Society, no. 52 (March 21, 1857), p. 234. [Fenton on Thomas Frederick Hardwich's paper "On the Manufacture of Collodion."]

L[acan], E[rnest]. "La photographie en Angleterre." *La Lumière* 7 (February 28, 1857), p. 33.

Liverpool and Manchester Photographic Journal, no. 4 (February 15, 1857), p. 35. [Mention of Fenton's contributions to Photographic Society exhibition.]

Liverpool and Manchester Photographic Journal, no. 4 (February 15, 1857), pp. 37–38. [The Reverend J. B. Reade on Manchester Photographic Society exhibition.]

"Manchester Photographic Society." *Liverpool and Manchester Photographic Journal*, no. 3 (February 1, 1857), pp. 28–29. [Exhibition review.]

Moigno, F. "Exposition de la Société Française." *Cosmos* 10 (February 6, 1857), pp. 116–22.

Notices of the First Exhibition of the Norwich Photographic Society. N.p., 1857. [Reprinted from the *Norfolk News*.]

"Photographic Art-Treasures." *Athenaeum*, no. 1529 (February 14, 1857), p. 198. [Advertisement.]

"Photographic Art-Treasures." *Athenaeum*, no. 1542 (May 16, 1857), p. 614. [Advertisement.]

"Photographic Art-Treasures. Part I." *Athenaeum*, no. 1524 (January 10, 1857), p. 54.

"Photographic Art Treasures. Part 2." *Photographic Notes*, no. 23 (March 15, 1857), pp. 104–5.

"The Photographic Exhibition." *Illustrated London News*, January 17, 1857, p. 41.

"The Photographic Exhibition." *Journal of the Photographic Society*, no. 51 (February 21, 1857), pp. 213–17.

Photographic Society. *Exhibition of Photographs, at the Gallery of the Society of Water Colour Painters.* London: Richard Barrett, 1857.

"The Photographic Society." *Athenaeum*, no. 1524 (January 10, 1857), pp. 54–55. [Exhibition review.]

"Photographic Society. Annual General Meeting. February 5, 1857." *Journal of the Photographic Society*, no. 51 (February 21, 1857), pp. 217–22. [Fenton on Archer Fund.]

"Photographic Society. Ordinary Meeting. December 3, 1857." *Journal of the Photographic Society*, no. 61 (December 21, 1857), pp. 101–2. [Fenton listed as vice-president.]

"Photographic Society. Ordinary Meeting. May 7, 1857." *Journal of the Photographic Society*, no. 54 (May 21, 1857), pp. 270–72. [Fenton on fund for F. Scott Archer.]

"Photographic Soirée at King's College." *Chemist* 4 (January 1857), pp. 255–56. [Fenton listed as an attendee.]

"Rapport sur l'exposition ouverte par la société en 1857." *Bulletin de la Société Française de Photographie* 3 (September 1857), pp. 250–72.

"Trésors de l'art photographique." *La Lumière* 7 (June 20, 1857), p. 98. [Brief mention of Fenton's photographs.]

1858

Architectural Photographic Association. *Exhibition of the Collection of Photographs for 1857, at the Galleries, in Suffolk Street, Pall Mall East. Catalogue.* London: Architectural Photographic Association, [1858].

"Architectural Photographic Association." *Builder*, no. 780 (January 16, 1858), p. 42. [Fenton's involvement with the Architectural Photographic Association.]

Art-Union of London. *Twenty-Second Annual Report of the Council of the Art-Union of London.* London, 1858.

"The Art-Union of London." *Art-Journal* 20 (September 1, 1858), p. 283.

"The Art-Union of London. Distribution of Prizes." *Art-Journal* 20 (June 1, 1858), p. 183.

"Association Photographique d'Architecture." [Signed H. H.] *La Lumière* 8 (January 23, 1858), p. 14. [Mention of Fenton's involvement with the Architectural Photographic Association.]

Athenaeum, no. 1597 (June 5, 1858), p. 709. [Advertisement for the *Stereoscopic Magazine*, with description of contents.]

Blanchère, H. de la. "Sur les images amphipositives." *La Lumière* 8 (January 30, 1858), pp. 18–19. [Fenton on amphipositives.]

Book of the Household. London: London Printing Company, 1858.

"The Exhibition." *Journal of the Photographic Society*, no. 66 (May 21, 1858), pp. 207–11.

"Exhibition of Photographs at the South Kensington Museum." *Liverpool and Manchester Photographic Journal*, no. 5 (March 1, 1858), pp. 61–63.

"Exhibition of Photographs at the South Kensington Museum." *Liverpool and Manchester Photographic Journal*, no. 7 (April 1, 1858), pp. 82–83.

"Exhibition of the Architectural Photographic Association." *Photographic News*, no. 16 (December 24, 1858), pp. 185–86.

"Exposition photographique de Londres." *La Lumière* 8 (May 29, 1858), p. 84.

"Exposition photographique de Londres." *La Lumière* 8 (July 3, 1858), p. 105.

Fenton, Roger. "The Law of Artistic Copyright." Letter to the Editor. *Journal of the Photographic Society*, no. 62 (January 21, 1858), p. 151.

"The Forthcoming Exhibition." Letter to the Editor. *Journal of the Photographic Society*, no. 70 (September 21, 1858), p. 31.

Hervé, C. S. "Copyright and Photography." Letter to the Editor. *Journal of the Photographic Society*, no. 66 (May 21, 1858), pp. 223–24.

Journal of the Photographic Society, no. 74 (December 11, 1858), p. 89. [Fenton listed as a society member who will exchange fifty prints.]

"List of the Medallists for Photography, at the Brussels Exhibition of 1857." *Photographic Notes*, no. 43 (January 15, 1858), p. 26.

Macduff, Sholto. "Important Discovery in Photography." *Notes and Queries*, 2nd ser., no. 125 (May 22, 1858), pp. 423–24. [Brief mention of Fenton's presiding over discussion of carbon printing.]

Newton, Sir William J., and Roger Fenton. "List of Subscribers to the Archer Testimonial Fund." *Chemist* 5 (January 1858), pp. 254–56. [See also Sir William J. Newton and Roger Fenton, "The Archer Fund," *Photographic Journal*, no. 85 (May 23, 1859), pp. 298–300.]

"The Photographic Exhibition." *Art-Journal* 20 (April 1, 1858), pp. 120–21.

"The Photographic Exhibition at the Crystal Palace." *Photographic News*, no. 3 (September 24, 1858), pp. 29–30.

"The Photographic Exhibition at the Crystal Palace." *Photographic News*, no. 4 (October 1, 1858), pp. 40–41.

"The Photographic Exhibition at the Crystal Palace." *Photographic News*, no. 5 (October 8, 1858), pp. 52–53.

Photographic Notes, no. 44 (February 1, 1858), pp. 34–35. [Brief mention of Fenton in Architectural Photographic Association.]

Photographic Notes, no. 46 (March 1, 1858), pp. 59–60. [Review of exhibition at Photographic Society, including Fenton's work.]

"Photographic Society." *Athenaeum*, no. 1582 (February 20, 1858), p. 246. [Discussion of Fenton's photographs.]

"Photographic Society." *Athenaeum*, no. 1596 (May 29, 1858), pp. 692–93. [Mention of Fenton's photographs.]

"The Photographic Society." *Literary Gazette, and Journal of Belles Lettres, Science, and Art*, February 20, 1858, pp. 185–86.

"Photographic Society. Ordinary General Meeting. December 7, 1858." *Journal of the Photographic Society*, no. 74 (December 11, 1858), pp. 90–94. [Mention of Fenton as chairman and a number of references to the actions of the chairman.]

"Photographic Society. Ordinary General Meeting. November 2, 1858." *Journal of the Photographic Society*, no. 72 (November 6, 1858), pp. 52–54. [Mention of Fenton as chairman.]

"Photographic Society. Ordinary Meeting. April 6, 1858." *Journal of the Photographic Society*, no. 65 (April 21, 1858), pp. 190–91.

"Photographic Society. Ordinary Meeting. March 2, 1858." *Journal of the Photographic Society*, no. 64 (March 22, 1858), pp. 170–72. [Fenton on Petzval's lens.]

"Photographic Society. Ordinary Meeting. May 4, 1858." *Journal of the Photographic Society*, no. 66 (May 21, 1858), p. 211. [Fenton announces death of Mrs. F. Scott Archer.]

"Photographic Society of Ireland." *Journal of the Photographic Society*, no. 66 (May 21, 1858), p. 215. [Members to receive a Fenton photograph.]

"Photographic Society's Exhibition." *Builder*, no. 785 (February 20, 1858), pp. 132–33.

"Photographs." *Athenaeum*, no. 1622 (November 27, 1858), p. 694. [Thomas H. Gladwell advertisement.]

"Rapport sur la section de photographie à l'Exposition des Arts Industriels de Bruxelles." *Bulletin de la Société Française de Photographie* 4 (March 1858), pp. 82–84. [Discussion of Fenton's position in English photography.]

Rejlander, Oscar G. "On Photographic Composition; with a Description of 'Two Ways of Life.'" *Journal of the Photographic Society*, no. 65 (April 21, 1858), pp. 191–97. [With Fenton's comments on Dr. Rejlander's paper.]

"Séances des sociétés de photographie. Société Française.— Séance du 15 avril 1858." *Cosmos* 12 (April 30, 1858), pp. 459–61. [Fenton donated prints to benefit Société Française de Photographie, Paris.]

"Société de Londres. Séance du 1er juin 1858.—Présidence de M. Roger Fenton." *Bulletin de la Société Française de Photographie* 4 (September 1858), p. 233. [Lists Fenton as chairman.]

"Société de Londres. Séance du 4 mai [1858].—Présidence de M. Roger Fenton." *Bulletin de la Société Française de Photographie* 4 (September 1858), p. 232. [Lists Fenton as chairman.]

"Société de Londres. Séance générale annuelle du 2 février 1858.— Présidence de lord Pollack." *Bulletin de la Société Française de Photographie* 4 (September 1858), p. 230. [Mention of Fenton as new vice-president.]

"La Société Photographique de Londres." [Signed H. H.] *La Lumière* 8 (March 27, 1858), p. 50. [Discussion of Fenton's landscapes.]

"Stereoscopic Magazine." *Literary Gazette, and Journal of Belles Lettres, Science, and Art*, no. 2153 (April 24, 1858), p. 408.

"To the Editor of the Photographic Journal." [Signed W.M'L.] *Journal of the Photographic Society*, no. 70 (September 21, 1858), pp. 30–31.

1859

Art-Union of London. *Twenty-Third Annual Report of the Council of the Art-Union of London*. London, 1859.

Athenaeum, no. 1628 (January 8, 1859), p. 55. [Mention of Fenton's landscapes at Suffolk Street exhibition.]

British Association. *Exhibition of Photographs, in the Music Hall Building*. Aberdeen, 1859.

Burty, Philippe. "Exposition de la Société Française de Photographie." *Gazette des beaux-arts* 1 (May 15, 1859), pp. 209–21.

"Conversazione of the Halifax Literary and Philosophical Society." *Photographic News*, no. 21 (January 28, 1859), pp. 249–50.

"The Exhibition in Suffolk Street." *Photographic Journal*, no. 77 (January 21, 1859), pp. 143–50.

"The Exhibition of the Photographic Society." *Photographic News*, no. 19 (January 14, 1859), pp. 217–18.

"The Exhibition of the Photographic Society." *Photographic News*, no. 20 (January 21, 1859), pp. 230–31.

"The Exhibition of the Photographic Society." *Photographic News*, no. 21 (January 28, 1859), pp. 241–42.

"Foreign Science. (From Our Special Correspondent.)." *Photographic News*, no. 33 (April 21, 1859), pp. 77–79. [Review of Palais de l'Industrie exhibition.]

"Foreign Science (From Our Special Correspondent)." *Photographic News*, no. 38 (May 27, 1859), pp. 137–38. [Review of Paris exhibition.]

Glasgow Photographic Society. *Catalogue of Their Exhibition of Photographic Works, Held in the Gallery of the Crystal Palace*. Glasgow: S. & T. Dunn, 1859.

"Glasgow Photographic Society." *Photographic Journal* (BJP), no. 95 (June 1, 1859), p. 139.

L[acan], E[rnest]. "Exposition photographique." *La Lumière* 9 (July 9, 1859), p. 109.

"London Photographic Society." *Photographic News*, no. 18 (January 7, 1859), p. 213. [Mention of Fenton as chairman.]

"London Photographic Society." *Photographic News*, no. 22 (February 4, 1859), pp. 261–62. [Discussion of Fenton's activities as chairman.]

"London Photographic Society." *Photographic News*, no. 31 (April 8, 1859), pp. 57–58. [Fenton on Mayall's discussion of lenses.]

"London Photographic Society." *Photographic News*, no. 35 (May 6, 1859), pp. 103–5. [Discussion of Fenton's actions as chairman.]

"London Photographic Society." *Photographic News*, no. 61 (November 4, 1859), p. 106. [Fenton on lenses.]

"Macclesfield Photographic Society's Exhibition." *Photographic Journal* (BJP), no. 89 (March 1, 1859), p. 60.

Newton, Sir William J., and Roger Fenton. "The Archer Fund." *Photographic Journal*, no. 85 (May 23, 1859), pp. 298–300.

"Notes on the Photographic Exhibition at Aberdeen. [By a Travelling Photographer.]." [Signed "Sel d'Or."] *Photographic Journal* (BJP), no. 108 (October 1, 1859), pp. 243–44.

"Nottingham Photographic Exhibition." *Photographic Journal*, no. 78 (February 5, 1859), p. 182.

"Nottingham Photographic Society: Exhibition at the Exchange Hall." [Signed F. R. F.] *Photographic News*, no. 20 (January 21, 1859), pp. 237–38.

"Nottingham Photographic Society's Exhibition." *Photographic Journal* (BJP), no. 87 (February 1, 1859), p. 36.

"Photographic Exhibition." *Art-Journal* 21 (February 1, 1859), pp. 45–46.

Photographic Journal, no. 80 (March 5, 1859), p. 203. [Appointment of committee to form a collection of photography.]

Photographic Journal, no. 84 (May 7, 1859), pp. 281–82. [Fenton's comments as chairman on technical process.]

Photographic Journal, no. 88 (August 16, 1859), p. 11. [Fenton reports additions to Archer fund.]

Photographic Journal (BJP), no. 85 (January 1, 1859), frontis. [Illustration of *The Undercliff near Niton, Isle of Wight* after Fenton photograph.]

Photographic Journal (BJP), no. 86 (January 15, 1859), p. 13. [Mention of Prince Albert's visit to Photographic Society exhibition at Suffolk Street gallery.]

Photographic Journal (BJP), no. 93 (May 1, 1859), p. 103. [Review of exhibition in Blackheath.]

Photographic Society. *Exhibition of Photographs and Daguerreotypes at the Gallery of the Society of British Artists*. London: Richard Barrett, 1859.

"Photographic Society." *Athenaeum*, no. 1629 (January 15, 1859), pp. 86–87. [Mention of Fenton's Orientalist studies.]

"Photographic Society. Ordinary General Meeting. January 4, 1859." *Photographic Journal*, no. 76 (January 8, 1859), p. 122. [Discussion of Fenton's actions as chairman.]

"Photographic Society. Ordinary General Meeting. Tuesday, November 1, 1859." *Photographic Journal*, no. 91 (November 15, 1859), pp. 72–74. [Fenton on lenses.]

"Photographic Society, London. Ordinary General Meeting. April 5, 1859." *Photographic Journal*, no. 82 (April 9, 1859), pp. 241–44. [Fenton mentioned as member of collodion committee.]

"The Photographic Society's Exhibition." *Builder*, no. 832 (January 15, 1859), p. 36.

"Photographic Society's Sixth Annual Exhibition." *Photographic Journal* (*BJP*), no. 87 (February 1, 1859), pp. 34–36.

"Pont-y-Pant." *Stereoscopic Magazine*, no. 11 (May 1859), pp. 161–64.

"The Present High Temperature." *Photographic News*, no. 45 (July 15, 1859), pp. 226–27.

Société Française de Photographie. *Catalogue de la troisième exposition de la Société Française de Photographie comprenant les oeuvres des photographes français & étrangers.* Paris: Société Française de Photographie, 1859.

"Stereoscopic Photography." *Athenaeum*, no. 1679 (December 31, 1859), p. 904. [Advertisement for *The Conway in the Stereoscope* by James Bridge Davidson, illustrated with Fenton's stereoscopic photographs.]

1860

"The Archer Fund. Additional Contributions." *Photographic Journal*, no. 97 (May 15, 1860), p. 243. [Announcement of receipt of prints from members, including Fenton, for distribution.]

"Architectural Photographic Association." *Builder*, no. 888 (February 11, 1860), pp. 87–88. [Fenton mentioned in a list of photographic classifications.]

"Architectural Photographic Association." *Builder*, no. 889 (February 18, 1860), p. 104. [Fenton's photographs mentioned.]

"The Architectural Photographic Association." *Photographic News*, no. 75 (February 10, 1860), pp. 265–67. [Exhibition of Fenton's photographs mentioned.]

"Architectural Photographic Association." *Photographic News*, no. 78 (March 2, 1860), pp. 307–8.

"Architectural Photographic Exhibition." *Photographic News*, no. 79 (March 9, 1860), pp. 319–20.

"Architectural Photographs." *Notes and Queries*, 2nd ser., no. 216 (February 18, 1860), n.p. [Advertisement lists Fenton's *Cathedrals of England*.]

"The Conway in Stereoscope." *Notes and Queries*, 2nd ser., no. 212 (January 21, 1860), n.p. [Advertisement for book by James Bridge Davidson, illustrated with Fenton's stereoscopic photographs.]

Davidson, James Bridge. *The Conway in the Stereoscope.* Illustrated with stereoscopic photographs by Roger Fenton. London: Lovell Reeve, 1860.

Donelly, Captain. "On Photography, and Its Application to Military Purposes." *Photographic Journal*, no. 101 (September 15, 1860), pp. 328–30. [Mention of Fenton's exhibition standards.]

"Exhibition of the Photographic Society." *Art-Journal* 22 (March 1, 1860), pp. 71–72.

"Exhibition of the Photographic Society of Scotland." *Photographic Journal*, no. 93 (January 16, 1860), pp. 130–32.

Figuier, Louis. *La Photographie au Salon de 1859.* Paris: L. Hachette et Cie, 1860.

"Government Competition with Photographers." *Photographic News*, no. 103 (August 24, 1860), p. 194. [Fenton quoted on confiscation of British Museum negatives.]

"London Photographic Society." *Photographic News*, no. 118 (December 7, 1860), pp. 379–80. [Fenton's retirement as vice-president.]

"London Photographic Society's Exhibition." *British Journal of Photography*, no. 111 (February 1, 1860), pp. 41–42.

"The Meeting of the National Rifle Association." *Illustrated London News*, July 14, 1860, p. 42 (ill. p. 25).

"The National Rifle Association. Inauguration by Her Majesty of the First Prize Meeting." *Illustrated London News*, July 17, 1860, suppl., pp. 17–18.

"Obituary." [Obituary for Marcus Sperling.] *British Journal of Photography*, no. 117 (May 1, 1860), p. 137.

Obituary for Peter Wickens Fry. *Photographic Journal*, no. 101 (September 15, 1860), p. 314. [Fenton mentioned.]

Parliament. House of Commons. *Report from the Select Committee of the House of Commons on the South Kensington Museum: With Notes.* London, 1860.

"The Photographic Exhibition." *Athenaeum*, no. 1682 (January 21, 1860), pp. 98–99.

"The Photographic Exhibition." *Photographic News*, no. 73 (January 27, 1860), pp. 241–43.

"The Photographic Exhibition." *Photographic News*, no. 74 (February 3, 1860), pp. 253–55.

"The Photographic Exhibition." *Photographic News*, no. 76 (February 17, 1860), pp. 282–83.

"The Photographic Exhibition." *Photographic News*, no. 77 (February 24, 1860), pp. 294–96.

"Photographic Exhibition. (From a Correspondent.)." *Photographic Notes*, no. 94 (March 1, 1860), pp. 68–69.

"Photographic Exhibition. (From a Correspondent.)." *Photographic Notes*, no. 95 (March 15, 1860), p. 86.

"Photographic Exhibition. (From a Correspondent.)." *Photographic Notes*, no. 96 (April 1, 1860). p. 98.

"Photographic Exhibition. (From a Correspondent.)." [Signed A. H. W.] *Photographic Notes*, no. 97 (April 15, 1860), pp. 112–14.

Photographic Journal, no. 100 (August 15, 1860), pp. 291–93. [Article on copyright, including mention of Fenton.]

Photographic Society. *Exhibition of Photographs and Daguerreotypes at the Gallery of the Society of Painters in Water-Colours.* London: Taylor and Francis, 1860.

"The Photographic Society." *Photographic News*, no. 70 (January 6, 1860), pp. 211–12. [Mention of Fenton's actions as chairman.]

"Photographic Society. Ordinary General Meeting. January 3, 1860." *Photographic Journal*, no. 93 (January 16, 1860), pp. 116–17. [Mention of Fenton's actions as chairman.]

"Photographic Society of London." *Photographic News*, no. 83 (April 5, 1860), pp. 374–77. [Fenton's actions as chairman.]

"Photographic Society of London. Ordinary General Meeting. December 4, 1860." *Photographic Journal*, no. 104 (December 15, 1860), p. 50. [Fenton's retirement as senior vice-president.]

"Photographic Society of London. Ordinary General Meeting. Tuesday, April 3, 1860." *Photographic Journal*, no. 96 (April 16, 1860), pp. 192–94. [Fenton's actions as chairman.]

"Photographic Society's Exhibition." *Builder*, no. 886 (January 28, 1860), p. 59.

"Photographs of Public Collections." Letter to the Editor. *Photographic Journal*, no. 102 (October 15, 1860), pp. 3–5. [Mention of Fenton's association with British Museum.]

"Photography and the Volunteers." *Photographic Journal*, no. 99 (July 16, 1860), pp. 269–71. [Fenton's activities at the Hythe School of Musketry.]

"Report of the Collodion Committee." *Photographic Journal*, no. 94 (February 15, 1860), pp. 151–55. [Reprinted in translation in "Rapport du comité chargé par la société de Londres de l'étude du collodion," *Bulletin de la Société Française de Photographie* 6 (March 1860), pp. 77–83.]

"Report of the Collodion Committee." *Photographic News*, no. 75 (February 10, 1860), suppl., pp. 278–80. [Discussion of Fenton's paper on collodion.]

"Review of the Volunteers by Her Majesty in Hyde Park." *Illustrated London News*, June 30, 1860, p. 628 [ill. pp. 624–25].

1861

"Address." *Stereoscopic Magazine*, no. 34 (April 1861), n.p.

Architectural Photographic Association. *Catalogue of the Fourth Annual Exhibition of English and Foreign Photographs.* London: Architectural Photographic Association, 1861.

"Architectural Photographic Association." [Signed S. H.] *British Journal of Photography*, no. 135 (February 1, 1861), pp. 50–51. [Exhibition review.]

"Architectural Photographic Society." *Builder*, no. 936 (January 12, 1861), p. 21. [Mention of Fenton's submissions.]

"'The Athenaeum,' January 19, 1861." *Photographic Journal*, no. 106 (February 15, 1861), pp. 117–18. [Reprint of review of Photographic Society exhibition in Pall Mall East.]

Beeton, Isabella. *The Book of Household Management . . . Also, Sanitary, Medical, and Legal Memoranda; with a History of the Origin, Properties, and Uses of All Things Connected with Home Life and Comfort.* London: Ward, Lock & Tyler, 1861.

"British Association." *Athenaeum*, no. 1767 (September 7, 1861), pp. 313–18.

"The British Association at Manchester." *Photographic Journal*, no. 113 (September 16, 1861), pp. 271–72. [Exhibition review.]

"British Association for the Advancement of Science. By Our Eye-Witness at Manchester." *British Journal of Photography*, no. 150 (September 16, 1861), pp. 330–31. [Exhibition review.]

"Chinese Curiosities." *Stereoscopic Magazine*, no. 34 (April 1861), p. 7.

"Chinese Ivory Casket." *Stereoscopic Magazine*, no. 34 (April 1861), p. 9.

"'A Copy of the Photographic Album' (Fading Photographs)." Letter to the Editor. *Photographic Journal*, no. 114 (October 15, 1861), pp. 285–86. [Mention of Fenton's *Birth of Saint John*.]

"The 'Court Circular,' February 9, 1861." *Photographic Journal*, no. 106 (February 15, 1861), pp. 118–19. [Reprint of review of Photographic Society exhibition in Pall Mall East.]

"Criticisms on the Exhibition." *Photographic Journal*, no. 106 (February 15, 1861), p. 116.

"The Exhibition of Architectural Photographic Association." *Photographic News*, no. 125 (January 25, 1861), p. 37.

"Exhibition of Photographs at Manchester in Connexion with the Meeting of the British Association for the Advancement of Science. By Our Eye-Witness at Manchester." *British Journal of Photography*, no. 151 (October 1, 1861), pp. 344–47. [Exhibition review.]

"Exhibition of the Architectural Photographic Association." *Photographic News*, no. 124 (January 18, 1861), p. 26.

"Exhibition of the Photographic Society." *Art-Journal* 23 (February 1, 1861), pp. 47–48.

"George Lance, Esq." *Illustrated London News*, December 21, 1861, 2nd suppl., pp. 647–68.

"'The Golden Age.' By G. Lance." *Illustrated London News*, February 23, 1861, p. 166.

"'Illustrated News of the World,' Jan. 19, 1861." *Photographic Journal*, no. 106 (February 15, 1861), p. 119. [Reprint of review of Photographic Society exhibition in Pall Mall East.]

"Lectures: Architectural Photographic Society." *Builder*, no. 943 (March 2, 1861), p. 145.

"London Photographic Society." *Photographic News*, no. 123 (January 11, 1861), pp. 18–19. [Mention of Fenton's position on the Council.]

"London Photographic Society." *Photographic News*, no. 127 (February 8, 1861), pp. 68–70. [Mention of Fenton's retirement.]

"London Photographic Society. Report." *British Journal of Photography*, no. 136 (February 15, 1861), pp. 69–72.

"London Photographic Society's Exhibition." *British Journal of Photography*, no. 134 (January 15, 1861), pp. 37–38.

"London Photographic Society's Exhibition." *British Journal of Photography*, no. 136 (February 15, 1861), pp. 67–68.

"London Photographic Society's Exhibition." *British Journal of Photography*, no. 138 (March 15, 1861), pp. 108–9.

"The Photographic Exhibition." *Photographic News*, no. 124 (January 18, 1861), pp. 25–26.

"The Photographic Exhibition." *Photographic News*, no. 125 (January 25, 1861), pp. 38–39.

Photographic Journal, no. 109 (May 15, 1861), p. 171. [Mention of Fenton as one of the "leading photographers."]

Photographic Society. *Exhibition of Photographs and Daguerreotypes at the Gallery of the Society of Painters in Water-Colours.* London: Taylor and Francis, 1861.

"The Photographic Society." *Art-Journal* 23 (July 1, 1861), p. 223. [Discussion of proposed placement of photographs in 1862 International Exhibition.]

"Photographic Society of London. King's College. Ordinary General Meeting. Tuesday, June 4, 1861." *Photographic Journal*, no. 110 (June 15, 1861), pp. 196–202.

"Photographic Society's Exhibition, Pall-Mall." *Builder*, no. 937 (January 19, 1861), p. 39.

"Photography as a Fine Art." *Photographic News*, no. 125 (January 25, 1861), pp. 41–42. [Mention of Fenton's landscape photographs.]

"Report of the Council of the Photographic Society." *Photographic News*, no. 128 (February 15, 1861), pp. 79–80. [Mention of Fenton's actions in founding the society.]

"Report of the Council of the Photographic Society." *Photographic Notes*, no. 118 (March 1, 1861), pp. 76–78. [Fenton's role in founding the society.]

"'The Sun,' January 24, 1861." *Photographic Journal*, no. 106 (February 15, 1861), pp. 119–21. [Reprint of review of Photographic Society exhibition in Pall Mall East.]

Thompson, S. "Notes on the Present Exhibitions." *Photographic Journal*, no. 106 (February 15, 1861), pp. 110–13.

"'The Times,' January 18th, 1861." *Photographic Journal*, no. 106 (February 15, 1861), pp. 116–17. [Reprint of review of Photographic Society exhibition in Pall Mall East.]

1862

Black's Picturesque Guide to Yorkshire. 2nd ed. Edinburgh: Adam and Charles Black, 1862.

Catalogue of the Photographs Exhibited in Class XIV. International Exhibition of 1862. London, 1862.

The Illustrated Catalogue of the Industrial Department, British Division. Vol. 2. International Exhibition of 1862. London, 1862.

"Mr. Fenton's Photographic Effects." *Photographic News*, no. 222 (December 5, 1862), p. 588. [Auction of Fenton's equipment.]

"Photography at the International Exhibition." *Photographic Journal*, no. 123 (July 15, 1862), pp. 79–82. [Award given to Fenton.]

"Report of Jurors. Class XIV. Photography and Photographic Apparatus." *Photographic Journal*, no. 128 (December 15, 1862), pp. 190–93.

"Retirement of Mr. Fenton from Photographic Pursuits." *Photographic Journal*, no. 126 (October 15, 1862), pp. 157–58.

"Ruined Abbeys and Castles." *Photographic Journal*, no. 121 (May 15, 1862), p. 57. [Review of publication, *Ruined Abbeys and Castles of Great Britain* by William and Mary Howitt (1862). Fenton's photographs, included as photographic illustrations, are mentioned by the reviewer.]

1863

Fenton, Roger, and J. Durham. "Report." *Photographic Journal*, no. 130 (February 16, 1863), pp. 220–21. [Report on medals awarded in exhibition.]

Law List for 1863. London: V. & R. Stevens, 1863.

Photograph Credits